—⚓ **Women and Children First** ⚓—

Women
&
Children
FIRST

Nineteenth-Century Sea
Narratives & American Identity

ROBIN MISKOLCZE

University of Nebraska Press

Lincoln and London

Publication of this volume was assisted by a grant from the Bellarmine
College of Liberal Arts and the Office of the Chief Academic Officer, Loyola
Marymount University.

Portions of chapter 4 originally appeared in "Transatlantic Touchstone:
The Shipwrecked Woman in British and Early American Literature," in *Prose
Studies* 22.3 (1999), and are reprinted with the permission of the publisher,
Taylor & Francis (http://www.tandf.co.uk).

Portions of chapter 5 originally appeared in "Holy Motives and Loyal Bodies:
Cross-Dressed Female Seafarers in Early American Popular Literature," in
the collection *Masquerades: Disguise in Literature in English from the Middle Ages to
the Present*, edited by Jesus López-Paláez Casellas, David Malcolm, and Pilar
Sánchez Calle, University of Gdansk Press, 2004. Reprinted with permission
of the publisher.

∞

Library of Congress Cataloging-in-Publication Data

Miskolcze, Robin.
Women and children first : nineteenth-century sea narratives and American
identity / Robin Miskolcze.
p. cm.
Includes bibliographical references and index.
ISBN 978-0-8032-3258-7 (cloth : alk. paper)
 1. Women and the sea—United States—History—19th century. 2. Seafaring
life—United States—History—19th century. 3. Women—United States—
Social conditions—19th century. 4. Women—United States—Social life and
customs—19th century. 5. United States—Social conditions—To 1865.
I. Title.
G540.M56 2007
910.4′508209034—dc22
2007017372

Set by Kim Essman.
Designed by Ashley Muehlbauer.

For K. J. and Eliza

Contents

List of Illustrations   viii

Preface   ix

Acknowledgments   xxi

1. Shipwreck Narratives in Early American Literature   1

2. Women and Children First   25

3. Women and the Middle Passage   66

4. Englishwomen and U.S. Shipwreck Narratives   99

5. Cross-Dressed Female Seafarers in Early American Popular Literature   131

Notes   167

Bibliography   193

Index   211

Illustrations

1. Sarah Allen kneeling on a rock   27
2. Emblem of Truth, Love, and Hope, who is leaning on an anchor   30
3. Emblem of Hope seated on a rock by the sea   31
4. Nathaniel Currier's *Mary*   37
5. Edward Augustus Brackett's sculpture *Shipwrecked Mother and Child*   40
6. Man and woman on a floating settee after a shipwreck   46
7. Currier and Ives, *My Child, My Child*   48
8. Currier and Ives, *They're Saved, They're Saved*   49
9. Herndon Monument   59
10. "Am I Not a Woman and a Sister?"   82
11. Eliza's leap across the ice   91
12. Lucy leaps overboard   93
13. Emmeline for sale   97
14. George Morland's *The Wreck of the Halsewell*   112
15. Eliza Fraser in captivity   119
16. Ann Saunders's shipwreck as depicted in *The Melancholy Shipwreck of the Frances Mary*   128
17. Ann Saunders appealing for rescue   129

Preface

Recently, tales of sea adventures have surfaced in various arenas of American popular culture. Building on the blockbuster success of the 1997 movie *Titanic*, television and film industries have produced shows and movies that often derive their central drama from a disaster at sea, whether it is the result of a whale's wrath (NBC's adaptation of the literary scholar Nathaniel Philbrick's *In the Heart of the Sea*, 2001), a plane crash (Tom Hanks in *Castaway*, 2000), or destructive weather (*The Perfect Storm*, 2000).[1] Best-selling nonfiction such as Erik Larson's *Isaac's Storm: A Man, a Time, and the Deadliest Hurricane in History* (1999) likewise reflects the reading public's interest in historical stories of survival at sea.[2] These contemporary manifestations of sea adventures are, I believe, rooted both in Americans' interest in their nation's history and in an anxiety over an inability to survive in the absence of technology.

In simple terms, we are drawn to survival stories set at sea because they expose "the naked truth" about ourselves and an American ethic of survival. This ethic is imagined to have been derived from the survival experiences of early Americans, and it is one we hope to share in as an audience. Early American immigrants are portrayed as having survived the unforgiving ocean and uncivilized wilderness while propagating an ethic of family and loyalty, and a self-reliance rooted in the hope for a better society. Likewise, many African American narratives, such as the print and film version of the story of the *Amistad*, Charles Johnson's *The Middle Passage*, Toni Morrison's *Beloved*, and John Edgar Wideman's *Sent for You Yesterday* work to interpret traumatic sea crossings and their influence on an ethic of survival among the historical and contemporary lives of African Americans.

Initially, I began this project exploring the historical foundation of Americans' interest in sea narratives. I found that contemporary critiques of eighteenth- and nineteenth-century sea stories and maritime culture commonly represent the sea as a frontier of masculinity. Traditionally, the sea has been read as the boundary between boyhood and manhood, ignorance and discovery. The 1967 assumption of W. H. Auden that the sea is a "state of barbaric vagueness . . . unless saved by the effort of gods and men" (6) remains rooted in later critics' assumptions as well.[3] Understandably, the narratives that result from "mastery" of the sea have traditionally been assumed to be by or about men exclusively.

And yet, during my research, I have been struck by the persistent presence of women and the feminine on the watery terrain seemingly reserved for men and masculinity. Historically, women, in form and in flesh, have been going to sea as ship figureheads; women have authored letters from aboard ship and accompanied their husbands who captained their floating homes; and women have played fictional roles as slaves, sweethearts, wives, mothers, and daughters. Women at sea contributed to the formation of an ethics of survival that helped to define American ideals. The exclusion of women from the sea and sea narratives is a twentieth-century construction.

This book focuses on American sea narratives that are very seldom explored, yet their one-time popularity and accessibility indicate the early American public's interest in defining itself as an exceptional community. As I uncovered images of women at sea in antebellum narratives ranging from novels, to sermons, to newspaper accounts and lithographs, it became clear to me how women and the sea narratives they occupied contributed to the construction of a national rhetoric of exceptionalism at a crucial time in American history. The argument of this book is that Anglo-American women who appear in antebellum sea narratives are often portrayed as models of American ideals derived from women's seemingly innate Christian self-sacrifice. These ideals, in conjunction with the maritime directive (originating in the first half of the nineteenth century) that one should attend to women and children first during sea disasters, in turn defined a new masculine individualism, one that was morally minded, rooted in Christian principles, and dedicated to preserving virtue. The early American nation used the "women and children first" maxim not only as a lifesaving procedure but as a principle to which its men would be held. The exceptional nature of America, a nation chosen by God, depended on this ideal.

My work develops a line of inquiry sparked by a number of Americanists who trace the interstices of the private and the public, race and gender, and the created definitions of self, family, and nation. In particular, I follow the lead of Dana D. Nelson, who has examined how nineteenth-century hierarchies of power influenced gender and race perceptions that coalesced into a national identity.[4] While contemporary literary critics currently analyze one or the other theme in relation to particular novels or cultural trends, this study shows how all of these thematic building blocks to national identity coalesce in representations of women at sea. All but one of the chapters explore a type of female character in sea narratives who reveals national anxieties about God's influence on America's progress, the moral risks inherent in masculine individualism, Anglo-American notions of racial difference, the moral implications of slavery, and male and female gender roles. Thereby I make the case that women in sea narratives serve as a new resource for critics' ongoing discussions of how representations of women contributed to national identity in early America.

The link between sea narratives and national identity has been explored by other American literary critics who see the maritime novels and stories of James Fenimore Cooper, Herman Melville, and Edgar Allen Poe as historically situated critiques of American ideals.[5] Critics of sea literature typically assume that while the sea has helped to define America, it has always been a space for predominantly male activities such as exploration, wars, whaling, and sailing. With the exception of the work of the historians Margaret Creighton, Lisa Norling, and Joan Druett, little attention has been paid to women's influence on sea narratives and the national ideals informed by such narratives. In 1973 *National Geographic* inaugurated a series called Men, Ships, and the Sea: with few exceptions, the associations implied in the title have held true.

Historians and literary critics are beginning to reread American maritime history and recover women's contributions. Norling examines how women's handiwork, clothing, food, letters, and self-sufficiency at home fostered the growth of the shipping and fishing industry in the nineteenth century. Creighton has focused on how the culture of sailors and officers was influenced by their perceptions of women. Druett uncovers forgotten historical examples of women at sea and reviews their sailing experiences as wives, mothers, and daughters. Haskell Springer interprets the rarely published private letters and correspondence between women and men at sea.[6] It is apparent that women are increasingly seen by scholars as participants in and contributors to American maritime culture and history. Unlike the subjects of these historians, the women in my study are not necessarily real women who go to sea. Instead, I am interested in the image of women at sea. How did publishers, engravers, newspaper reporters, and male and female authors represent women at sea, and what do those representations say about the hopes, desires, anxieties, and goals of the United States at a volatile time in the nation's history?

The antebellum era, which in this study refers to the several decades before the Civil War, was a time when the explosion of print culture, pride in the sea, westward expansion, and unstable gender roles converged to create images that sketched the contours of the nation's moral nature. It was an immensely fertile and volatile age. The United States grappled with the memories of two wars with England during which many of its own citizens had been disloyal to the new nation. Additionally, within a span of a few decades, the states and territories experienced Indian removal, religious awakening, increased abolitionist agitation, an industrial revolution, economic instability, increased immigration, and railroad expansion. The impact of a perceived "manifest destiny" even brought a war with Mexico.[7] Necessarily, the young nation's commitment to, and understanding of, a consistent set of ideals was tenuous at best.

Responding to the fluidity of social change, the nation's literary output, in the form of novels, newspaper accounts, sermons, and broadsides, often carried messages that reinforced certain notions of American exceptionalism.[8] American exceptionalism, as recently defined by Wai-chee Dimock, is the antebellum version of the Puritans' belief in America as the new Jerusalem. According to Dimock, after the Revolutionary War, faith in supposedly American institutions like "truth and justice" contributed to Americans' notion that they composed an exceptional nation (13).[9] Presuming to have been chosen by God as torchbearers of civilization, Anglo-America saw commitment to truth and justice as an obligation to God, family, and the nation.[10] This belief surfaced in the pages and images of sea narratives, populated by men and women whose natures were tested by the sea, by God, and by one another. The test was all the more consequential when women were on board. The recognition, or lack thereof, of the individual's obligation to God, family, and the nation sent messages to readers that either challenged or affirmed America's exceptional nature. Whether they were passengers, female slaves, Englishwomen portrayed by American publishers, or cross-dressed mariners, the antebellum women and men examined in this study expose national anxieties about the fragility of America's definition of itself as exceptional.

National dramas were staged on land. But as the following chapters demonstrate, America's oceanic frontier consistently served as center stage for the dramatization of American character, particularly when women were involved in the story. Though landscapes shaped the stories of early Americans, the presence of the sea in their lives was profoundly influential as well. In the early nineteenth century, when the United States began building a navy, packet ships became regular mail carriers, and whalers prospered, the sea proved to be integral to the young nation's multiple identities. As the path for the slave's Middle Passage or route of escape, or the freed black sailor's source of subsistence, or the immigrant's desired site for transition from old world to "new," the sea maintained a presence in the lives of many Americans. The War of 1812, America's second war of independence, was essentially instigated by the American desire for freedom at sea. In particular, as illustrated by President Madison's list of reasons for the War of 1812, many Americans recognized the sea as central to the nation's identity.[11]

By the start of the nineteenth century, serious construction of a U.S. navy began as a response to North African rulers who demanded exorbitant tributes in exchange for freedom at sea.[12] These wars with "Barbary," as most North African countries were labeled, were later celebrated in patriotic songs, including "The Marine's Hymn." Preceding the Civil War, American ships "carried close to seventy-five percent of the country's foreign trade" (Springer, Introduction 13), enabling Americans to see themselves as a nation whose principles of life and liberty touched shores all over the world. As such, the sea is not only a source of pride and American economic and military power in the early nineteenth century but also the stage where the American character was enacted in national dramas. The draw of the sea and its potential to help define, develop, and reflect a desirable national identity was so strong that fictional and real imperiled women were yanked from the domestic setting of the parlor and tossed aboard a ship to become characters destined to test the nation's own self-image.

Representations of women at sea served as a repository for Anglo-American anxieties about exceptionalism and the desire to fulfill both its promise of individual liberty and its special covenant with God. The chapters that follow examine how images of women at sea attended to the nation's crisis of identity. In the first chapter, I trace American foundations of the sea narrative; the "sea-deliverance" stories from which later nineteenth-century shipwreck narratives evolved. The chapter outlines sea narratives from Columbus's claim that he threw his account of discovery overboard in a barrel when imperiled by the ocean, to William Bradford's written version of the Pilgrims' *Mayflower* landing. Seventeenth- and eighteenth-century Americans often heard or read sermons or accounts of the English immigrant's struggles at sea. The first nine chapters of the well-known *Remarkable Providences* by Increase Mather tell stories of struggle and survival during the crossing to America and how such "remarkable sea-deliverances," as Mather termed them, earned many immigrants a rite of passage as a Christian and "New World" citizen.

This chapter builds on Donald P. Wharton's reading of sea-deliverance narratives from 1610 to 1766.[13] Wharton argues that shipwreck tales pointed to the hand of "Providence" as the source of salvation and served as proof that the Puritans were "a people especially called to a historic mission" (8). Wharton suggests that for Puritan Americans, such narratives confirmed God's hand in their destiny. With Wharton as a point of departure, I consider how early Americans shifted from seeing solely the hand of Providence at work in their lives to more rationalistic interpretations. By the end of the eighteenth century, rationalism and optimism in human potential took root, producing a new focus for sea narratives—the value of human effort. While Providence never disappears from shipwreck narratives, narratives such as Olaudah Equiano's auto-biography illustrate how the individual's choices and efforts are instrumental in God's design. If Providence and human effort both contributed to survival at sea when disaster struck, then there was no especial grace to be bestowed on Americans. The final section of the chapter proposes that the key to the perpetuation of American exceptionalism was the growing presence of morally minded Anglo-American women within sea narratives, women who bridged the gap between Providence and human perseverance, the holy and the human.

Chapter 2 recovers forgotten narratives by and about antebel-lum female shipwreck victims. These stories, some fictional, some based on actual shipwrecks, come in a variety of forms, such as published eulogies, letters, popular anthologies of disaster stories, and even a fashion plate, and are central to the concept of American exceptionalism. Largely unexplored by literary critics and historians, these narratives demonstrate how images of men saving women at sea served as moral lessons, cautionary tales, and reminders of the nation's covenant with God and the necessity of controlling the self-interested passions so dangerous to a democracy.

It is no coincidence that the oft-repeated cry of "Women and children first!" became a culturally sanctioned maritime custom during the antebellum period. The relative success of crew and male passengers to ensure the safety of women and children became a gauge of a national moral character at a time when individualism threatened the ideal of a national community. In accounts of the wreck of the *Helen M'Gregor* (1830), the *Home* (1837), the *Pulaski* (1838), the *Ocean Monarch* (1849), and the *Central America* (1857), men who risked their own lives to save women during a crisis at sea were depicted as saving faith in God, loyalty to family, and commitment to community. As such, these accounts reveal that American men were not just rescuing women and children first but also securing America's exceptional nature. Anglo-American women facilitated the belief that Americans were uniquely moral beings, and American exceptionalism was exemplified by the reaction to this endangered, sanctified female at sea.

The inherent moral virtue of Anglo-American women also served abolitionists, who attempted to associate the suffering of slave women during the Middle Passage with suffering Anglo-American women. Middle Passage journeys, during which hundreds of thousands of Africans died of starvation or disease, are mostly undocumented, yet they are the most apparent sea narrative of the antebellum era. Nearly every institution functioning in the United States by 1861 was connected to the Middle Passage, which brought over the hands that both physically and psychically built the nation. As Cynthia Griffin Wolff says, the Middle Passage was essentially the "*beginning* of every 'slave narrative'" (emphasis in original, 27). In studies of African Americans and the sea, such as W. Jeffrey Bolster's *Black Jacks* and Paul Gilroy's *The Black Atlantic*, however, black women and the sea have been overlooked. The few narratives about the Middle Passage experience that survive were written by African American men; none are explicitly recounted by African American women.

In chapter 3, the Middle Passage is interpreted as a crucial trope for African American women whose writing helped shape an American moral character. First, I look at how some African American women writers transformed the cultural legacy of the Middle Passage into a source for self-determination. The first section of the chapter traces the trope of the Middle Passage in African American women's writing, particularly Harriet Jacobs's *Incidents in the Life of a Slave Girl* and Nancy Prince's *Narrative of the Life and Travels of Mrs. Nancy Prince*. Though neither woman traveled the Middle Passage herself, it is recalled as a cultural touchstone in their narratives. For example, in Harriet Jacobs's *Incidents*, the author escapes slavery and hides in a nine-feet-long, seven-feet-wide, and three-feet-high attic space. Jacobs watches her children grow up, from a distance, through a small hole in the wall of these tight quarters. Such positioning recalls the cramped berths of the slave ships, and the peephole provides a kind of symbolic, porthole perspective of loss as experienced by slave women during the Middle Passage. Yet images of the Middle Passage are subverted even as they surface. Jacobs labels her peephole a "loophole" and uses it to mastermind her own and her children's futures. African American women writers such as Jacobs interpreted the cruel realities of the Middle Passage as both a symbolic route of transfiguration and a source for persuasive rhetoric demonstrating the God-given morality of their desires and summoning the respect and liberty afforded Anglo-American women.

Secondly, I trace how the suffering of slave women and the Middle Passage were linked to the moral directive "women and children first" to become the core of abolitionist polemics. Abolitionists like Lydia Maria Child and Harriet Beecher Stowe represent women and the Middle Passage as a spectacle of suffering, the epitome of the unnaturalness of slavery. These writers argue that perpetuating the Middle Passage legacy of physically abusing slave women and separating them from their children was a violation of white womanhood as well. Abolitionists attempted to convince men that they were violating the directive that women and children should have precedence by scolding sea captains and slaveholders for separating slave mothers and their children, and insisting that such suffering would never be tolerated in white women's lives. Abolitionists warned that white manhood would be threatened if the sanctity of enslaved women and children's humanity were not validated. In simple terms, abolitionist rhetoric posited that the mistreatment of black women was essentially an exercise in emasculation.

American abolitionists understood how the idea that women and children should come first could be used to rhetorically join the suffering of slave women and Anglo-American women. However, saving black women from suffering does not exclude the fact that Americans were anxious about maintaining the mystique of American exceptionalism and, by extension, superiority over, not just African Americans, but all nonwhites. Chapter 4 examines another group of shipwreck narratives that attempted to link ethnic rather than racial identity when Anglo-Americans perceived themselves as threatened by nonwhite populations. The preservation of national identity, which often took Anglo-American women as its emblem, unfolds in unexpected ways in several popular sea narratives in which Englishwomen are the victims. The fictional accounts of Maria Martin and Eliza Bradley were immensely popular. Their tales of shipwreck and captivity by North Africans appeared in over a dozen editions. The fictionalized female narrators are represented as British ladies, yet their narratives were issued exclusively by American publishers. Two other shipwreck tales, written by Eliza Fraser and Ann Saunders, feature captivity among Native Americans and cannibalistic passengers, respectively, and are purportedly nonfiction. The narratives were altered when republished in the United States; these alterations reflect national attitudes toward race and gender.

Transatlantic tales of women in crisis have been overlooked by critics.[14] However, these popular stories contribute to the construction of an American character as distinct from other, less exceptional or downright "godless" nations. Post-Revolutionary and early antebellum Anglo-Americans saw the plight of these Englishwomen as their own. Using Etienne Balibar's notion of "fictive ethnicity" to describe Anglo-Americans' seemingly "natural" ties to an English ethnicity, I illustrate how American audiences identified with English women like Eliza Bradley, Maria Martin, and Eliza Fraser, whose popular narratives define an Anglo-Christian ethnicity against the North African "Moors," with whom the United States was in constant conflict, or the natives of other lands, who are constructed to resemble the characterization of Native Americans in captivity narratives. The Anglo-American identification with English ethnicity made it possible for white Americans to project a hierarchy on those who didn't share Anglo-American cultural assumptions, namely, North Africans, African Americans, and Native Americans. The plight of British ladies at sea and in captivity demonstrated for Americans the dangers posed by nonwhites at home and abroad while emboldening a sense of Anglo-American exceptionalism. Additionally, the American publishers' alterations of Eliza Fraser's and Ann Saunders's narratives reflect the perceived desires and expectations of a race, gender, and class-conscious American public. Identifying the shipwrecked English woman's miseries assured Anglo-Americans that, though the umbilical cord to England had been cut, they could still believe their "natural" English ethnicity was superior to all others.

The question of American exceptionalism and anxiety over commitment to God, family, and the nation is raised in yet another type of female character: the cross-dressed female sailor. This character appears in popular fiction such as *The Female Marine* (1815), *Fanny Campbell, the Female Pirate Captain* (1844), and most of James Fenimore Cooper's sea fiction, including *The Pilot* (1824), *The Red Rover* (1827), *The Water-Witch* (1830), and *Jack Tier* (1848). In an era of the self-made man and expansionism, when the Constitution's promotion of individual liberty was put to the test, interactions with cross-dressed female characters indicated qualities in men worthy of loyalty or condemnation.

The women in these (likely) fictional stories dress as sailors or marines to earn a living, fight for their country, or pursue a lover or husband. Though the women are cross-dressed, their identity as loyal servants to God, family, and the nation shines through all disguises. These stories address anxieties over what lies beneath American men's clothing—selfless virtue or greed and self-advancement. Cross-dressed female mariners serve two purposes: they chart the best qualities of the American male, or they provide a warning to Anglo-American men in danger of dismantling American claims to exceptionalism. Looking like men and acting as a model of manhood, these female characters remind men of their nobler nature and obligation to God, family, and the nation.

Cross-dressing mariner narratives are one way of foregrounding the precariousness of a self-ascribed American exceptionalism. The woman in distress at sea challenged America: questions about American character lay in the response. What is the role of the individual in a community believed to be sanctioned by God? Does capitalist America's promotion of the self-made man dissuade men from sacrificing themselves for their families, communities, and God? Does black women's suffering emasculate white men? Is white America's ethnic identity and cultural superiority a fiction? And finally, do efforts at self-advancement affect the founding ideals of the nation? As the faces of Americans changed and men's loyalties became unstable in the face of the potential profits to be gained by expansionism, putting women and children first was not just an act of selflessness but a call for the citizenry to inhabit the cloak of virtue and honor its profound commitment to God, family, and the nation.

⊸ Acknowledgments ⊶

Grants from the University of Nebraska–Lincoln, the Northeast Modern Language Association, and Loyola Marymount University allowed me to complete the research and writing of this book. My deepest appreciation goes to Sharon M. Harris for inspiring me to study women in literature and for responding to the earliest and messiest stages of this book. I also want to thank Joy Ritchie, Stephen Behrendt, and Dane Kennedy for their suggestions. Father Mike Engh, dean of the Bellarmine College of Liberal Arts of Loyola Marymount University, has been especially accommodating and supportive, providing time and funding that allowed me to complete my work.

The two anonymous readers for the University of Nebraska Press offered detailed suggestions that led me to significantly rewrite portions of this book; I greatly appreciate their time and insights. I am also very grateful to Ladette Randolph, editor at the University of Nebraska Press, for believing in this project. Ladette's enthusiasm and care for me and my work has been truly uplifting. Beth Ina's editing skills are also much appreciated.

I feel fortunate to have such wonderful friends and colleagues who have read portions of the book, responded to various moments of despondency, or distracted me with their good humor and wit. Theresia de Vroom participated in all three of these, and is a good friend and mentor. My thanks also to those who read a chapter draft for a colloquium: Mel Bertolozzi, Sharon Locy, Stuart Ching, K. J. Peters, and Linda Bannister. Thanks to Kelly Younger and Pam Felcher for responding to a draft of my introduction, and thanks to Linda Bannister for encouraging me to teach a course on shipwreck literature, a class that contributed to another chapter in this book. Akira and Miya Lippit have always offered real enthusiasm and encouragement for this project. Several research assistants tried to keep me organized: thanks to all of them, and, most recently, Jenny Lower and Shannon Gleason for assistance in tracking down sources, illustrations, and permissions.

To my family, I offer love and appreciation. Thank you to Judy Hill for taking the time to read through my manuscript and listening to me all these years. My parents, Penny and Bob Miskolcze, have had a great impact on my life. My mother and grandmothers' boldness has continually inspired me, and my father, who loved to be on the water, is sorely missed. Thank you to my best friend and sister, Amy, and to the rest of the Battaglias, Sam, Jamie, Marissa, and Gino, for taking time to look for a Currier print during their precious (sweaty) vacation. Thank you to Marvin and Elda Peters for their patient support of my work. My book contract arrived a week or so before my proudest moment, the arrival of Eliza. This book could never compete with a kiss and smile from you. Finally, to my husband, K. J., I offer apologies for taking up so much of your time with this project. You are the most generous, loving person I know, and without your intelligent revision suggestions, encouragement, and personal sacrifices, I simply would never have written this book.

Women and Children First

Shipwreck Narratives in Early American Literature

One of the most enduring stories in Euro-American mythology is that of Columbus, sailing home to Lisbon after discovering the "New" World, watching in horror as waves and wind threatened to overwhelm and perhaps destroy his flotilla of ships. Believing the ships would soon founder, Columbus wrote the story of his "discoveries" on parchment, sealed it in wax, and placed it in a barrel. He tossed the lot into the raging sea with the hope that his glorious success would not go down with the ship, and that someone, somewhere, would recover the account and show others. In the midst of what the captain and crew believed to be the wreck of their ships, the first "American" shipwreck narrative was written.

One of the successes Columbus may have recounted and sent off in the barrel was his story of the founding of a new colony in the "new" world. One of the earliest colonies would never have existed had, on Christmas Eve 1492, the *Santa Maria* not wrecked on a sandbank off the north shore of Hispaniola. Setting a precedent for what would appear in many future shipwreck narratives, some of Columbus's men became so enamored of the women and lifestyle of the kind natives that they begged permission to stay. Columbus saw their willingness to remain as a perfect opportunity to establish the beginnings of a colony. To build this colony, he used the fragments of the wrecked *Santa Maria* to erect a tower that was to be part of a new fortress—a new bastion of European power and promise. With the occasion of the shipwreck and the

European materials made available to Columbus by the fractured vessel, Columbus endeavored to construct a colony that had been, so to speak, manufactured in Europe. The logic of European colonizers insisted that the ship, at once displaying emblems of Christianity (the cross) and national origin (the flag), could simply be transplanted (like her timbers) in a new world. Shipwreck, then, provided both the narrative and literal materials out of which the myth of the settlement of America began; as symbol, it is woven into what Djelal Kadir calls the "complex web of certain notions, cultural forms, and conditioning ideas" that sprung from the "cultural phenomenon" of Columbus (x).

By the end of the 1690s, Columbus's landing had become such a "cultural phenomenon" that the Puritan leader Cotton Mather interpreted it as "one of three shaping events of the modern age" (Bercovitch, *Rites* 68), in part because American colonists saw themselves as transplanting their own enterprise from the old to the new world. It is understandable, then, that shipwrecks and stories of survival were some of the first written narratives published in Puritan New England. The stories of explorers like Columbus in which shipwreck shadowed discovery prompted future emigrants to America to believe that from shipwreck springs discovery and settlement of a new world. The sea, ships, and shipwreck proved to be a resilient undercurrent in American literary and cultural history.

Throughout the seventeenth, eighteenth, and early years of the nineteenth century, ships and the sea became part of the fabric of U.S. national narratives because they contributed to America's efforts to imagine herself as a viable, if not exceptional, community in relation to the rest of the world. This chapter provides the background to future chapters of this study by tracing some of the ways in which early American ships and sea narratives contributed to national ideals in the years leading up to the nineteenth century. Following the lead of Columbus, Pilgrims and Puritans perceived their migration across the Atlantic as a rite of passage to settle a new world, and ships became emblems of the Puritan colony. In the late seventeenth and early eighteenth century, shipwreck narratives were used to prove that Puritans were "chosen" by God to settle New England, and by the end of the eighteenth century, the new republic's pride in the shipping trade and the increasing availability of printed materials led to a more widespread appreciation of these stories. With the end of the century, however, came the age of Enlightenment, when the moral character of the individual and his actions preoccupied American intellectuals. Though Anglo-Americans were now convinced that God had chosen them, there was unease over what exactly constituted the character of an American deserving of this status as citizen of a morally exceptional nation. This unease surfaces in sea narratives. The final section of this chapter proposes that the key to the perpetuation of the sea narrative as proof of American exceptionalism was the growing presence of morally minded Anglo-American women, who bridged the gap between the holy and the human.

From the start, sea voyages and ships served as representations of what Pilgrims and Puritans perceived as their divinely ordained mission. As many early American literary historians have shown, the sacred goal of the seventeenth-century Puritan migration was to heed the call to commence an "errand into the wilderness" of America (34), a land perceived as "God's New Israel" (Bercovitch, *Rites* 35).[1] The symbolic significance of the means of transportation the early colony used for this errand, however, is often overlooked. Ships shaped Pilgrims' and Puritans' self-definition. In their stories, as in Columbus's, the ship endured as an emblem of religion and nation, witnessed the formulation of governmental policies and social codes, and became a character in abiding myths such as the now-famous story of the landing on Plymouth Rock.

One of the primary examples of a ship enduring throughout American history is the *Mayflower*, a replica of which still draws thousands of visitors every year to Plymouth, Massachusetts. The *Mayflower* was the settlers' first new world. After the Pilgrims anchored in Provincetown Harbor, William Bradford describes how they gave thanks to God for being able "again to set their feet on the firm and stable earth" (61), even though their feet had not yet actually touched American soil.[2] They remained aboard the

Mayflower for a couple of months; thus, their first recognition of what it meant to be on American soil was actually a pronouncement of what it meant to be at sea and aboard the *Mayflower*. Also, the ship, rather than the land, influenced the title and terms of their new government. The first Anglo-American constitution of sorts was not pieced together in a church or city hall; rather, the Mayflower Compact of 1620 was imagined and approved aboard a ship whose name would forever be a part of the document guiding the early settlers.[3]

The compact made among Pilgrims on how to govern and be governed relies on a covenant theology that became even more pronounced a decade later by the Puritans aboard another ship. Not long after the Mayflower Compact came into existence, one of the most famous Puritan sermons utilized the image of the lost ship to emphasize the dangers of breaking the covenant with God as His chosen colony.[4] Once again, a ship bore witness to the covenant. When the *Arbella* brought nearly four hundred people to America, the Puritan leader John Winthrop articulated what was expected of new world citizens. In a sermon aboard the *Arbella* in 1629,[5] Winthrop anticipated the construction of a "Citty upon a Hill [where] the eyes of all people are upon us" (233). To build and maintain such a holy city, however, the citizens would need to fulfill their covenant to God: "to doe Justly, to love mercy, to walke humbly with our God," or else, warns Winthrop, "the Lord will surely breake out in wrathe against us, be revenged of such a perjured people, and make us know the price of the breache of such a Covenant" (233). The price, claims Winthrop, is nothing less than a "shipwracke" (233).

Winthrop equates the colony with a ship, for if the colony breaks its covenant with God, he claims the colonists will be "shipwrecked." Revealing his training in law, Winthrop argues that perjury and breach of contract will wreck the new colony's holy ship of state.[6] Winthrop's listeners need only, he asserts, look around to see that God's ship appears to be the reward for their loyalty to the terms of the sacred contract. The ship is a promise from God of deliverance, but if and only if the covenant is not broken. If it is broken, the "holy" colony, represented by the faces listening to Winthrop's sermon as the Arbella aimed for the shores of the promised land, will become nothing more than the remains of a shipwreck. A human breach of a sacred contract will draw the most devastating, in body and soul, of God's punishment.

Their ship and its potential destruction, then, were important components in the symbolism of early religious leaders' covenant theology. Likewise, early governors and preachers such as William Bradford and Increase Mather recognized that stories of perils at sea could be used both to highlight the colony's chosen status and to foster colonists' commitment to the community. The way they portrayed the landing of the Mayflower reveals the colonists' conviction that their settlement was preordained by God. William Bradford provides the most well-known depiction of the Pilgrims' landing, characterizing the settlers as saints and their landing as fated. Though his comparison is often overlooked by contemporary critics, Bradford explicitly likens the spiritual challenge of the Pilgrims' landing to the situation faced by the shipwrecked apostle Paul in Acts 28.2. According to Bradford, the Pilgrims faced a predicament much like Paul in that "what could they see but a hideous and desolate wilderness, full of wild beasts and wild men . . . If they looked behind them, there was the mighty ocean which they had passed and was now as a main bar and gulf to separate them from all the civil parts of the world" (62). Representing Pilgrims as Christian figures of shipwreck, Bradford mingles their identities with an apostle of Christ surrounded by a heathen wilderness and a barbarous ocean, wanted by neither but needed by all. As He did with Paul, God had chosen the Pilgrims for this mission.

The security of the Pilgrims' Christian beliefs and practices aboard the ship is shaken by their landing. After this, the ship would no longer be their city hall, or bed, or church; thus, Bradford represents the condition they are left in as that of shipwreck survivors. It was an apt metaphor in that what follows from shipwreck is a rebuilding of civic (city hall), familial (house), and religious (church) institutions that mirror the duties of the newly landed Pilgrims. Identifying themselves as shipwreck survivors strengthened the

Pilgrims' Christian convictions that they were a people chosen to endure threats of destruction to their community in the old world so that they could transplant that community to a new world. As prophets chosen by God to be tested by shipwreck, Pilgrims like Bradford could believe their situation to be more of a Christian allegory of faith than a tale of destruction by wild seas, wild beasts, and wild men.

Even the mythical landing of the Pilgrims on Plymouth Rock is affected by shipwreck, and is cast as a moment of destiny. What carried the first of the Pilgrims to Plymouth Rock was not the *Mayflower* but one of her small boats, a shallop. This shallop, tossed about by wind and waves, landed where it did purely out of the necessity to salvage life and limb from shipwreck. Bradford writes:

> the wind increased and the sea became very rough, and they broke their rudder, and it was as much as two men could do to steer her with a couple of oars . . . the storm increasing, and night drawing on, they bore what sail they could to get in, while they could see. But herewith they broke their mast in three pieces and their sail fell overboard in a very grown sea, so as they had like to have been cast away. Yet by God's mercy they recovered themselves . . . And though it was very dark and rained sore, yet in the end they got under the lee of a small island and remained there all that night in safety. (71)

Later, the small group of men "sounded the harbor and found it fit for shipping, and marched into the land and found . . . a place (as they supposed) fit for situation" (72). Two things from these passages are important. For one, as the Bradford scholar Samuel Eliot Morison reminds us, the anticlimactic sounding of the harbor and the weary hike on land is the only contemporary account of the landing of the Pilgrims on Plymouth Rock (72). It is clear from the narrative that the *Mayflower* did not make the landing, for it was still anchored in what is now Provincetown Harbor. But because this ship has become an emblem for the origins of Anglo-America, it has replaced the small shallop in the imagination of most Americans. Drama trumps historical fact when the past is reconstructed.

Secondly, the Pilgrims appear to land where they did because fate drew them there, and once again, shipwreck is involved in their tale. The party's small shallop was breaking up in the storm (a sign from God), and they needed protection. According to Bradford's story, they took shelter under a lee and stayed there safely all night. With their ship nearly destroyed, the land of the new world protects them. This small slice of coast seemingly saves their lives and thereby becomes the site of settlement. In the Puritan scheme of interpretation, they didn't choose the land, the land chose them. The idea that America was God's gift of salvation would strengthen the foundation of Puritan self-definition for decades to come.

While Americans began to construct themselves and their government as chosen by God, shipwreck narratives became increasingly popular devices for Puritan religious leaders, who tried to intensify colonists' ties to the rest of their community. Influential leaders such as Increase Mather understood the symbolic potential of the ship of state and the lessons to be learned when that ship was threatened with destruction. The entire first chapter of Mather's *Remarkable Providences Illustrative of the Earlier Days of American Colonisation* is a catalogue of nine examples of "remarkable sea-deliverances" that illustrate the ways in which Providence has favored New Englanders. Even if the testimony did not result in survival of the most faithful, as Patricia Caldwell stresses in her study of Puritan conversion narratives, "the whole experience" of such hardships as a tumultuous sea passage "could be turned into one huge 'evidence' or 'effect' of grace" (130).[7] As Mather emphasizes at the start of the catalogue, God's grace is reserved for these new settlers. He explains that his aim is to "confine [himself] unto things which have happened either in New England, or wherein New England vessels have been concerned" (2). Though he could have reported on shipwrecks occurring all over the world, Mather is interested only in shipwrecks off of New England's coast. Mather uses these wrecks to teach lessons of submission and loyalty crucial to the viability of the colony.

The first lesson is from a story that serves as the model for how an American should behave during a shipwreck—and within the colony itself. When Anthony Thacher's boat breaks up as the waves dash it to pieces against the rocks off of the New England coast, his family makes no attempt to save their own lives. As his wife and children cling to one another, Thacher attests that "there was not one screech or outcry made, but all as silent sheep were contentedly resolved to die together lovingly" (5). Unlike the selfish population that exists beyond America, God's chosen New England flock, the Thachers, know they must resign to His will aboard ship as on land; or at least that is what readers and listeners were expected to glean from these narratives.[8] As Sacvan Bercovitch has suggested, the Puritans' legacy includes "a set of rituals of anxiety that could at once encourage and control the energies of free enterprise" (35). Shipwrecks had the potential to call forth base impulses to survive at the expense of others. Thus, shipwreck narratives such as that of the Thachers begin *Remarkable Providences* as a means of ritualizing the appropriate Puritan behavior when self-advancement competes with the survival of the community. As a family unit, and as a group belonging to the larger colony of New England, the Thachers' actions are made to reveal a simultaneous resignation to God's will and commitment to community values. No one will survive without the others.

The Thachers' wish to die together enacts the words of the *Mayflower Compact*: to follow the laws of the godly leaders "as shall be thought most meet and convenient for the general good of the Colony, unto which we promise all due submission and obedience" (Bradford 76). Like the family of silent sheep who are resigned "to die together lovingly" as members of Christ's flock, so too must the colonists submit to the best interests of a colony presented to them by God. Mather, always concerned about keeping the religious community intact, utilizes their story and those of other shipwreck victims throughout *Remarkable Providences* to build a social imaginary committed to the covenant with God and one another.[9]

Puritan leaders recognized that stories about their ships and experiences at sea could be used to teach colonists how to define themselves as Americans, and in so doing, to redeem themselves from the ways of the old world, as Donald P. Wharton suggests

("Colonial Era" 35). The heads of the colony recognized that they could manipulate stories of sea travel and shipwreck to make it appear as though any event were ordained by God, thereby reinforcing the notion that God chose them to settle New England. In turn, as Wharton suggests, the audience of sea deliverance shipwreck narratives "were called on to bear witness to God's Providence in the experience of the writer and in the life and history of the community" (33). God guided them aboard their ships as they planned how to govern themselves when on land, and God guided their commitment to one another during trials at sea. The compact the colonists made carries the name of the ship that brought them there, and early settlers were warned that a breach of the contract made between God and the "city on the hill" would result in the sinking of their ship—the symbol of their government, their families, their religion, and their community. Thus, stories of ships and trials at sea found their way into origin myths and the sermonizing of early American leaders eager to define the moral ideals of a community believed to be exceptional.

⸺⧼⧽⸺

The experiences of early Americans were formulated into lessons that taught colonists to submit and remain obedient to an all-powerful God, for to do so was to ascribe to the idea that God had chosen them as the settlers of the new world. Throughout the following decades, such didactic lessons were not always consistent, but the interest in sea narratives did not abate after the Puritans were firmly established on land. With the rise of print culture throughout the eighteenth century, sea adventure and shipwreck accounts appeared in newspapers, magazines, anthologies, broadsides, and plays. Maritime dramas, such as William Congreve's *Love for Love* and Tobias Smollett's *The Reprisal*, were performed in New York and Philadelphia, respectively, in the middle of the century. Isaac Bickerstaffe's operetta *Thomas and Sally*, which contains nautical characters, was produced seven times in Philadelphia in the latter half of the century, and J. C. Cross's comedy *The Purse; or, The*

Benevolent Tar was produced eight times between 1795 and 1797. Americans contributed their own nautical drama with the New York production of *The American Citizen* in 1787, which told the tale of the *Empress of China*, the first U.S. ship to fly the American flag in Chinese waters. These dramas perhaps influenced the publication of the earliest American example of prose fiction containing nautical themes, including shipwreck, *The History of Constantius and Pulchera; or Constancy Rewarded*, published in Boston in 1794.[10] By the early 1800s, James Fenimore Cooper launched his first bid at popular success with nautical novels of shipwreck and intrigue (*The Pilot*, *The Red Rover*, *Water-Witch*), while Edgar Allan Poe and Herman Melville took readers to sea with "Descent into the Maelstrom," "MS in a Bottle," *Narrative of Arthur Gordon Pym*, *Typee*, *Mardi*, and *Moby-Dick*.

Both Americans and Britons were consistently interested in shipwreck narratives, which were often published at the same time in both America and England. John and Jasper Dean and Miles Whitworth's account of the wreck of the *Nottingham Galley* was published in Boston in 1726, as was Joseph Bailey's tale of shipwreck (New York, 1750), Nathaniel Pierce's account of the wreck of the *Portsmouth* (Boston, 1756), Barnabas Downs's narrative of his shipwreck aboard a privateer (Yarmouthport, 1786), Jonas Clark's account (Boston, 1788), and Benjamin Stout's *Narrative of the loss of the ship Hercules* (Hudson NY, 1798).[11] By 1806 nearly two hundred shipwreck narratives were made available to the American public.[12] Some shipwreck narratives were so recognizable that an American periodical, *The Portfolio*, swiftly identified in 1822 the shipwreck section in the second canto of Lord Byron's *Don Juan* as being "plagiarized" from such shipwreck narratives as *Loss of the ship Hercules*, *Loss of the Centaur man of war*, and *Wreck of the ship Sydney*, to name but a few.[13] The Briton William Falconer's long poem *The Shipwreck* (1762) had appeared in the United States in at least twenty-four editions by 1843. One of the most famous shipwreck narratives of the time, James Riley's *Authentic Narrative of the loss of the American brig Commerce, wrecked on the western coast of Africa*, was read by a young boy named Abraham Lincoln and is said to have influenced his opinion of slavery (Huntress 106). Exaggerated "sea yarns," including shipwreck narratives, were commonly available in the popular journals of the first half of the nineteenth century, such as *Knickerbocker*, *Burton's*, *Graham's*, and *Ladies Companion* (Egan 72).

Though Puritans saw ships and shipwreck imagery as important components of their sermons, the proliferation of eighteenth and nineteenth-century sea narratives arose for both secular and nonsecular reasons, especially after the American Revolutionary War. For one, most Americans lived along the Atlantic seaboard. Families were left ashore for months at a time while a husband, father, son, and sometimes mother or sister made a trip to the West Indies, Europe, England, or even China, or simply up and down the coast. It was an age when families waited for letters and news about friends or family from Africa, Germany, Ireland, England, and other European countries and a time when the emigration experience was still fresh, if not ingrained, in the minds of many Americans. In fact, shipwreck accounts may have influenced emigrants' decision to sail for the United States. Widespread reporting of shipwrecks in nearly every newspaper may have caused the ebb in emigration to the United States in the late 1830s (Koch 81), a rare phenomenon during the nineteenth century. Shipwreck narratives served as sources of information, showing how others met with perils at sea. Readers could even learn survival strategies, such as lashing oneself to a mast during a storm to keep from falling overboard, or that light patches of water signaled land or dangerous shoals nearby.

Aside from their practical appeal, shipwreck narratives had the potential to build community among an audience. Shipwreck was a disaster everyone experienced in some way, either directly or by way of family and friends, and the accounts of these disasters facilitated a shared sympathy among Americans. These were the types of stories that united disparate backgrounds into a common experience. A New England broadside of 1792, *The True Account of the Loss of the Ship Columbia*, makes explicit the communal need to collectively sympathize with shipwreck victims:

From hence this lesson learn, that all our joys
Are but delusive, vain and empty toys,
Yet 'tis allow'd the sympathetic tear,
Must drop, and yield to natures tender care.
(Qtd. in Wharton 52)

Much like earlier Puritan versions of shipwreck narratives, which persuade audiences to preserve the colony's covenant with God, sentimental eighteenth-century versions such as this poem suggest that audiences should sympathize with one another. Influenced by the growth of sentimentality, post-Revolution American readers were prompted to feel sympathy for fellow Americans who had died in a shipwreck, thus preserving a kind of covenant to the community.

This sympathy for shipwreck victims derived some of its efficacy from the attitudes toward the ships themselves. Ships were as important to the lives of many Americans as those who went aboard them, and they were likewise celebrated in literature. By the end of the eighteenth century, most residents along the Atlantic were likely to have had an economic investment in ships, shipbuilding, and/or trade. The U.S. shipping industry came to hold such international prominence that American-made ships were used to fight in the Revolution under British flags. American naval technology extended to undersea crafts when American David Bushnell invented a one-man, hand-powered submarine, the Turtle, which allegedly attempted an attack on the British HMS Eagle in New York harbor in 1776.[14] When President Madison listed five reasons for going to war with England the second time around, four of the reasons "involved illegal acts at sea" (Egan 64). Any kind of challenge to mobility, or commercial interests counter to American trade practices, then, were possible causes for war. This protective pride likewise reveals itself in nationalist literature connecting American mercantilism and the sea, initially in the form of poetry by writers such as Philip Freneau.

As one of the earliest American popular poets, Freneau often chose ships and sea narratives as topics for his writing. Not surprisingly, he was influenced by William Bradford's writing and was so fascinated by Columbus's explorations that he constructed his own version of Columbus's landing in "The Rising Glory of America." This popular poem, taking a cue form Bradford, perpetuates the Puritan belief in the "chosen" status of Americans.[15] Throughout his life Freneau published sea songs and poetry derived from his experiences with the sea and ships, including his final edition of poetry appearing in 1815. Thus, his biography tells us that both his reading and firsthand experiences relied on ships and the sea as touchstones to an American experience, and his chosen subjects solidify connections between himself and Columbus and Bradford, two of the earliest American mythmakers.[16] Overall, most of Freneau's poetry about ships illustrates how post-Revolutionary writers distilled America's chosen status into the commercial success of its ships.

In "The Rising Glory of America," Freneau conflates America's status as a maritime culture with fifteenth-century Spain's and asserts the colonialist supposition that the indigenous peoples are unsophisticated compared to a nation reliant on sea trade. According to Freneau, the natives are:

unskill'd to raise the lofty mast,
Or force the daring prow thro' adverse waves.

His theory becomes more explicit later in the poem, when he pronounces:

Strip Commerce of her sail, and men once more
Would be converted into savages—No nation e'er grew social and
   refined
Till Commerce first had wing'd the adventurous prow.
(11)

Freneau identifies sea commerce as an activity Anglo-Americans excelled in from the very beginning of their shipbuilding efforts, representative of the road to nationhood. In Freneau's line about the "savages," the road to nationhood is assumed to be paved by the unbalanced opposition between the civilized and the savage.

As long as commerce by sea is a nation's primary objective, says Freneau, America will not revert back to a "savage" state.

These sentiments, as Robert Berkhofer Jr. explains, "became a staple of American literature," beginning with Freneau, and contributed to later "romantic" convictions that the Indian was fading from view because of "the onslaught of civilization" (88). Though at times Freneau attempts a critique of colonization, he interprets shipping as evidence of Anglo-America's, and not Native America's, inevitable progression toward nationhood. He is clearly filled with pride for the United States, a nation best represented by her ships. In a gesture of patriotism, Freneau describes the awesome presence of the U.S. frigate *Alliance* and its imagined effect on other countries like France and Spain, who see the ship's name as a fitting representation of the "union" of the United States. Furthermore, the ship's American flag serves to "[i]nvite the old world to the new" (35). As Freneau makes clear in this poem and others, American ships are American beacons, the emblem of the transfer from old to new. And as the ship's name indicates, the ship is emblematic of unity, of community, of nation.[17] Eighteenth-century pride in America's ships extended the trajectory of early Puritan leaders who saw their settlement as a ship of state ordained by God. Their conviction was fortified by nationalist writers like Freneau who claimed the United States' was an exceptional civilization, superior to natives and other nations alike, because of its lofty masts and commercial success at sea.

Clearly then, as Freneau's work and the hundreds of shipwreck narratives, plays, and novels published in the early nineteenth century illustrate, the Atlantic and America's ships began to be characters in a developing drama of Anglo-American progress and success. I use the identifying mark of "Anglo-American" because for the most part, published African American stories of disasters at sea were rare, though, as I argue in an upcoming chapter, the suffering during the Middle Passage represents an American experience like no other. As Carla Mulford's definition makes clear, a nation, or social imaginary, is not necessarily unified or homogenous, and the narratives that contribute to a national identity may likewise be derived from notions of nationhood different from the dominant group's.[18] The writer and activist Olaudah Equiano saw the symbolic potential for the shipwreck narrative, a potential that could launch his own drama of success in the African American and transatlantic abolitionist community.[19] By dramatizing his own individual strengths during shipwreck to his audience, Equiano not only strengthens the abolitionist cause but also provides one of the best illustrations of the changes emerging in shipwreck narratives taking place by the end of the eighteenth century. Equiano's survival represents both an abolitionist message of confidence in the natural capacities of all black people and the growing Enlightenment conviction that individuals have power over their own fate. It is not surprising, then, that Equiano's story provides the foundation for future African American autobiography in the nineteenth century (Gates xii–xiv) and serves as an early precedent for a new theme in successive shipwreck narratives: the power of the individual.

Equiano's existence was consistently connected to the sea. Though his life at sea begins involuntarily when he is taken aboard a slave ship, his narrative reveals an ongoing attachment to sailing aboard ships, even after he buys himself out of slavery. For a man who could barely describe the "scene[s] of horror almost inconceivable" aboard the slave ship, he would one day choose to work aboard ships, very often of necessity, but a remarkable choice nonetheless (41).[20] Equiano likely went to sea for various reasons, not the least of which was the fact that working aboard ships was one of the few lines of work open to free black men in the eighteenth and early nineteenth centuries.[21] He was familiar with life aboard ships from his days as a slave and though always potentially in danger of being illegally sold into slavery again on the high seas, Equiano perhaps saw taking that risk as preferable to low-paying and menial jobs ashore.

Also, ships shape Equiano's character throughout his life. His first time aboard a ship as a slave prompts him to redefine the conceptions of place and community that would later serve him well during his travels as a seaman. When he is captured in Africa as a boy, as Sharon M. Harris points out, it is aboard the slave ship that Equiano experiences the "impetus for his own redefinition of place as a specific sense of community" (17). Place becomes an idea defined by a mental geography rather than a physical one. As idea, Equiano's community—his family and friends in Nigeria—need not be left behind or replaced solely by his fellow prisoners, who are forced by circumstance to exist within an oppressed community. Rather, the space of the ship and Equiano's misery require him to identify a place where "the manners and customs of my country had been implanted in me with great care, and made an impression on my mind which time could not erase, and which all the adversity and variety of fortune I have since experienced served only to rivet and record" (qtd. in Harris 18). Later, when Equiano is free and takes to the sea as a career, this sense of himself as rooted in community emerges when he reinforces his ties to Africans during a challenging test of his will and commitment to community—a shipwreck.

Soon after a voyage that proves Equiano to be a knowledgeable navigator, Equiano sets sail for Georgia with a cargo of slaves. Earlier in the voyage, Equiano had cursed at the ship while doing the exhausting work of pumping water. When the sloop becomes wedged in rocks and appears to be about to sink along the Bahama Banks, Equiano claims his sins "stared me in the face," for he believed "God had hurled his direful vengeance on my guilty head for cursing the vessel on which my life depended" (113). He believes it is his fault when the captain orders the hatches to be nailed down on the slaves in the hold, who would then be trapped and drowned when the ship went under. Risking punishment for insubordination, Equiano steps forward and claims that the captain's bad navigation has led to the ship's distress. Following Equiano's complaint, the hatches are not nailed down.

While the rest of the crew gets drunk, Equiano and several others go to work putting together the small boat brought along for such emergencies. By morning, Equiano and only four others willing to help—three black men and a Dutch creole sailor—volunteer to row toward a small island. This is arduous work, for they often must get out and carry the boat onto the shallow reef, which tears the flesh of their hands. Nevertheless, Equiano returns to the ship five times to haul away the drunken lot, for he feels that "God would charge me with their lives" if he did not help them (115). Not a single person dies. Reflecting on the rescue, Equiano tells the reader: "I could not help looking on myself as the principal instrument in effecting our deliverance"(114).

Several images ring both familiar and dissonant in this section of his autobiography, which has essentially become a shipwreck narrative. In the context of the typical shipwreck narrative, the recognition of God's hand in the wreck and repentance for one's sins is a familiar characteristic. Like most narrators of shipwreck stories, Equiano consistently worries about the costs of displeasing God and expresses regret for any past sins. The human reaction aboard the slave ship is another common feature of shipwreck narratives. Equiano makes it clear that the captain secured the slaves in the hold so the lifeboat would be available for the captain and officers only, while the crew gets helplessly drunk. Equiano's appeal for God's forgiveness in the midst of human cowardice is typical of many eighteenth-century representations of shipwreck.

But Equiano was an intellectual man of the Enlightenment who wrestled with the competing theories of predestination and the role of good deeds in the salvation of one's soul. Before the shipwreck, he says he had always lived his life as a "predestinarian," though he found it difficult to accept this position if his "fate" was to be enslaved (88). So he addresses this dilemma by praying and "us[ing] every honest means, and endeavor[ing] all that was possible" to gain his freedom (89). He embodies this philosophy during the shipwreck: Equiano believes God is punishing him with shipwreck for cursing His name, yet he feels driven to take action to save all aboard. Though Equiano would eventually come to identify with Methodists and the doctrine of salvation, he represents his experiences from the perspective of both a Calvinist and an individual conscious of his own self, independent of God's will.[22]

Equiano's behavior during the shipwreck highlights how shipwreck narratives can teach not just lessons of providential power, as in the Thacher shipwreck when all submitted to God's will, but also the power of individual will. Equiano takes action and criticizes the captain for his bad judgment and for his failure of duty toward the ship and crew. Equiano proceeds to take personal responsibility for every person's survival aboard his ship. Most significant is how he casts his and the others' survival. Whereas the previous generation of shipwreck victims would see God's hand in their survival (or failure to survive), Equiano congratulates *himself* for saving the ship, her crew, and the passengers. He calls himself "the principal instrument in effecting our deliverance" (114). He clearly sees his own actions as the primary reason the rest of the people on the ship survived, even using the word *deliverance*, a heavily loaded term usually associated with the will of God, not man.

Along with most critics, I read Equiano's narrative as spiritual autobiography (Sollors, Potkay) antislavery propaganda (Gates, Ito), and travel narrative (Murphy), but in the context of this study of sea narratives, I see the climax of the autobiography arising out of the shipwreck narrative portion of his autobiography. This section of his story dramatizes the moments that cause him to act for the sake of the community aboard the ship and the larger community of black slaves when he serves as the "principal" actor in their rescue. This rescue is the climax of his story because nearly all of the autobiography's personal and political issues converge: from the opening scene on the slave ship when he redefines his space as a place of community, to the defining moments when he is named twice, to his abolitionist hope that audiences will read his actions as proof of the potential of all black people. Equiano's awareness of the importance of his actions during the wreck illustrates how shipwreck narratives were beginning to foreground human will and courage rather than the role of Providence in survival.

As discussed earlier, Equiano's capture aboard the slave ship at the beginning of his story was an assault on his body. But Equiano explains that he brought with him the memories of his fellow Nigerians, the idea of which sustains him in the enslaving space of the ship by convincing him he is part of a larger African community. Later, in the climactic shipwreck scene when Equiano takes control of the rescue, the slaves aboard the ship are reminders of his past enslavement. He identifies with their entrapment below the decks and takes on the responsibility of getting all safely to shore. Even though working aboard a slave ship would have required Equiano to distance himself from the slaves' plight (if he was to remain in the employ of the captain), he nevertheless works for the slaves when the ship is wrecked. The space he once saw as confining but connected to his friends and family he now sees as extensions of his past that must be rescued. His efforts reveal his connection to a black community larger than himself and his willingness to sustain the connection by rescuing other Africans.

In turn, the recognition of his own power to save himself and an entire community of people is symbolized by his names. Equiano lives up to his African name and personalizes his slave name during the shipwreck scene. Early on in his narrative, Equiano describes the significance of his African name. He explains that Olaudah "signifies vicissitude or fortune also, one favored, and having a loud voice and well spoken" (27). His second name, Gustavus Vassa, is given to him by his new master aboard a ship bound for England, a name he initially protested. As Adam Potkay recounts, Vassa was a "sixteenth-century Swedish patriot who freed his country from Danish tyranny" and was made into a much hallowed and famous figure by Henry Brooke's play, *Gustavus Vasa, the Deliverer of His Country* (684). Britons such as Samuel Johnson "viewed Gustavus as a hero who stands firm against tyranny and corruption; who puts the political good of his people above all else" (684–85). Both names are in the title of Equiano's book, which suggests that they are meaningful to him, and both names surface in his shipwreck narrative.

As the ship founders and Equiano's rescue begins, he embodies his African first name, Olaudah. He has a "loud voice" and is "favored" as the savior of others. As the ship gets tossed about on the rocks and the captain orders the hatches to be nailed down, Equiano can not keep silent. As mentioned earlier in the summary, he tells the captain "he deserved drowning for not knowing how to navigate the vessel," and it is implied that Equiano's protest is what keeps the hatches from being nailed down (113). He fulfills the meaning of his African name; his well-spoken protest saves others from being drowned. What Equiano couldn't do during the Middle Passage, he does aboard a ship in another time, another place. As well-spoken as he is, he also typifies "one who is favored." Alluding to Christian symbolism, Equiano is at times reminiscent of Christ. For example, as he saves each individual aboard the ship, even those who have been sinful, his hands bleed when scraped against the reef. Like Christ, who was favored by God to save humankind with his crucifixion, Equiano's injurious rescue efforts illustrate his favored status as the "principal instrument" in the "deliverance" of those on board his ship.

Equiano's actions allude to the legacy of his adopted name as well. While fulfilling the definition of a well-spoken and favored man, he also embodies the identity of the historical Gustavus Vasa known for defeating tyrants and putting others' needs before his own. The African Gustavus defeats the tyrannical captain by defying orders to lock the slaves below deck, thereby putting the good of his people above all else. In more ways than one, then, Equiano proves he can live up to his name and that his will is equal to the will that imposed on him the name of Gustavus. During the shipwreck, Equiano defines himself—names himself—through his actions. It is appropriate, then, that the only two illustrations in his autobiography are his portrait and a sketch of his shipwreck. Both define who he is.

While his actions during the wreck define the contours of his identity, Equiano's story also has far-reaching implications beyond his own flesh. The autobiography was published during the second half of the eighteenth century, when scientific racialism and a belief in inherent racial characteristics were beginning to challenge the predominant view that "mankind in general was capable of indefinite improvement" (Horsman 104). Though most philosophers and anthropologists were convinced human beings were of the same species, a growing number of thinkers perpetuated the idea that blacks exhibited innate physical and character traits that made them inferior to Caucasians.[23] Philosophers such as Immanuel Kant were proclaiming, "[T]he Negro is . . . lazy, soft and dawdling," while others categorized blacks as inherently "indolent, negligent . . . [and] governed by caprice."[24] Although "chosen" Europeans believed the shipwreck was their stamp of Christian authenticity, Equiano uses the shipwreck narrative to show his audience that a black man can also be strong, self-sacrificing, stricken by conscience, and chosen by God to be tested. Furthermore, his account proves that blacks can act on Christian values, have a sense of personal and communal responsibility, and can be good "citizens;" therefore, they can be free.[25] Though these messages were indeed bold, the elements of a shipwreck narrative—premonitions of doom, the chaos on deck during shipwreck, appeals to Providence, and methods of survival—provided familiar themes to an audience perhaps uncomfortable with Equiano's message. Equiano surreptitiously utilizes the tradition of the shipwreck narrative to articulate antislavery appeals through a description of the actions of a black man. His rhetoric is in his actions, which are motivated by morals that are then assumed by the entire black community.

Equiano's narrative is essential to a study of American sea narratives because his tale artfully exposes the seeming contradiction between Calvinist theology and Enlightenment faith in human potential, and provides the opportunity for showcasing an individual's moral responsibility to his community. His actions serve as proof to late eighteenth-century rationalists of man's "innate goodness, free will, and reasonableness" (McLoughlin 99). Though post–Jonathan Edwards eighteenth-century religious thinkers would continue to assert man's inherent depravity and the necessity of God's grace, other American rationalist writers such as Thomas Jefferson claimed "the human constitution was . . . endowed with a comfortable combination of sense, reason, morality, and capacity for improvement in the favoring American environment" (Curti 103). By the late eighteenth and early nineteenth century, sea narratives often depicted these seemingly contrary perspectives.

As the nineteenth century began, representations of storms at sea and shipwreck typically highlighted either God as the sole determinant of one's fate at sea or the power of the individual to influence his own survival through intelligent and moral choices.

In a broadside describing the wreck of the *Charles* in 1807 off of the coast of Portland, Maine, Thomas Shaw mentions "GOD" (in capital letters) over a dozen times in his short poem, where God's hand in the wreck is made explicit:

> *Young men and maidens did the same [fall into the sea and die],*
> *And lost their lives, and wealth, and fame.*
> *Thus young and old together went,*
> *As if it were GOD's great intent*
> *That they should die, and be no more*
> *Upon this life's tempestuous shore.*

Shaw's emphasis on God as an all-powerful source of shipwreck is mirrored in a review of *Robinson Crusoe* in an early American periodical. A reviewer of a new edition claims that "the dormant fancy of thousands" was aroused by DeFoe's "warm, simple, and beautiful reference of all the events of life to a gracious and over-ruling Providence; patience under misfortunes; the whole circle of such Christian duties as could be practiced in so contracted a sphere."[26] Here again, Crusoe, thrown from a ship and forced to survive like a shipwreck victim, is interpreted as a man whose life is determined by Providence.

However, as Olaudah Equiano's narrative illustrates, God's influence on shipwrecks was often tempered by the rationalist impulse to identify the effects that human reason and morality had on an individual's survival. For example, the anonymous poem "The Voyage" aims at giving advice to a young man about to emigrate to England. The poet advises that when the sea is calm, "The light of Heaven / Smiles on it," but when the seas roar, "the wise *may* suffer wreck, / The foolish *must*." These lines suggest one's own intellect can determine the fate of a ship; wisdom improves the odds of survival. The poem goes on to suggest that the young man must learn from those knowledgeable of the sea that morals can likewise keep one's boat afloat. The narrator claims the individual must learn "[t]o station quick-eyed *Prudence* at the helm, / To guard your sail from passion's sudden blasts, / And make firm *principle* your magnet guide" (53).[27] Rather than relying on God, an individual must be a principled and prudent passenger to survive the perils of life at sea and, implicitly, on land as well.

As revealed in these reviews, poems, and shipwreck narratives, sea and sea narratives had taken on a new shape by the end of the eighteenth century. Originally appearing as narratives proving God's hand in the settling of America by Anglo colonists, stories of sea disasters began to reflect evolving philosophies of human potential. Writers like Olaudah Equiano and poets publishing in newspapers and magazines began to credit (or discredit) the character of ship-wreck victims, holding them partly responsible for the choices they made when disaster struck. On one hand, post-Revolutionary Americans were more invested than ever in relying on stories that reflected their special nature to other nations, especially England. On the other hand, ironically, the shipwreck narrative as national narrative, as it was used in the colonial age, was in danger. Surviving shipwreck no longer indicated a covenant with God, because an individual's fate was no longer seen as solely in the hands of God; instead, it was under the influence of other human beings. Humans, as Equiano expresses so frankly, could indeed see themselves "as the principal instrument in effecting our deliverance." Such a shift could very well have sent the lessons learned from seventeenth and eighteenth-century narratives of calamity at sea to the dustbins of nationalistic rhetoric. The logic could have gone like this: If Providence is on comparable footing with humans when disaster strikes at sea, there is no especial grace to be bestowed specifically on Americans. Being that the early nineteenth century was a time when the United States could little afford losing such a self-ag-grandizing myth, the American metaphor of the shipwreck was in danger of falling apart, even though ships were more important than ever and shipwrecks increased in number. How could the role of Providence be revised in a narrative that once depended on it for its nationalistic import? How could the genre accommodate God's control of one's destiny and the individual's will to survive?

What eventually came to be key to the perpetuation of sea narra-tives as a form of nationalistic rhetoric, and was likely also respon-sible for their increasing popularity throughout the first half of the nineteenth century, was the growing presence of women within them. Increasingly, women appeared in shipwreck narratives as passengers, companions, wives, and emigrants at sea, and waiting maidens and widows ashore. Women were already part of the vocabulary of both the sea and the nation; ships and country were represented by a feminine pronoun. Within paintings, poems, and tales of peril at sea, in firsthand accounts and in works of fiction by both men and women, women came to embody, in a variety of ways, both Providence and nation, both godly and human virtue. As women literally became more visible in maritime dramas, they affected the nation's attempts to imagine itself as an exceptional community.

2

Women and Children First

In an early nineteenth-century published letter to her sister in
Boston, Sarah Allen narrates a tale of a frightful calamity at sea
and on land. In *A Narrative of the Shipwreck and Unparalleled Sufferings
of . . . Sarah Allen*, dated July 2, 1816, Allen describes how her journey
from New York to New Orleans to join her husband takes a terrible turn. When a storm batters the already leaking ship during
the evening and drives it on a rock, the vessel is forced to lie nearly
on its side. Soon thereafter, another burst from the storm rights
the ship, but since it is badly damaged and about to sink, Allen
and the others struggle in the darkness to get to the rocky shore.
Amazed to have survived such a harrowing disaster, everyone in
the party drops to their knees to "offer up [their] thanksgivings
to Heaven, for having still preserved [them] alive even in such a
deplorable situation" (8). They go on to ask "Providence to complete
its miracle" by assisting them in finding a safe place to stay (9).
The wonder and thrill of their survival do not last long, however,
for new challenges face them. Allen claims that they landed on a
"wild and probably uninhabited coast" (most likely the coast of
Florida) (9–10), and the party of survivors, of which she is the only
woman, must attempt to "penetrate a wild and pathless forest"
(11). Finally, after nearly succumbing to swelling bug bites, the
weary party is found and taken in by friendly Native Americans
who feed them and take them to a town where they gain passage
to New York.

Allen's narrative is a harrowing tale of terrible personal trial. Though this female-authored shipwreck narrative is one of the first of its kind, the shipwreck narrative as a genre had been around for a long time. As illustrated in chapter 1, hundreds of shipwreck accounts were published by the mid-nineteenth century. Pre–Revolutionary War audiences looked for signs that God had chosen survivors to justify their perceived status as the "elect." However, by the end of the eighteenth century, Enlightenment philosophy and the rise of individualism began to alter American perceptions of God's providence. Humans were now believed to be capable of reason and intelligence, which made individuals responsible for their own actions. Though audiences continued to search for God's presence in sea narratives, they also began to scrutinize the moral choices people made when their own and other passengers' lives were at risk. These moral choices were even more freighted when women were aboard.[1]

By the middle of the nineteenth century, middle-class Anglo women were consistently conceived of as the moral and Christian strongholds of the home. When their lives were imperiled at sea, women became holy surrogates for God, and the suspense of shipwreck narratives arose over men's choice of whether to save women—who represented America's covenant with God—or themselves. The desire to judge men's behavior toward women and children in distress was a response to increasing anxiety over whether American men could maintain control of the self-interested passions that could endanger a democracy. In demonstrating the necessity to suppress selfish passions and save "women and children first," shipwreck narratives dramatized the need to preserve the nation's covenant with God and citizens' bonds with each other, as the post-Revolution country moved forward with a government that stressed the rights of the individual. In other words, saving women and children first became analogous to saving the exceptional nature of the nation.

Sarah Allen's shipwreck account, most likely fiction, was seemingly molded to allude to America's historical covenant with God.[2] Her story echoes Puritan sermons reminding Americans of their

1. Sarah Allen kneeling on a rock after her shipwreck. Frontispiece from *A Narrative of the Shipwreck and Sufferings of Mrs. Sarah Allen*, 1816. Courtesy of the Nantucket Historical Association (RB910.452 A429 1816).

covenant and the qualities necessary to the young nation's survival. First, the rendering of the passengers' experience reads like the Pilgrims' landing on Plymouth Rock, a story enjoying a great deal of attention by the turn of the nineteenth century.[3] The harkening back to New England myths of origin is apparent in the first image we see of Sarah Allen. The frontispiece to the book displays a woman on shore praying on a rock, while behind her, a ship founders. Like the pilgrims of William Bradford's narrative and those surviving the shipwrecks in Increase Mather's *Remarkable Providences*, Allen proclaims that she is thankful God has chosen her for this calamitous test, during which she "resigned [her] life to the Being who had lent it" (6). The rocky shore and the rock she kneels on to give thanks in the frontispiece are subtle reminders of the story of the Pilgrims' landing on Plymouth Rock.

Furthermore, Allen repeatedly explains that they are left to face a "wild coast," "wild beasts," and a "pathless forest," again recalling Bradford's famous description of the Pilgrims' first sight of a "hideous and desolate wilderness, full of wild beasts and wild men" (62).[4] Facing the same coast as her forefathers, Allen asks God to "complete its miracle" by preserving their lives and helping them find a "hospitable dwelling," or, rather, a clearing in the wilderness, the same thing desired by her Pilgrim ancestors (6). Though the party suffers in the wilderness, they remain determined to survive and refuse to abandon Allen even when she feels too weak to move on. Finally, the local tribe of Native Americans comes to their relief. Much like the Puritans, these shipwreck survivors give thanks to God on landing, confront a wilderness, form bonds of group loyalty, and receive aid from the natives.

Allen makes clear that the nation's historical covenant with God can be rehearsed again and again when Americans, particularly women, are in distress. But why is it that Allen, and, as we shall see later, Anglo women, were the ones prompting the memory of this covenant? Why doesn't the captain or a crew member tell the story of survival? Sarah Allen's frailty as the rescued woman summons male heroism. Further, as a female narrator, she suits nineteenth-century readers' expectation of the sentimental narrative style. Though Allen stresses that she did her best to press on once she survived the wreck, it was the crew and captain who never let her quit. With Allen as narrator, the story can emphasize the camaraderie and loyalty the men show her throughout the ordeal, whereas if the men had told the story, they would risk sounding like braggarts. Also, a female narrator could use sentimental vocabulary and images to portray the men's loyalty. For instance, Allen claims the captain and crew shed tears for her suffering. When she collapses and feels like she will die, the captain "took [her] hands between his, and pressed them with the utmost tenderness" and assures her that he will not abandon her (19). The tears, the hand-holding, and the tenderness add sentimental coloring to the admirable behavior of Allen's fellow male survivors. The audience would find these men all the more appealing for the tender way they made Allen's life their responsibility, putting her welfare before their own. Their actions as characterized from a woman's perspective reveal how the covenant with God is upheld by her community.

Such heroics might not recall that covenant were someone other than a woman being saved. The salvation of women at sea symbolized America's apparent devotion to preserving women's role as cultural icons. In saving women, Americans were preserving the nation's covenant with God. By the beginning of the nineteenth century, middle- and upper-class Anglo-American womanhood was evolving into a sentimentalized metaphor for America's seemingly innate Christian character. White women came to represent hearth and home, and the accompanying values of loyalty to family, faith in God, and heartfelt morality. However, little critical attention has been paid to how these values gained cultural currency through representations of women at sea.

A good place to begin the discussion is through looking at the simple visual representations found in emblem books, because these were commonly found in middle-class homes and the emblems within them were likely recognizable to a wide audience. Similar to the emblem books popular throughout western Europe in the fifteenth, sixteenth, and seventeenth centuries, emblem books published in the United States in the nineteenth century most often presented a series of emblems that appeared as drawings and were accompanied by a short poem or explanation of the scene pictured as the emblem.[5] A look at some of the emblems reveals a consistent theme of women's loyalty to husbands and God in images connecting them to the sea.

Often, women are sketched as emblems of Hope or Faith, figures who keep men—and the nation—anchored to Christian principles. In an oft-reprinted antebellum emblem book, for instance, Hope, a woman, is one of the "symbols of Christian faith" (13), and as such, she leans on (and is equated with) an anchor.[6] The purpose

Till we all come in the unity of the Faith.   Ephes. iv. 13.

SYMBOLS OF CHRISTIAN FAITH.

See on the right, all glorious *Hope* doth stand,
And gives to heavenly *Truth* the plighted hand :
With Seraph's wings out-spread, *Love* stands between :
And binds their hearts with his celestial chain.
These are *Faith's* emblems ;—These its Parents three :
To produce Faith, *Hope, Truth,* and *Love* agree.

2. Emblem of Truth, Love, and Hope, who is leaning on an anchor. From *Religious Emblems*, by William Holmes and John W. Barber (Cincinnati: Henry Howe, 1855). Courtesy of the University of Chicago Library.

Which hope we have as an anchor of the soul, both sure and steadfast.
Heb. vi. 19.———*For we are saved by hope.*   Rom. viii. 24.

HOPE.

On Truth's substantial rock, Hope takes her seat,
While waves tumultuous dash against her feet;
The sky with blackness now becomes o'erspread;
The tempest threatens her devoted head:
Louder, and louder still, the thunders sound;
The lightning flings its fearful glare around;
Creation trembles; but fast anchored there
Hope sits unshaken, never in despair;
With eyes turned upward, whence her help descends,
She waits expecting, till the tempest ends.

3. Emblem of Hope seated on a rock by the sea. From *Religious Emblems*, by
William Holmes and John W. Barber (Cincinnati: Henry Howe, 1855). Courtesy
of the University of Chicago Library.

31

for her pose with an anchor is further explained in figure 3, where Hope is seated on a rock by the tempestuous sea, "unshaken, never in despair; / With eyes turned upward, whence her help descends." The emblem's caption deems it appropriate for Hope to lean on an anchor because "the world is like a tempestuous sea." Though the storm rages on, if the ship is "seaworthy" and "the anchor bites . . . into good holding ground," the ship will "ride out the gale" (89). Like a good American woman who keeps her husband and family anchored during life's storms, the anchor Hope "does not remove trouble; it sustains the soul in the time of trouble. The anchor . . . does not dispel the storm; it does not quiet the roaring waves, arrest the rolling thunder, nor bid the winds be still: but it enables the vessel to ride out the fury of the gale" (89).

It is evident throughout this depiction that women's perceived strengths conjoined nicely with images of the sea. Though simplistic, the messages in these emblems supported contemporary theories about women's character. The emblems suggest women's role in the "American Experiment": though women did not have the all-controlling powers of God to "dispel the storm," nevertheless, as moral beings, they could provide spiritual stability and hope for the preservation of the souls of their loved ones. Although women were not a replacement for God at sea, they were certainly holy surrogates. Such an emblem of feminine faith is expressed in the Reverend E. P. Rogers's sermon after the wreck of the *Central America* in 1857. He proclaims that belief in God provides an "anchorage for Faith, a place where she can cling, and look up amid the jarring elements, and say, 'Even so, Father, for so it seemeth good in thy sight'" (17). Faith, a female, is likewise the emblem of the anchor of belief, who holds steady the connection between the physical and spiritual worlds.

Thus, when Sarah Allen's fellow shipwrecked souls save her life and sustain her will to live—in a setting reminiscent of the landing at Plymouth Rock—they are exhibiting much more than kindness. They are saving the image of women's unwavering faith in God, loyalty to family, and commitment to community—a covenant believed to have been at the core of the Pilgrims' mission. Similar to the Pilgrims, the captain and crew withstood the journey to safety by sustaining the life of hope and faith. They were rescuing the heavily touted quality of "virtue" and sending a message about national priorities.

Preserving female emblems of national virtue would be at the core of most of the antebellum shipwreck narratives that followed Allen's. Allen's narrative recounts a story of success, a model of good American behavior, but many true shipwreck narratives involving women imparted much more complicated lessons made urgent by accounts of tragedy. Often, women in shipwreck narratives didn't survive; in fact, some of the most famous (and infamous) shipwreck accounts listed hundreds of women among the dead. Thus, narrators were presented with a dilemma that went something like this: what is to be made of the virtue of the nation when its symbol of faith, hope, and loyalty is allowed to perish in a disaster at sea? How does the death of a woman at sea affect America's self-image, its self-imposed contours of historically validated virtues? These anxious questions led to one of the most famous maritime and, by extension, cultural mantras of the nineteenth century: Women and children first. The maritime practice became an injunction that would solidify Anglo women's position as holy surrogates of God's grace on America and provide a standard for manhood and the nation.

⸺⁂⸺

To understand what was at stake when women were lost during shipwreck, let us first turn to some of the shipwreck accounts to see how women were represented during sea disasters. In published sermons, nonfiction accounts, and lithographs, the shipwrecked woman both titillated and taught. The dead shipwrecked woman had the potential to draw audiences intrigued by another's suffering and to teach moral backsliders that their time on earth was tenuous. Such was the case in a lithograph and published funeral sermon following the real wreck of the steamboat *Swallow*, which occurred on April 7, 1845. The wreck was of particular interest because a large number of women were lost. Of the approximately 259 people on board, nearly all of the drowned were women. In addition to newspaper accounts, two other lasting responses to the wreck surfaced. Around the same time that the Reverend William B. Sprague published a sermon he delivered at funeral services in Albany, New York, for four of the female victims, Nathaniel Currier printed a lithograph that reveals the titillation prompted by vulnerable middle-class ladies in distress. Juxtaposing the stories told by both word and picture provides a close look at how nineteenth-century culture interpreted female shipwreck victims.

Religious leaders utilized the female shipwreck victim as a pedagogical tool. In Reverend Sprague's sermon at the funeral of four female victims of the wreck, the pastor suggests that the death of these women serves as a lesson to others who are too self-interested to fear God and live a life of pious selflessness. Sprague uses a list to remind listeners of the tenuousness of their material good fortune. His list includes: "the brevity of human life—the uncertain and unsatisfying nature of earthly enjoyments—the dread realities of the eternal world—the relations of the present as a scene of trial to the future as a scene of retribution—[and] the importance of being always ready for the momentous change" (6). Underlying these lessons is an anxiety that Americans are too focused on themselves and will be too self-involved to interpret the moral consequences of their present-day lives when they find themselves in "the eternal world."

Sprague emphasizes that the recent shipwreck is "a scene of trial to the future." He renders the female shipwreck victims as models for his audience's future lives in eternity. Sprague takes these ladies to new heights, so to speak, by imagining the dead women's speeches from Heaven, where they celebrate their heavenly homecoming. The preacher imagines the two women to say: "'[I]f you knew how light a thing we found it to die, and how glorious a thing it is to live and reign here in the palace of the Great King . . . You could not weep'" (17). Likewise, Sprague suggests the audience should look up to (literally and figuratively) the dead shipwrecked women as models of pious selflessness for their lives on earth. In a description of two female victims, who were sisters, Sprague claims that they both "lived in the fear of God all the day long . . . lived . . . in habitual and intimate communion with Heaven" (16). Their piety serves as the foundation for their elevation to sentimental heroines. As is the case for the sentimental heroines of nineteenth-century novels, as Jane Tompkins has defined them, for these women, "the kingdom of heaven on earth [is posited] as a world over which women exercise ultimate control" (141). Thus, these sentimental, angelic sisters not only reigned on earth as heavenly beings but also "live and reign" in God's palace. They are not just subjects of the "Great King"; they reign along with him. Representations of American female shipwreck victims, then, make it appear that women's spiritual selves did not sink with the ship, for their devotion to God on earth landed them a berth in heaven.

In *Sentimental Democracy*, Andrew Burstein posits that a culture of sentiment and sympathy arose as "rational Christianity dissuaded many from a resort to miraculous cures or mere resignation to God's will . . . [and] a new emotional system took hold . . . [of] hope for progress from the scientific mind, a mastery over nature" (301). Though such an emotional system did indeed, as Burnstein suggests, turn away from a "mere resignation to God's will," representations of shipwrecked women make clear that pious women were an apt replacement for those experiencing a creeping doubt in Providential mastery. What made this cultural transition less threatening, especially when the seeming punishment of shipwreck invaded people's lives, was the growing reliance on the idealized woman to model both hope in a life on earth and hope for a life beyond. It was a method of "feminization" of antebellum religion, a process characterized by "a stress on feelings over reason, and a decline in harsh Calvinistic doctrines" (Haynes, "Women" 301).

The feelings evoked by shipwrecked women gained efficacy partly from the image of the dying woman. The dying woman in literature and art had the potential to elevate earthly misfortunes, such as shipwreck, to the realm of the sacred.[7] This way, when a ship went down, Providence would not wholly disappear. The shipwrecked woman, representing pious holiness akin to God, stimulates the audience's emotional attachment to a providential presence in their lives. In the case of the Swallow, when pious Anglo women died during a shipwreck, the mourning was as much for God's surrogates as it was for females from New York.

Sprague specifically remarks on the character of three of the young ladies, including Mary Anne Torrey, who possessed a most "exalted piety" (21). Though Mary's piety is appealing, or perhaps *because* her piety was appealing, the shipwrecked "lady" was likewise fascinating for the titillation that she provided. The well-known artist Nathaniel Currier created a lithograph, entitled *Mary*, that depicted the wreck of the Swallow. This 1845 portrait depicts a woman of leisure standing in what appears to be a drawing room or parlor. Her genteel suffering, signified by her slight lean on the chair, her handkerchief in hand, and her head demurely turned away from the painting on the wall, is contrasted with the shipwreck scene of chaos and horror in the painting in the background, which is entitled "Swallow." There is a kind of trebled voyeuristic agenda to this plate: the audience is looking in on a woman in the privacy of her parlor while the woman is acutely aware of the sight behind her. When Mary, the shipwreck victim, is recalled while looking at Currier's lithograph, the two Marys are transposed. The audience may have made a connection between the Mary of the print and Mary Anne Torrey, over whose body Sprague sermonized, and would perhaps be tantalized by the idea that just such a middle-class "lady" as Currier's Mary had been tossed about by the sinking ship and drowned. It may have been titillating to imagine the scenario of the suffering of a middle-class lady: her gown removed or wet and flattened against her body, her hair disheveled, her refinement reduced to base human reactions to a life-or-death emergency. Even the portrait subtly enacts the attraction/repulsion an audience might experience while looking at it. Though the painting evidently drew her into the room, the woman does not look at it; like her audience, she experiences a conflicted fascination with dead young women.

Though my reading of the appeal of Currier's lithograph is grotesque, the desire buried in the mourning for dead, innocent women

4. Nathaniel Currier's *Mary*, 1845. On the wall behind her is a picture of the wreck of the *Swallow*. Courtesy of the Mariners' Museum, Newport News VA.

was common in the nineteenth century. As Nancy Isenberg and Andrew Burstein explain in their study of death in early America, "[T]he social body of the state, constituted by common feelings and shared sympathies," expressed a "fascination with dead women. 'Stolen innocence' evoked the fear of sexual transgression and the peril faced by unprotected women" (8). The Swallow disaster killed innocent young women who could not be protected from disaster. Though their dead bodies were a source of mourning, so too was men's inability to protect them. Sprague emphasizes that the two sisters were unmarried and devoted to their father, Dr. Wood. The sisters wore rings given to them by their father; when he identified their bodies, he found them with these rings still on their fingers. Though rings given by a father symbolize a kind of marriage to his protection, he was unable to protect them from their own death, and their innocence was stolen from them by the perilous wreck. In addition to the young ladies' loss of life, the audience likely mourned the father's impotence when they needed his protection most: Though safe in her domestic sphere of parlor and home, Currier's Mary is nevertheless shadowed by a scene of "stolen innocence" and masculine helplessness behind her on the wall; the handkerchief dangling from her fingers may have just dabbed her eyes over the sadness of it all.

The admiration, fears, and anxieties surrounding shipwrecked females such as those aboard the Swallow originated in Anglo-American assumptions about piety, class, and race. In the nineteenth century, "women and children first" rarely applied to women of color or a lower class, as long as there were middle- and upper-class white women aboard. Class is apparent in Sprague's sermon. In describing the victims, he points out that Dr. Wood's two daughters were "young ladies of the most amiable and deserving characters, and had diligently and successfully improved every opportunity for the cultivation of their minds" (16). Likewise, Miss Mary Anne Torrey is described as "a young lady of excellent education of the most amiable dispositions and of exalted piety" (21). Clearly of the educated class, yet not so serious as to be of a strict disposition, Miss Torrey and the other victims are "deserving characters," made even more worthy of admiration by their class ranking among the refined and educated.

In addition to having the proper manners and education of white, middle-class women, these young "ladies," particularly the sisters, exemplified another attribute of the typical female shipwreck victim: loyalty. Torrey is reputed to have exhibited an "exalted piety," while the dead Wood sisters were both found wearing a ring given to them as a gift from their father. One of the sisters was even discovered with Mary Lundie Duncan's memoir clutched in her hand (!), a memoir Sprague describes as "a delightful book" written by a "beautiful model of Christian character" (16).[8] Dedicated to God and father in their hour of need, the sisters, in death, assume a martyrdom that projects the virtue of a goodly/godly middle-class Anglo-American woman.

This martyrdom was not just the work of Christian leaders. Secular accounts of shipwrecked females reified white middle-class values as well. Women's behavior at sea, especially that of mothers and wives, is almost always represented as selfless. Though young ladies like the Torrey sisters were commended for their angelic behavior,[9] mothers and wives possessed a similar sentimental currency. A male survivor commended the wives and mothers aboard the sinking steamship *Helen M'Gregor* (1830): "[T]he ladies exhibited a degree of firmness worthy of all praise. No screaming, no fainting; their fears, when uttered, were for their husbands and children, not for themselves" (Howland 128). Some women apparently could not survive the wreck without their husbands and children, as one account, subtitled "Conjugal Affairs," made clear. While watching her husband drown, one woman cried out: "'I'm coming, my husband' . . . and leaping on the railing of the deck, plunged headlong into the sea" (*American* 22). Mothers are even more sacred than wives, and a mother's love is portrayed as of this earth but timeless in nature.[10] A mother aboard the *Home* in 1837 is described as sustaining "in a noble manner the character, which in all ages has distinguished maternal affection. Her infant was in her arms, pressed close to her bosom . . . a wave wrested the infant from her grasp and hurled it into the foaming waters . . . before the

5. Edward Augustus Brackett's sculpture *Shipwrecked Mother and Child*, 1852. Worcester Art Museum, Worcester MA. Gift of Edward Augustus Brackett.

relentless surge could hide her lost one for ever, she sprang among the breakers and perished" (263). The mother has no influence over her children's life or death aboard the ship ironically named after her sphere of influence, the *Home*. Too overcome by the loss of her child and role as mother, she follows her child to death, a gesture of dramatic note to the author of the account.

A woman's selfless physical devotion to motherhood sanctified her and assured the nation that her holy love, like God's, would never truly depart. During the burning of the *Lexington*, the narrator highlights a mother who tried to keep the flames away from her child by wrapping him/her in her veil. It is "the last act of that passion which ceases only with life,—a mother's love. Ceases, did we say? Never! It is of heaven, heavenly,—allied to the essence of deity, and co-eternal with the soul which never dies" (Howland 222). Devoted mothers of the earth form a holy alliance with both God and eternity, an assumption molded into marble by the well-known American sculptor Edward Augustus Brackett. His *Shipwrecked Mother and Child*, consistently on exhibit throughout the 1850s, is an act of a mother's devotion frozen in time. Her motherhood is as immortal as her devotion to God, toward whom her face is tilted.[11] Good mothers, shipwreck narratives suggest, are innately holy and eternally present in people's lives—both profoundly important reasons why they should be protected when crisis is at hand. Saving them is saving motherhood, essentially a symbol of the grace of God. When shipwreck narratives constructed female victims as the embodiment of everything the nation needed to see itself as exceptional, it became imperative that they be protected by others.

Imperiled women at sea served as God's surrogates. However, alleviating their suffering was not the responsibility of other women or God: it was the burden of men. During much of the antebellum era, when the unwritten maritime code of "women and children first" became the assumed procedure during shipwreck, Americans were likewise struggling to be seen as first among other nations on the scale of moral superiority. Yet concerns about human nature produced anxieties about the capabilities of the American man. Brought to the forefront in the debates between Federalists and anti-Federalists, questions about the nature of the individual were essential to the origins of American democracy. A central point of debate bandied about by Thomas Jefferson, Alexander Hamilton, and John Adams was based on Adam Smith's assumption that men are driven by selfish desires. Were men, these thinkers asked, too corrupted by self-interest to govern themselves? Such a question became increasingly relevant as capitalism took root and expanded to the western territories. The laws of capitalism prompted the individual to compete for economic success, potentially at the expense of others and the nation itself.

Religious beliefs mirrored secular trends. Much as the path to wealth was lined with individual choices, religious movements authorized the individual to direct his or her own path to salvation. The Second Great Awakening produced religious leaders such as Charles Finney, who claimed man was a "moral free agent" responsible for making appropriate choices for his own spiritual benefit (Kimmel 22). The self-interest inherent in the competitive spirit of capitalism backed by this moral free agency prompted concern that Americans would become too self-centered to care about anyone but themselves. If Americans could not control their selfish behavior, people worried that "'the rising glory' of America," as William L. Hedges puts it, "might prove to be a mere soap bubble" (109).

Americans wanted to believe that selfishness could be checked by a moral nature born in every American. The sea was often the stage on which this character was tested, in a scene where material and spiritual choices had to be made when the ship (a stand-in for the nation) was in distress. There was no better space than the ocean to remind the nation of its virtues and warn of its shortcomings. The ocean was the state of nature (soon to be taken up by images of the prairie) where American men's faults and merits would supposedly be separated from the influence of convention. In her study of political philosophy in America, Catherine H. Zuckert explains that "the state of nature can represent a setting in which certain truths about human beings become evident" (1–2). Antebellum novelists, claims Zuckert, were interested in exploring the moral questions that arise when such truths become self-evident: "Do human beings retain a loyalty to their community and obey its laws primarily on the basis of a calculation regarding mutual self-interest? Or do they continue to live together primarily on the basis of sentimental ties developed over time?" (4). A ship battered by the elements or foundering after a wreck furnished the quintessential state of nature. Because seafaring was such a strong part of the national experience and memory, the ship at sea served as the perfect setting in which to test Americans' devotion to either themselves or their community.

Men's behavior at sea appeared to reflect their true nature, and their true nature was perceived as a reflection of America's true character. Men's deeds were judged more closely when women were involved. As will be illustrated in the examples that follow, failure to save females from shipwreck was interpreted as a loss of control over self-interested passions and as a violation of the

United States' covenant with God and community. Heroic reactions provided an opportunity to redeem men's morality from their baser impulses. As Barbara Cutter explains in her theory of "redemptive womanhood," antebellum culture "always implicitly or explicitly labeled men as nonredeemers or destroyers of the nation's moral and religious fiber" (8). As rescuers responding to their moral and religious obligations, men could therefore be redeemed from such perceptions. Though it is true that women's bodies became "vessels for male salvation," which Lara Romero explains is a product of "domestic ideology" (22), images of shipwrecked women were also facilitating a more expansive, far-reaching salvation. Those who enacted loyalty to others, especially the bodies of women, were preserving America's hope in its own exceptionalism.

The sea as a state of nature, then, tested men's commitment to something other than the pursuit of wealth. First, the shipwrecked woman appealed to (or awakened) the self-made man's attention to the needs of others. In capitalist America, the aggressive self-interest required to prove one's manhood provoked fears that the nation would be piloted by selfish men driven only by ambition for their own material gain, as had been proven by the mass exodus to the West to find gold in the 1840s and 1850s. Secondly, saving women during a sea disaster required a feat of physical prowess. Observers of American culture feared that the wealth gained by individual men would lead to dissipation and "vice," producing a nation of "effeminacy, intoxication, extravagance, vice and folly," as John Adams put it in 1819.[12] Shipwrecked women in distress tested men's masculinity on a physical level rather than through their bank accounts. The nation needed to hear about mothers, wives, and young women who were not abandoned and left to their own fate, and women rescued from shipwreck fit the bill.

By the middle of the nineteenth century, the notion that to succeed financially, men in the United States had to look out for themselves was widespread. By the third decade of the century, men had little impetus to empathize with the rest of the population. The term *self-made man* originated in 1832, and by the 1840s and 1850s, when many shipwreck narratives appeared, the self-made man had become a recurrent topic in the publishing industry (Kimmel 26). The ideology that underlay the term suggested that a man could improve the material circumstances of his life without the aid of others. Further, a man's world of wealth could be constructed only through his own efforts. Caring for anyone other than family involved in those efforts was a marginal concern; as E. Anthony Rotundo explains, "[a]mbition, rivalry, and aggression drove the new system of individual interests, and a man defined his manhood not by his ability to moderate the passions but by his ability to channel them effectively" (3). Ambition, rivalry, and aggression do not engender selfless passions.

Though the self-made man served as a model for attaining status in a capitalist democracy, his presence also endangered the moral character of a nation that had relied on "communal manhood" as the glue that kept a social imaginary intact. In the seventeenth century and most of the eighteenth century, as Rotundo explains, "a man's identity was inseparable from the duties he owed to his community. He fulfilled himself through public usefulness more than his economic success, and the social status of the family into which he was born gave him his place in the community more than his individual achievements did" (2).[13] By the mid-nineteenth century, however, men were more likely to direct their passions toward themselves, thus endangering Americans' pride in their professed exceptional commitment to God, their communities, and their nation.

Sentimental depictions of women's suffering at sea redirected men's self-interested passions. In many narratives, women's suffering appears to prompt empathy and emotion from men. In fact, to be involved in the rescue of such an eternal icon was cause for an emotional and spiritual awakening for male rescuers and the nation. As the *Ocean Monarch* burned in 1849, a rescuer named Reverend Remington appears nearly overwhelmed by the emotional experience of helping to lower a woman and her niece into a lifeboat: "I felt for the first time something of the suffering that must have been endured by the poor creatures in that ill-fated ship. I had been greatly *excited* before—but now I could *weep*—before all was horror—now all *sympathy* and *tenderness*—the *terrible* and *awful* gave place to the free scope and exercise of the *tenderest emotions* of my *heart*" (emphasis in original, *Burning* 20). It is not until he sees the struggles of the woman and her niece—"woman and child"—that Remington's heartstrings are bound to the sinking ship. In fact, this was the case for the whole city of New York; Frederick Jerome, a naturalized American citizen, was presented with the Freedom of the City of New York award for saving the woman that brought Remington to tears. On this day, Miss Mary Crook and her niece sat near the preacher's pulpit in front of an "immense crowd collected at the Mariner's church in Roosevelt street" (29).

Mary Crook, the saved, and Frederick Jerome, the savior, are as close to the altar as it is possible to get; they are heroes of the church and heroes of the city. The emotional attraction to such heroism was clearly not experienced by Remington alone; the entire city was drawn to worship at a literal altar of suffering and self-sacrifice, instead of at the feet of the self-made man. Other people were saved from the *Ocean Monarch*, but it was the woman and child and their rescuer that the city celebrated and invited into its churches. The shipwreck narrative appealed to audiences who were looking for exhibitions of men's effort and responsibility toward other passengers, particularly women. There was no room for the self-interested man on Remington's boat, or at the altar.

A woman's life on the line called forth fantasies of passionate men driven by devotion to women instead of wealth or personal success. Self-made men were irrelevant to women in distress, for neither money nor family connections could make a difference to female shipwreck victims. When women's lives were in danger, America wanted to believe that men would redirect their passion toward women, and that such passion would manifest in physical heroics. This was a fantasy, because on land, such obstacles as wealth and status often determined the viability of heterosexual relationships. Typically, suitors were powerless before the whim of a young lady and the judgment of her family, both of which, as Lombard explains, would determine the extent of the man's "self-restraint" and "devotion before they would marry" (177). In

6. Man and woman on a floating settee after a shipwreck. From *Steamboat Disasters and Railroad Accidents in the United States*, by S. A. Howland (Worcester: Warren Lazell, 1846), p. 85.

a nation where masculinity was continuously tested by aggressive competition, and it was believed that such a system would produce the best man ("may the best man win"),[14] "[c]ourtship was risky to men's self-esteem, and many expressed ambivalence toward the women who held the power to reject and wound them" (176).

Shipwreck narratives assured men that women wanted to be rescued, regardless of the male suitor or rescuer's class. Likewise, rescuing women bolstered the fantasy that men did not have to hide their passions for women in order to appear to have "self-restraint." In an account of the wreck of the *Pulaski* that can hardly be true but had to be a sensational source of interest, shipwreck was the occasion for a male rescuer not only to save a woman's life but also to make her his wife. The wreck features a man who saves a woman from drowning by pulling her onto his life raft, which happens to be a floating settee (a kind of sofa). This instant parlor scene becomes the setting for a passionate exchange of vows. The exhibition of the man's selfless passion begins when the woman worries that the float will not hold them both. Her rescuer's response is: "'We live or die together'" (Howland 84). When a small boat floats by, the woman refuses to go without him. By the end of their third day together aboard the settee raft, rendered in one of the few drawings included in the anthology version, the man has found that "her good sense, her fortitude, and presence of mind at the most perilous moment, and particularly her readiness to meet and share with him the fate which awaited them, excited on his part an attachment which was neither to be disguised nor conquered" (85). She is likewise enamored by him, and so "they pledge their mutual love" and vow to stay together if they are saved (86). Indeed, they are rescued, and in a final act of loyalty, the woman insists on maintaining their engagement even though he confesses he is in "poverty to his very lips" (86).

The unnamed couple is represented as an exemplar of perfected American values, and the soon-to-be-groom wins a bride even though he is no self-made man. Male anxiety about courtship is allayed by the symbolic dimensions of the story. The woman is not "pursued" by a suitor; rather, she is "saved"—heroically pulled onto their makeshift life raft by the sheer selfless will of the male shipwreck survivor. Thus, when the male suitor is commended for saving her, he is also rendering her incapable of dismissing him as too passionate or poor after their courtship. The narrator reports that when the suitor sees that the woman was willing to share his fate, he did not have to "disguise" or "conquer" his "attachment." In essence, he never had to hide his passions and suppress his desires—or his poverty—as men were expected to do during courtship; instead, he reaped the rewards of rescue, an act that inherently prompted devotion at sea, on the settee, and at home, in the parlor.

Portrayals of the rescue of shipwrecked women also reveal a cultural desire for men to put their bodies, not just their capital, at risk for the safety of women. Shipwrecked women tested men's masculinity on a physical rather than a material level. Currier and

7. Currier and Ives, *My Child, My Child*. Engraved and published by John C. McRae, NY, ca. 1855. Courtesy of the Library of Congress (LC-USZ62-136505).

Ives chose to depict such physical prowess in dual prints of a female shipwreck victim.[15] The mother in figure 7 holds her child above her head, out of harm's way and toward the heavens. In figure 8, a man has swooped down to rescue them and, notably, is in a pose of sacrifice that resembles a crucifix. His muscular back dangles before the viewer, and another man, who is also faceless, holds the other end of the rope. In effect, the rescue transforms one man's efforts into emblems of the power of masculine effort in saving what is holy. As illustrated by the rescuer's pose, the very effort is an exhibition of Christian fortitude. The faces of the rescuers are not depicted because their identity as individuals is not relevant; they are the fantasized American everyman. In contrast, the woman's identity is very clear; in figure 7, we see her anguish as she holds up her child to be saved, even if she herself drowns. Her identity is revealed for sentimental appeal; the audience sees the woman and child up close so that her image incites in the viewer a reaction

8. Currier and Ives, *They're Saved, They're Saved*. Engraved and published by John C. McRae, NY, ca. 1855. Courtesy of the Library of Congress (LC-USZ62-136506).

similar to the "tenderest emotions" felt by Reverend Remington during the rescue of the woman and child survivors of the *Ocean Monarch*. And as was the case with the sensationalism underlying Currier's print of the wreck of the *Swallow* (figure 4), the audience is also drawn to the eroticism of the half-naked man of muscle wrapping his arm around the waist of a woman whose filmy, wet gown barely keeps her clothed. His body is all the more heroic for rescuing not just an innocent child but also its mother, the icon of the nation's moral virtue.

As discussed in chapter 1, early nineteenth-century Americans were experiencing a shift in their assumptions about the role of Providence in their lives. An individual's fate was no longer seen as solely in the hands of God, but rather as influenced by human beings. If Providence is on comparable footing with humans when disaster strikes at sea, there is no especial grace to be bestowed specifically on Americans. Currier and Ives's lithographs, like other shipwreck narratives, reflect this dilemma in which God seems to be missing. Both the mother and child in figure 7 reach out to the heavens, but those heavens are dark, foreboding, and seemingly unresponsive. It is not God's intervention but a strapping young man's arms that save the woman and child. Though human intervention is welcome in this scene, the print also dramatizes the fear that God is indifferent to the loss of human life.[16] Most preachers could give no explanation for why God seemed to be absent during shipwrecks. Reverend Remington acknowledges the dilemma when he observes that "[God] suffers others to fall victims, without exercising over them any particular interposition" (*Burning* 18). Others claimed that God witnessed the suffering but could not interfere with "the order of Nature," as Reverend S. G. Bulfinch puts it (*Narrative* 24), or the "consistency" of the "elements of nature," as labeled by John Weiss (8).

The suspicion that God could not be counted on to make "any particular interposition" in the lives of those in crisis was potentially devastating, for Anglo-Americans wanted to believe that they were chosen to build a nation out of Christian principles. However, shipwreck narratives taught that there was a correlative alternative that would secure America's chosen status. Tales of male heroism at sea in response to women in distress suggested that national character was defined by the personal responsibility individuals assumed for others, particularly women and children. It was assumed that such an undertaking of personal responsibility would be reciprocated by women, who would then be loyal to fathers, brothers, and husbands. Americans were defining themselves through the actions of men and women in crisis who sacrificed self for the sake of others. When men did not take on responsibility for others as well as themselves, especially when women were concerned, the chastising and mourning that followed reveals the nation's anxiety over the very components of the success story it claims made America exceptional: self-reliance, wealth, progress. Men were blamed for a selfish disregard for authority and a misplaced reverence for money, power, and speed.

When Ralph Waldo Emerson published "Self-Reliance" in 1841,

he called for Americans to become "nonconformists," to resist what was expected of them by institutional authority and to make their own judgments as to what is right and what is wrong (141, 144). The irony, of course, is that Emerson was looking to reform the integrity of the mind (141), not to propose a way for men to become selfish in the marketplace or on board ships. Nonconformity for selfish reasons put lives at risk at sea. Aside from the military, nowhere else but aboard a ship is the hierarchy of power more clearly defined. The second mate must follow the orders of the first mate, and the first mate must carry out the orders of the captain. The rest of the officers are hierarchically arranged, and all must fulfill the wishes of the captain. There is no room for misapplying Emerson's rhetoric to the deck of a ship. Resisting the captain's orders might result in punishment by death, since one weak link in the chain of command could cause injury or death to both crew and passengers. When orders were not followed and loss of life ensued, especially the lives of women, nineteenth-century shipwreck narratives served as poignant reminders of the misdeeds of a nation taking Emerson's suggestion too far. If personal success was one's only goal, then loyalty to countrymen and women sank out of sight.

This condemnatory note rang particularly true when two significant shipwrecks occurred within two years of one another. It took the wreck of a British ship in 1852 to teach Americans a lesson two years later when they suffered their own devastating shipwreck. In 1852 the British ship Birkenhead struck a reef off of the coast of South Africa and broke in two with approximately 650 people on board. According to reports, the five hundred or so British soldiers aboard the ship did not panic or rush for the boats; instead, they followed the captain's orders and helped the women and children into the lifeboats in an orderly manner. These reports of the men on board showing little regard for their own survival were widely circulated in both England and America. Many of the soldiers, according to the accounts, stood at attention as the ship went down. Though only 192 people survived, nearly all of the women and children lived (Huntress 158). Maritime historians point to the men's actions aboard the

Birkenhead as the inauguration of England's "unwritten maritime code" that women and children should come first (Brown 167).

The behavior of those British soldiers would come to haunt Americans. Two years later, the U.S. vessel *Arctic*, the fastest ship in the world in 1854, collided with a French steamer in thick fog off the coast of Newfoundland. Though the American steamer remained afloat for more than four hours, there was a general panic on board, and little regard was given to the captain's order that women and children be saved first. Only eighty-six of around four hundred passengers were saved: "seventy per cent were crewmen, thirty per cent passengers." Not a single one of them was a woman or child (Brown 167). According to accounts of the disaster, the most appalling thing about the wreck of the *Arctic* was the loss of women and children, which was attributed to the crew's and passengers' selfishness and lack of deference to order. Compared to the image of the *Birkenhead*, with its obedient soldiers standing at attention as the ocean waters rose over their heads and the women and children rowed safely to shore, the loss of women's lives on the *Arctic* was shameful. With not a single safe woman or child to consecrate, citizens vocalized doubt in the capability of Americans to maintain ties with each other and uphold their sacred covenant with God. It is not surprising, then, that historians point to the *Arctic* disaster as the origin of a more explicitly urgent protocol that women and children were to be rescued before anyone else.[17]

It is clear from the rhetoric surrounding the wreck that not only the material reality of the wreck was horrifying—the tremendous loss of life—but also the symbolic implications of the ship's demise and the death of so many women. The *Arctic* was interpreted as a floating symbol of the United States. In a sermon in his Brooklyn church, the renowned Reverend Henry Ward Beecher described the scene as the *Arctic* departed from Liverpool: "[T]he national colors streamed abroad, as if themselves instinct with life and national sympathy" (qtd. in Howe 338). The ship's very size symbolized the fast-growing proportions of the United States. The *New York Post* proclaimed the *Arctic* to be "the most stupendous vessel ever constructed in the United States, or the world, since the patriarchal days of Noah" (qtd. in Brown 17). The ship (and in turn, the United States) is rendered as a historical achievement of biblical proportions, while the name itself alludes to America's antebellum efforts to explore a little-known region of the world, the Antarctic.[18]

The behavior of those aboard this symbol of a nation was interpreted as an indicator of national values. Liverpool saw the national glory of the *Arctic*'s departure from its port, and Americans were embarrassed by how the shipwreck likely tarnished their image in British minds. Newspaper accounts and published sermons about the wreck of the *Arctic* alluded to Americans' anxiety about their potential moral inferiority in comparison with the British. In his sermon, Cortlandt Van Rensselaer proclaimed that the saving of every woman and child on board the *Birkenhead* was Britain's highest military achievement and warned that "American commercial discipline . . . must exhibit sterner stuff than at the wreck of the Arctic, in order to secure public confidence" (17). To secure public confidence in America's exceptional nature, American men would need to check their selfish desires and their basest instinct for survival. If they did not, America's public image, or "commercial discipline," as Van Rensselaer puts it, would lag behind that of the British.

By the mid-nineteenth century, railroads delivered Americans faster and farther west, new territories were annexed, and trade and production increased. Through force and industry, U.S. geographic boundaries and wealth increased rapidly. The wreck of a fast-moving technological achievement such as the *Arctic* was perceived as a sign of danger and a rebuke for the escalating greed for money, power, and speed. Americans believed the demise of the *Arctic* was the consequence of a speed-obsessed captain who did not choose to slow the steamer when he first encountered fog. Such a heedless act prompted doubt in Americans' motives for success. Might men's desire for advancement create a society neglectful of God's presence, one that preferred success in the material realm to success in the spiritual world? As the nineteenth-century minister Elam Smalley mournfully asked, should Americans apply their "ingenuity and wealth" to "the problem of annihilating time and space?" (25). Selfish behavior is equated with men behaving as if they are more powerful than God, subverting the sacred hierarchy that is reflected on a smaller scale aboard a ship. Beecher bemoaned the selfishness and betrayal aboard the sinking ship for similar reasons: "All command was lost. The men heeded but one impulse, and that was the desperate selfishness of an aroused and concentrated *love of life*. They abandoned their posts. They deserted their duty. They betrayed their commander. They yielded up to death more than two hundred helpless souls committed to their trust" (qtd. in Howe 339). Beecher's words suggest that men's "love of life" renders the hereafter irrelevant to their lives and that their selfishness is a desertion of duty to fellow Americans. In not saving women and children, men eliminated God and community from their lives.

When such a thing happened, Americans ran the risk not just of appearing selfish but also of appearing less than human. As the Unitarian minister John Weiss proclaims, the men aboard the *Arctic* turned into "animal men [who] must resign life with the frenzy and reluctance of the animal, and [who] leave us only the revolting legacy of their shrieks and selfishness" (12). When men cannot stay loyal to a "natural" order of command and will save only themselves, they are nothing more than selfish beasts, not the moral human beings deserving of their status as Americans. Becoming beasts means losing what defines them as human—their souls. The preachers suggest, as Van Rensselaer notes, that "the transition is natural from the shipwreck of the body to that of the soul" (25). An anonymous verse in the *New York Herald* makes the connection as well:

> *God! Can it be so? In an hour like this,*
> *Can things in our clay shapen, thus forget*
> *That woman bore and nursed them—that her blood*
> *Runs pulsing through their arteries, even yet?*
> *Are men like these our brethren? Are they framed*
> *As we are? Have they hearts, or merely bone*
> *And soulless reservoirs of life, that hold*
> *No more of feelings than the insentient stone?*
> (Qtd. in Brown 245)

Americans did not want to claim the male passengers and crew of the Arctic as fellow citizens, or "brethren." As Van Rensselaer's sermon and the poem suggest, the men's behavior indicates soullessness, a frightening existence in the minds of Christian Americans.

The poem just cited asks God if it is possible for men to forget that women "bore and nursed them," suggesting that their selfish behavior is an affront to motherhood itself. This question prompts repulsion, especially when men's reaction to the wreck is compared to women's. Mothers are depicted as pious devotees of God rather than as soulless. Reverend Beecher tells his audience that "there were mothers there, that, when the first shock was over, settled their face to die, as if it were to dream in peaceful sleep. Maidens were there, who looked up in that tremendous hour as the bride for her bridegroom" (qtd. in Howe 340). Similarly, Reverend Van Rensselaer imagines the reaction of the heaven-ascended woman who reflects on the shipwreck of the Arctic: "Methinks I see her, that noble Christian woman, with habits of life arranged for heaven; sorrowing, indeed, for loved ones left behind, but smiling for a welcome from her Saviour gone before . . . with eyes undimmed for eternity" (23–24). Like the women in Reverend Sprague's sermon on the female victims of the Swallow, the female Arctic victims are as immortal and holy as Heaven itself, in profound contrast to the hearts, or "soulless reservoirs," of men.

When women died because of men's moral failings, the passengers and crew were not the only ones in danger: America's claim to exceptionalism was jeopardized as well. As illustrated thus far, Anglo-America believed itself an exceptional nation because of its self-proclaimed covenant with God. This covenant was weakened when symbols of piety—middle- and upper-class Anglo-American women—were not saved. As land and labor promised more and more wealth, Americans began to see themselves as God's preferred recipients of prosperity. As Arnon Gutfeld explains in American Exceptionalism, Americans believed that they were not just spiritually exceptional but materially blessed as well and that the two were interconnected. As Gutfeld explains, antebellum Americans were frequently exposed to a "rhetoric of consensus" that claimed

America was "bestowed with two powers—material and spiritual" (60). Americans and their democracy were unique in that these powers fed from one another, forming "a bridge between the individual's right to personal success and his social obligations" (60). Such a bridge between the two powers served as "a tool that sanctified the theory and the practice of democratic capitalism" (60).

This rhetoric of consensus was put at risk when, for the sake of their own advancement, men did not uphold their social obligations to women. Such behavior severed the desired relationship between the ideals of individual rights and selfless loyalty to a larger community of Anglo Christians. Aware of the danger of this division, those who responded to the wreck of the *Arctic* saw ripple effects on a national scale, not just within maritime practices. John Weiss proclaimed that from that day forward, Americans would have to display "a national quality of moderation penetrating every body's business, making prudence respectable, and success consistent with it, a remedy that shall result from a deliberate education of the private heart . . . *It rests with each man to make the sea and land secure by regulating the speed of his desires*" (emphasis added, 17). Weiss does not comment on the shipwreck itself but on the endangered national character. He intimates that the recent debacle at sea is indicative of a larger flaw in American men's character. Tapping into the rhetoric of consensus, Weiss suggests that an individual desire to be the best—the fastest at sea and the wealthiest on land—is detrimental to prudence and moderation, character traits that help maintain ties to the larger community. When the community was forgotten, Americans could not claim the material or spiritual exceptionalism that girded democratic capitalism.

When American males did succeed in regulating their desires so that they could rescue women and children first, it produced a national sensation that culminated in celebratory news reports, sermons, and monuments. The most prominent antebellum example of this was the wreck of the *Central America*, which was carrying men, gold, and a few dozen women and children. This particular shipwreck was so pedagogically valuable because of the origins of its passengers and the material wealth on board. The self-made man of the 1830s was known for accumulating wealth in the cities, seaports, and plantations along the eastern coast, while the self-made man of the late 1840s and 1850s often earned the title by competing with other men to find gold and other opportunity out west. It was truly a male-dominated endeavor of unprecedented proportions: approximately "200,000 men came to California in 1849 and 1850 alone, composing 93 percent of the state's population" (Kimmel 61–62). Americans were aware that men's competitive behavior out west was far from the public scrutiny of the populated east, and prospectors' and businessmen's desires and dirty deeds could exist without women's censure or prohibitions. As General H. McLeod notes in the popular *Godey's Lady's Book* in 1847, the west is a place where "liberty is ever degenerating into license and man is prone to abandon his sentiments and follow his passions. It is woman's high mission, her prerogative and duty to counsel, to sustain, ay, to control him" (qtd. in Kaplan, *Anarchy* 24). So when news of the wreck of the *Central America*—a ship loaded with men returning with their fortunes in gold and the women who loved them—made its way to print, Americans held their breath to see whether the wreck would besmirch the nation's self-image or polish it to perfection.

Not only did the male passengers and crew of the *Central America* save every single woman and child when the ship was destroyed by a hurricane, but it was believed that they also prioritized the lives of women over the fortunes in gold they were carrying home from California. The numbers astonished the nation. Thirty women and twenty-six children were saved, while passengers lost a quarter of a million dollars in gold. All told, 423 of 572 persons on the ship perished in the disaster (Coulter 472). The high number of passenger deaths made this 1857 shipwreck the worst marine disaster in American history. The lost gold was equally remarkable. It was estimated that more than 1.3 million dollars drifted to the bottom of the sea (474).

Reports focused on the male passengers' inattention to the loss of their gold. As the male passengers and crew transferred women and children to the badly damaged brig, the *Marine*, men rid themselves of extra weight by emptying their pockets and carpet bags of thousands of dollars of coins and gold dust. One New York journal reported that "carpet bags were opened by men, and the shining metal was poured out on the floor with the prodigality of death's despair" (qtd. in Coulter 459). Such disregard for wealth and personal gain so as to save women and children was what prompted the admiration of another survivor, who saw "five hundred men with death yawning before them at any moment, [who] stood solid as a rock, nor made a movement for the boats until the women and children had been all safely transported to the brig" (461). Furthermore, there was no "instance of self-devotion," only "coolness, and manliness seldom excelled, if equalled" (461). The *Federal Union* reported that everyone's behavior during the disaster was "irresistibly in favor of the high tone of the American mind. Their country ought to be proud of them; all Christendom will praise them" (477).

This rhetoric indicates the correlation between two ideals that made the United States appear to be exceptional: a belief that selfless American men had the capacity to balance the demands of the material and the spiritual, and a belief in America's superiority as a Christian nation favored by God. The men aboard the ship exhibited no "self-devotion," behavior the report associates with "manliness." Furthermore, the account suggests that selfless manliness is measurable, for American masculinity cannot be "equalled." The United States could be proud of this selfless masculinity unique to American men and even deserved to be revered by all "Christendom." Clearly, the men's behavior was worthy of attention from other nations as well as their own country. All Christian nations should admire American men, further evidence that the United States saw itself as the standard for the rest of the Christian world.

This attention to the manliness and Christian selflessness inherent in "the American mind" was brought to a tight focus when turned on the captain of the ship. The descriptions of Captain Herndon's words and behavior during the disaster provided seeds for the blossoming of a legend. Herndon's priority was to keep the

9. Herndon Monument on the campus of the U.S. Naval Academy. Courtesy of the U.S. Naval Academy Photography Laboratory, Annapolis MD.

passengers calm and unload the women and children first. It was reported that passengers were so respectful of his fortitude and authority that he never had to use his pistol to maintain order. As the ship went down, the captain encouraged everyone around him to remain hopeful. The sight of his posture while sinking with his ship is the perfect material for myth-making; witnesses said he went to the bridge in his best uniform and "with the utmost coolness and courage, [he] calmly smok[ed] his cigar as he sank beneath the waves" (qtd. in Coulter 461). Later, when efforts were being made to raise money for the captain's wife, the editor of the *New York Times* proclaimed that for saving women and children first, Herndon "well deserves a place in the heart of every woman who would honor herself by doing honor to courage, to loyalty, and to devotion"(479).

The newspaper suggests that the highest reward for Herndon's (and all men's) selfless masculinity is women's honor and respect. His prudence and moderation, so essential to John Weiss's vision of American character, inspired fund-raising efforts on behalf of the man who put women and children first. A monument erected in his memory still stands today. Over a dozen feet high, the Herndon monument on the U.S. Naval Academy campus in Annapolis, Maryland, stands as stiff and formal as Herndon apparently did during the sinking of the *Central America*. It is certainly a tribute to "manliness" in its phallic dimensions, and it is located on property traditionally occupied exclusively by men training to be selfless when the endangered or unprotected need saving. When women and all of the values they stand for needed rescuing, that masculine selflessness exhibited by Herndon and all of the men on board was equated with Christian codes embedded in the "high tone of the American mind." The reports of the wreck reveal that women and children were not all that was saved: a national rhetoric of exceptionalism was salvaged as well.

By putting this message in relief, shipwreck narratives helped define developing national ideals that reinforced earlier notions that America was chosen by God. Also, shipwreck narratives such as those recounting the wreck of the *Central America* celebrated the ways in which individuals could contribute to the nation's exceptional nature. These lessons were not limited to shipwreck victims' friends and family and were not confined to the maritime community; "women and children first" was a generic model intended to set a national standard. The lessons learned when females were involved in a sea disaster carried so much national import that the first self-proclaimed national ballad in the United States was about a female and a shipwreck. One of the most famous poems to come out of the nineteenth century, Henry Wadsworth Longfellow's "The Wreck of the Hesperus" is a prophetic warning to the nation. Filled with vivid and tragic imagery, the ballad tells the tale of a captain, too proud to heed an oncoming storm, and of his daughter, made holy by her innocence. The captain and his fair daughter, "[h]er cheeks like the dawn of day," and "her bosom white as the hawthorn buds" of springtime (6–7), sail aboard the schooner *Hesperus*. When the skipper is warned by another sailor that a hurricane is coming on, his response is to take a puff from his pipe: "And a scornful laugh laugh'd he" (20). A few stanzas later he tells his daughter not to worry about the storm because he claims he "'can weather the roughest gale / That ever wind did blow'" (31–32). As the winds blow fiercely and the water churns, the skipper lashes his daughter to the mast. His daughter urges him in repeated stanzas first to pay heed to the fog-bells, then to the guns of distress sounding through the blizzard, and finally to the light on shore; all three warn of the proximity of the rocky coast. By her third observation, her father is unable to respond to her question, for the freezing storm has turned him into a "frozen corpse" (48).

As the ship heads for rocks, the girl "thought of Christ, who stilled the wave / On the Lake of Galilee," hoping she would be saved (55–56). However, the *Hesperus* wrecks on the reef of Norman's Woe, and at daybreak a fisherman sees the dead girl floating offshore, still tied to the mast:

> The salt sea was frozen on her breast,
> The salt tears in her eyes;
> And he saw her hair, like the brown sea-weed,
> On the billows fall and rise.
> (81–84)

During the years of 1840–41, Longfellow composed "The Wreck of the Hesperus" with the intention, as he explains in a letter to George Washington Greene, of writing a national ballad. He chose this form because he believed "[t]he National Ballad is a virgin soil . . . and there are good materials," namely, an actual shipwreck in December 1839 that caught Longfellow's attention (Letters 2: 203).[19] Rather than paint a rose-colored portrait of life in America for his national ballad, Longfellow chose to portray the gruesome deaths of a skipper and his daughter in a shipwreck. Why a shipwreck? Moreover, what possessed the famous American poet to base a national ballad on ghoulish descriptions of a young girl's death in a sea disaster?

Given the symbolic potential of distressed women at sea, Longfellow's story is more than a tale of a tragic accident; it is a morality tale designed to teach men a lesson about their responsibility toward women and, in turn, their nation. First, Longfellow taps into the nineteenth century's conception of the pure and pious female as God's surrogate for the nation. Although the young girl's future is determined by her father's actions, she believes in Christ's power to save her. In fact, she evolves into something of a Christlike figure herself; her bondage to the mast recalls a crucifixion. Secondly, this common lesson— "put your trust in God"—and the girl's similitude to Christ fall alongside the ballad's allusions to a specific biblical story that directs the lesson toward selfish men. When an early nineteenth-century audience envisioned the unforgettable image of the daughter floating offshore with "salt sea . . . frozen on her breast" and "salt tears [frozen] in her eyes," they might have been reminded of Lot, his wife, and their escape from Sodom and Gomorrah.[20] During the escape, Lot's wife is turned into a pillar of salt for looking back at the city. Longfellow's images revise the biblical story so that the skipper and his daughter are frozen solid by the salty sea and winds; the skipper cannot help his daughter because he is a frozen corpse, while his daughter, tied upright to the mast, is frozen into a pillar of salt to pay for her father's sinfulness. The skipper is like the citizens of Sodom and Gomorrah; he is filled with pride, overconfident in his individual power, and careless of others' lives in pursuit of his self-centered goals. In other words, he is effectively a caricature of the self-reliant American individualist gone awry. When the skipper wrecks the ship, he wrecks his daughter, the sanctity of Christian belief, and the exceptional nature of the nation, all figuratively and physically bound to the *Hesperus*.

This same lesson could not have been taught so effectively had those warnings came from one of the sailors rather than the daughter. In fact, it is clear that Longfellow was well aware that a vision of youthful innocence and Christian faith would be preferable to his readers than any other character, male or female. Though he based his poem on the discovery of a fifty-five-year-old woman's dead body found lashed to the windlass bitts of a wrecked schooner,[21] he chose to transform her into a girl for his ballad. Longfellow sensed the sentimental appeal of a young girl facing death, a character type fast becoming typical in nineteenth-century literature. As Catharine E. O'Connell explains, children's deaths "resonated in significant ways with both the literary and social conventions of the antebellum period . . . The beautification of childhood, coupled with women's increasing self-definition as nurturing mothers, gave the death of children intense social meaning, both painful and poignant" (29). Though the "social meaning" of many young girls' deaths depicts "the agony of parting from loved ones and the need for reassurance that the dead will rest in peace," as Joy S. Kasson theorizes is the motive for nineteenth-century cultural representations of dead girls (107), the skipper's daughter plays a much more admonishing role to those left behind. Like the soon-to-be famous holy Eva in *Uncle Tom's Cabin*, who dramatized how "the pure and the powerless die to save the powerful and corrupt" (Tompkins 128), the drowned daughter appears to be crucified for others' sins. The audience, like the fisherman in the poem who first spots the dead girl tied to the mast, should stand "aghast" at such a sight.[22] Standing "at the intersection of the pious and the perverse," as Lynda Zwinger so eloquently describes sentimentalized daughters (41), the gory body of the skipper's daughter and her naively prophetic words of warning should provoke shame in any American who ever fell victim to hubris.

The skipper's pride is all the more sinful because he is selfish at the expense of a young girl. When composing the poem, Longfellow crossed out a stanza that makes it clear that such selfish pride was a violation not just of social mores but of God's law. The skipper proclaims in the marked stanza, which appeared immediately after the skipper's initial scornful laugh at the hurricane warnings,

> I would not put into yonder port,
> Nor yet into yonder bay
> Though it blew a gale, with fiery hail,
> As on the Judgment day![23]

In the published form of the ballad, the daughter represents the consequences that must be faced when a prideful man is so confident in his own individual strength as to ignore the powers of Nature and his obligation to his daughter's safety. The crossed-out stanza indicates that he imagined the skipper's defiance to be aimed as much at God as it was his paternal obligation, though perhaps it was too blasphemous a stanza to include. Either way, the idea that destroying the girl, a model of national virtue, was a violation of women's and God's trust was clearly on Longfellow's mind.[24]

Longfellow's national ballad, then, was unlike most others. One would expect a national ballad to celebrate the virtues of the United States. Yet Longfellow's ballad, like its church bells, guns, and lights on shore, is a warning to a nation, not a celebration. As the first chapter of this book illustrates, seventeenth-, eighteenth-, and early nineteenth-century populations repeatedly narrativized the importance of shipwreck to their origin, survival, and moral code, all of which, they believed, made them superior to the rest of the world. If Anglo-American cultural memory recalled shipwreck as the moment when God's covenant with the nation is revealed, the shipwreck of an American schooner with no survivors and no favors from God would have been disturbing indeed. A female body is destroyed and God's favor threatens to disappear altogether. When men renege on their social and Christian covenant, they put America's exceptionalism in danger. Shipwreck narratives, and America's underlying expectation that women and children should be put first, brought the dangers posed by individualism, democratic capitalism, and the self-made man to the forefront. And as the next chapter will show, stories of women suffering at sea demanded a critical look at another American institution that would crumble by the end of the Civil War: slavery.

3

Women and the Middle Passage

There is an historical circumstance, known to few, that connects the children of the Puritans with these Africans of Virginia, in a very singular way. They are our brethren, as being lineal descendants from the Mayflower, the fated womb of which, in her first voyage, sent forth a brood of Pilgrims upon Plymouth Rock, and, in a subsequent one, spawned slaves upon the Southern soil,—a monstrous birth, but with which we have an instinctive sense of kindred, and so are stirred by an irresistible impulse to attempt their rescue, even at the cost of blood and ruin. The character of our sacred ship, I fear, may suffer a little by this revelation; but we let her white progeny offset her dark one,—and two such portents never sprang from an identical source before.

—Nathaniel Hawthorne, "Chiefly about War Matters" (1862)

There is no place you or I can go, to think about or not think about, to summon the presences of, or recollect the absences of slaves; nothing that reminds us of the ones who made the journey and of those who did not make it. There is no suitable memorial or plaque or wreath or wall or park or skyscraper lobby. There's no 300-foot tower. There's no small bench by the road. There is not even a tree scored, an initial that I can visit in Charleston or Savannah or New York or Providence or better still, on the banks of the Mississippi.

—Toni Morrison, "A Bench by the Road" (1989)

66

When Nathaniel Hawthorne ruminated about the origins of America, he could not articulate such a beginning without an African presence and their "monstrous birth" as slaves. Hawthorne could not conceive of a "ship of state" without the image of slave ships, and yet 127 years later, Toni Morrison would lament that there is no marker of this birth. Has it become too easy to limit the slave experience to a generation now gone? Or, are markers missing because the United States has limited the memory and impact of the slave trade to the years when slave ships made the Middle Passage? Morrison's sense that "a dark, abiding, signing Africanist presence" shadows American literature suggests that the markers are not gone; they are overlooked (*Playing* 5). If this is the case, then Carl Pedersen's call to "widen the symbolic dimensions of the Middle Passage" ("Sea Change" 44) is not merely a request for literary insight but for the recovery of a memorial that will summon us to think about the history of the people who made the Middle Passage, even after such voyages came to an end.

With the exception of a collection of essays about black Caribbean women writers,[1] the "symbolic dimensions" of antebellum American writing about this sea passage have been overlooked. Recent analyses study how the cultural memory of the Middle Passage contributed to twentieth-century notions of modernity (Gilroy) or explore the Middle Passage experiences of eighteenth- and nineteenth-century black male writers like William Wells Brown (Mulvey) or Olaudah Equiano (Rice). Concurrent with these studies, contemporary novelists such as Toni Morrison and Charles Johnson have created characters whose stories are intertwined with the Middle Passage, while critics and theorists have recently begun to think about how the stages of such a crossing have influenced contemporary black consciousness.[2] However, little attention has been paid to the relevance of the Middle Passage in antebellum writing by and about black women.

Most people think about the Middle Passage in terms of its historical dimensions. Approximately 9.5 million Africans made the crossing from Africa to the Americas during the international slave trade (Franklin and Moss 41).[3] From 1518 to 1865, Africans crossed the Atlantic in horrifying conditions, imprisoned in the filthy holds of slave ships. It is estimated that nearly half of the Africans taken captive aboard slavers headed for the West Indies, America, or Britain died of disease, starvation, or dehydration (Mannix 124). As real as the historical facts of the Middle Passage is its travel within cultural memory, even for those African Americans born in the states as slaves, or those who were born free. The memory is not bound to texts that use the term *Middle Passage* or include a slave ship. The Middle Passage can appear in texts without an explicit reference: it is present in the narrative flow, the selection of images, and the casting of experience.

If, then, we are to take seriously Werner Sollors and Maria Diedrich's call to uncover "the values, the images, and the vocabulary [early African American] people developed in their survivalist endeavors to familiarize themselves with the unfamiliar—to reinvent, rediscover, and redefine America from a black perspective" (6–7), an analysis of the recasting of the Middle Passage in women's writing is a legitimate response to their suggestion. As I will show, the Middle Passage as a cultural memory appears in Nancy Prince's story of her return to Boston from Jamaica, and it surfaces again in the crawl space of Harriet Jacobs's grandmother's shed. Prince's and Jacobs's use of the Middle Passage likewise informs this book's exploration of women's presence in sea narratives and their influence on national identity. The virtuous behavior exhibited by women such as Prince and Jacobs as they recollect or allude to the punishing sea voyage of their ancestors sends forth a message to a nation indifferent to the slaveholders' principle that black women are tools for reproduction rather than moral, virtuous women. Jacobs's and Prince's stories, combined with a study, to be found in the second half of this chapter, of how white abolitionists used the legacy of women's abuse as it originated in the Middle Passage, expose the hypocrisy of Americans' belief in their exceptional moral nature. The United States could not claim to be blessed materially and spiritually when its self-imposed moral directive of "women and children first" was refused to those women whose lives were most powerfully afflicted by the legacy of a sea voyage—African American women.

Even though Nancy Prince was born a free black woman, the Middle Passage begins her autobiography, *A Narrative of the Life and Travels of Mrs. Nancy Prince*. In the opening pages of her story, Prince reveals that she was raised on her grandfather's stories of "how he was stolen from his native land" and her stepfather's stories of his Middle Passage and captivity (5). The tales of her seafaring stepfather, first as a slave then as a shanghaied sailor, supply Prince with the personal and family history lost to so many who made the Middle Passage.[4] These stories of escape provide her with the tools and themes to frame her own narrative.

When the slave ship he was on set anchor off the shore of a free state, Prince states that her stepfather and another slave swam to shore in the dark. This escape signaled the end of his Middle Passage, and a never-forgotten moment of freedom handed down from father to daughter. Though he died many years before she wrote her narrative, Prince recalls that "I have heard my [step]father describe the beautiful moon-light night when they two launched their bodies into the deep, for liberty" and then landed naked on the shore as the day dawned (6).[5] As she recounts his story in her own narrative, Prince's voice changes into her stepfather's easily recalled voice by reproducing a scene and dialogue between her stepfather and a man who finds them on shore. In essence, her story becomes his story for a while.

These family stories of ships, the Atlantic, and the Middle Passage do not merely represent a life long past for Prince, but also an "arrival," one of the three stages in the Middle Passage.[6] Prince never made the passage, but to imagine that her family's stories about it did not affect the way she experienced travel by ship, even as a free woman, is inconceivable. Slavery required continuous, disorienting transformations for her stepfather: from freedom, to captivity aboard a ship, to dehumanization and commodification as cargo, to risk of life in hostile waters, to liberty in an alien land. All of these transformations are echoed in Prince's narrative. "The Atlantic," as Carl Pedersen asserts, "was a different kind of space . . . [that]

constituted a transformative Middle Passage where an African past
and the American future, one in danger of fading from memory,
the other imposing its hegemonic will, were constantly in conflict over contested spheres of power" ("Sea Change" 43). Prince's
transformative Middle Passage experience on the Atlantic and the
Mississippi River surfaces when she tells stories about being at
sea as a passenger in a leaky ship or as a black woman marooned
in hostile ports.

Prince is a free woman when she pays for her passage home to
Boston, but boarding the ship has an imprisoning effect on her.
For African Americans, notes Paul Gilroy, "[s]hips immediately
focus attention on the middle passage" (4). The tie between slavery,
ships, and the Middle Passage emerges when Prince feels she has
become a spectacle to those around her aboard several ships. On
the voyage home from Jamaica, while white passengers disembark
for four days of fresh air and refreshments during an unexpected
stop in Key West, she and five other black passengers will not go
ashore for fear they will be abducted (75). Even worse, when they
leave port, a storm blows the ship haphazardly for thirty-six hours
and a steamer has to tow them to New Orleans for repair. Again,
the "poor blacks are obliged to remain on that broken, wet vessel" while the white passengers go ashore (75). This time, Prince
notes that she could see slaves "laboring and toiling" all around
her. The gaze is turned back on Prince when the ship reaches the
dock: a crowd gathers at first in awe that the ship had not sunk,
and then to stare at Prince, who describes herself as "there on the
old wreck a spectacle for observation" (76).

Prince's entrapment aboard the battered vessel recalls her stepfather's Middle Passage. Prince is free and remains aboard the ship
by her own decision, yet this decision reflects how quickly and
easy it was for whites to commodify her as if she were a slave when
gazing at her aboard a ship. In essence, her free will is reduced to
that of a slave, because to act on her will and leave the ship would
most likely result in a loss of freedom. Paradoxically, as long as
she does not move like a free person, she remains free. Like her
stepfather, Prince is anchored in a port full of people whose pow-

ers of observation restrict her freedom of mobility. Rather than sneaking to shore at night as her stepfather had to, Prince, now a spectacle in port, faces the crowd.

Prince does, however, reclaim her liberty through speech. Aboard the ship in a New Orleans port, which becomes a kind of pulpit, Prince speaks as a free woman and defuses the power of the classificatory gaze. As a group of African Americans chained together walk by the docks, Prince begins arguing with the assembled white crowd over their assumed right to rule over others. Prince's words are assertive and smart, while her onlookers' arguments are cast as one-dimensional:

> I asked them if they believed there was a God. "Of course we do," they replied. "Then why not obey him?" "We do." "You do not; permit me to say there is a God, and a just one, that will bring you all to account." "For what?" "For suffering these men that have just come to be taken out of these vessels, and that awful sight I see in the streets." "O that is nothing; I should think you would be concerned about yourself." "I am sure," I replied, "the Lord will take care of me; you cannot harm me." (78)

Her words are apparently so confident and threatening that her observers react with the impotent response, "[W]e do not want you here" (78). After she responds to a rude question with a precise quote from the Bible, "they made no answer, but asked the Captain how soon he should get away" (79).

It may seem difficult to see the correlation between the escape of Prince's stepfather and Prince's shipboard oratory. The stepfather breaks his bonds by leaving the ship. Prince is free, yet remains on her ship. However, if both events are viewed as more than mere physical action, the similarities between them become apparent. Prince's stepfather's swim to shore announces that he is not a slave; he is not what his captors think he is. Escape is an obvious strategy of resistance. Prince also deploys a strategy of resistance when she casts her voice, her reason, and her dignity ashore, refusing to be what the audience wants her to be. Prince perceives that she is interpreted as a spectacle, a commodified one at that, by the crowd who gathers at the docks and sees her as an object to be abused. Even though she is dressed like a lady, she might as well have been as naked as her father was when he swam to shore. The people gathered on shore see only her race. When she speaks, however, she radically revokes the status assigned to her as a black woman and the one-dimensionality of the spectacle imposed on her.

Prince initiates an examination of conscience in her audience, using arguments grounded in the most authoritative text of her time, the Bible, to outwit and exasperate the crowd. Her sophisticated responses to their taunts make them look foolish and dimwitted. As Cheryl Fish describes this scene, Prince "uses her voice as the unbound lash of verbal retribution, 'killing' her taunters with rhetoric" ("Voices" 485). Prince's father escaped in the night to evade the role of slave, while Prince, exposed in the daylight, cuts through and "kills" the crowd, literally silencing them when "they [make] no answer" to her argument. Prince presents herself not as an object "for audience consumption," the passive position most spectacles are forced to occupy (Glenn 3),[7] but rather as a minister speaking from a pulpit and exposing the hypocrisy of her audience.

Prince's ship leaves port and heads out to sea again, en route to Boston. Her time at sea is a reminder of the historical and contemporary reality of slavery. In nearly every instance in which Prince discusses her condition aboard the ship, she brings to view other African Americans in distress. For example, as the rescue ship tows her wrecked ship up the Mississippi River, Prince states, "I was made to forget my own condition, as I looked with pity on the poor slaves, who were laboring and toiling, on either side, as far as could be seen with a glass" (78). Later, when Prince's replacement ship and a slave vessel are towed side by side down the river and a storm kicks up, she looks over the side of the ship at the "awful sight" of the slave vessel "laying at the side of our ship!" (81) As Prince relates, "[T]he deck was full of young men, girls, and children, bound to Texas for sale!" (82). As the emotional tone and emphatic punctuation indicate, Prince is painfully aware of those young slaves on the ship next to her. The image of her ship connected by a tow rope to a boat filled with slaves symbolizes a kind of psychic tie to her father's story and imprisonment at sea during the Middle Passage. She is tethered to these experiences; she cannot escape memory as long as she is aboard such a ship.

Nancy Prince's ocean travel is tied to her family's Middle Passage experiences again and again. Gretchen Holbrook Gerzina asks that we look at the liberatory potential of the ocean travel of free African American writers such as Prince. Using Nancy Prince and Olaudah Equiano as examples, Gerzina asserts: "If the ocean was the site of diasporic travel and therefore symbolic of danger, displacement, and death, it also represented self-determination and the route to independence" (43). However, Prince's story is not one of liberatory potential, for her mobility is still restricted by what Cheryl Fish calls "laws, luck, and location" ("Journeys" 226). She may have built a temporary bulwark against the ignorant gaze of the New Orleans crowd, but she is still entrapped aboard a ship and confronted with the reality of slavery on the ocean. The ocean brought on a reality akin to the Middle Passage, one that recalls her stepfather's story. Like the slaves who experienced their own passages, Prince sees the United States as a punishing land and her journey as one that nearly stripped her of dignity.

Like her stepfather, a willing castaway who swims to shore naked after a horrifying experience at sea, Prince sees herself as a kind of castaway, though an unwilling one. When she finally gets to New York and then Boston, she has been so abused and so victimized—her money and her belongings were stolen during her ordeal—that she even calls herself a "castaway" (85). Returning to port and facing even further losses (her business fails, she is forced to move), she writes: "This has been my lot. In the midst of my afflictions, sometimes I have thought my case like that of Paul's, when cast among wild beasts" (85).

By telling a story that parallels both the biblical Paul's and her stepfather's castaway status, Prince again reshapes memory and the Middle Passage in at least two ways. In Saidiya Hartman's study of slavery and identity, she characterizes memory as a "trace" that "function[s] in a manner akin to a phantom limb, in [that] what is felt is no longer there" (73). In Prince's narrative, the echo of her stepfather's Middle Passage story surfaces in her depiction of her castaway status. His memories are sutured into her story. Prince senses his experiences like the ghost pains of a severed limb. Hartman calls such memory "a sentient recollection of connectedness experienced at the site of rupture, where the very consciousness of disconnectedness acts as mode of testimony and memory" (73–74). In reinventing herself as a castaway, in her stepfather's image, Prince claims him as a part of her and aligns herself with missing stories of the millions of slaves before her whose Middle Passage unceremoniously dumped them on land.

Secondly, as a mode of "testimony and memory" comparable to Paul's, Prince's representation of her travels and suffering appear as sacred as they are ancestral. According to Hartman, practices that recall the Middle Passage, practices I believe Prince's narrative exemplifies, provide a "space [that] becomes ineffably produced as a sacralized and ancestral landscape" (72). Prince's "landscape" is the very landscape encountered by Paul. Both she and Paul were "cast among wild beasts" and lost everything—she by theft and misfortune, he by shipwreck. Her journey, then, is sacralized through the comparison to St. Paul. Also, her stepfather's story is her Middle Passage story as well, as we have seen from her use of images and dialogue while aboard ships in port. Thus, when she identifies herself with Paul, she identifies her father and all slaves in port or at sea with this sacred, sainted traveler.

For abolitionists, the rhetorical value of Prince's story is the moving way she aligns her suffering with her enslaved forefathers' condition as well as that of the contemporary slave community; though the slave trade was abolished, slaves were still being traded along bodies of water like the Mississippi. Her story pokes holes in America's assumptions that the institution of slavery somehow stands outside of the lives of free individuals. Prince illustrates that slavery not only victimizes women—women as intelligent and virtuous as she—but that it breaks a covenant with God. If free Americans do nothing to save African Americans, who, Prince suggests, are the suffering shipwrecked "Pauls" of the nation, then they are ignoring the lessons of God's word. Like the representations of white women stranded at sea, Prince challenges the moral superiority of a nation that is too selfish to recognize that as long as slavery exists, all black women are cast away, ignored by the moral directive of "women and children first" intended to keep the nation's priorities in order.

Prince's narrative demonstrates Cynthia Griffin Wolff's assertion that the Middle Passage necessarily serves as a symbolic preface to all slave narratives.[8] As Prince illustrates, however, the Middle Passage is also woven into the memory of those who experienced it, and those who were handed the stories. The same is true of Harriet Jacobs's *Incidents in the Life of a Slave Girl*. What is missing in most critical analyses of *Incidents* is a tracing of the strong allusions to both cultural memories of the Middle Passage and western cultural icons such as the castaway Robinson Crusoe. Tracing these allusions in turn exposes one of the routes Jacobs takes in her abolitionist argument, a route that stresses her resilience, intelligence, and maternal affections, all qualities that were disavowed by anti-abolitionists.

At first glance, Jacobs's journey to freedom would seem to have little to do with ocean travel. Yet, a passage by sea is immediately alluded to in Jacobs's move to her grandmother's attic. After running away from the Flints, Jacobs hides for some time beneath the floorboards of a friend's kitchen. Her only way of knowing where she might be headed comes from the hints dropped by Betty, the black servant who walks back and forth over Jacobs's hiding place and sings or talks to herself about the goings-on of the day. The scene is comparable to that of a slave below deck listening for any indication of her/his fate. A passage at sea is further alluded to when Jacobs's friends arrange for her to walk through the streets in "sailor's clothes" (90). She is guided by a male relative to a ship that will conceal her while her hiding place ashore is prepared. She then moves dressed as a sailor through the streets once again and is sequestered in a crawl space above a shed near her grandmother's house. Though Jacobs spends no time at sea, she is dressed as a man of the sea, passing from woman to man, from ship to crawl space.

Jacobs's encounters with hiding, transporting, and listening for clues about her fate elicit comparisons to the similar encounters of those before her about to embark on the voyage across the Atlantic. Like Prince, who boards a ship and triggers a connection to her past, Jacobs's assent into the attic launches a symbolic voyage that harkens back to the Middle Passage.[9] This chapter in Jacobs's account plays a central role in determining Jacobs's passage between slavery and freedom. Jacobs names the attic and her experience within a "loophole of retreat," her title for chapter 21. This "retreat" is no withdrawal from her life. Some of the most significant action of the book, such as the coordination of her children's and her own escape, are orchestrated from this space.[10] Though Jacobs is in a forced retreat, as if she were in the bowels of a slave ship, she creates a space for her life beyond this passage.

The dimensions of the attic and Jacobs's experiences in it allude to slaves' experiences aboard slave ships. The attic is a "very small garret" measuring "only nine feet long and seven wide. The highest part was three feet high, and sloped down abruptly to the loose board floor" (91–92). Jacobs explains that she could sleep on her side, "but the slope was so sudden that I could not turn on the other without hitting the roof" (92). The air in the garret is "stifling; the darkness total"; she is not able to determine whether it is day or night. The heat is "intense" during the summer months. As she lies there, "rats and mice ran over [her] bed" (92). Her food is passed to her through a "trap door" in the floorboards (92).

All of these images recall the horrors of the Middle Passage. In one respect, the description of the space calls to mind the abolitionist reports of the overcrowded ships of the slave trade. The drawings of the tightly packed slave ships, which played a major role in abolishing the slave trade in England, made their way into an abundance of abolitionist propaganda in the United States.[11] Even though the slave trade was abolished in 1807 (though it continued clandestinely until the war), the diagram of cross sections of ships picturing slaves lying back to back, row by row, was consistently reprinted throughout the years leading up to the Civil War (Lapansky 203). The image of the tightly packed ship is identified as one of the three images from the late eighteenth-century abolitionist movement that "greatly influenced the illustrated propaganda of the abolitionists of the 1830s" (203). Descriptions of the limited space aboard slavers are found throughout abolitionist literature; Lydia Maria Child refers to a testimony of a Dr. Walsh who reported that the slaves were packed into spaces three-feet and three-inches high, the space being so low that "there was no possibility of lying down, or changing their position" (162). Aside from the lack of space, it is obvious that Jacobs suffers other conditions similar to those that slaves on ships endured: there is no light or fresh air, the heat is excessive, there are rodents running over her body, and her food is passed up to her in her hold, the garret, much as food was passed down a hatch to the slaves in a ship's hold.

Jacobs's experience mirrors that of her fellow slaves from the past, who were transported on land and boarded in cramped quarters aboard a slave ship. Yet, as with Prince's portrayal of her experience in the port in New Orleans, Jacobs's forced retreat to the attic results in a reshaping of the cultural memory of the Middle Passage. Primarily, her story of confinement—her Middle Passage—transforms the story of another well-known castaway, who, like the biblical Paul in Nancy Prince's narrative, was cast on a hostile landscape. Jacobs writes: "One day I hit my head against something, and found it was a gimlet . . . I was rejoiced as Robinson Crusoe could have been at finding such a treasure" (92). She uses the tool to bore a hole through which she keeps track of her children's lives, and she uses the light from it to write letters to Dr. Flint. She gives the letters to a seafaring male relative, who then sends them to Flint from New York, causing the doctor to believe she has escaped North. After seven years of letter writing, Jacobs boards a ship captained by a man sympathetic to her desire for freedom, and she finally does escape to the North, all the while Flint thinks she has been there for years.

Though most critics have followed Valerie Smith's lead in showing how Jacobs "invokes a plot" of the sentimental novel (41), few have noted that Jacobs also compares herself to the most famous castaway figure in English literature, Robinson Crusoe. In likening herself to Robinson Crusoe, Jacobs recasts the symbolic potential of her garret, which now evokes a series of new images. Once akin to a ship's hold, the garret is now a spot of land that Jacobs must make her own. As Crusoe, she vacates the ship and launches the drama of the quintessential castaway, known for his ingenuity, self-reliance, and physical and spiritual transformation.[12] Likewise, Jacobs ingeniously devises a ruse to fool the Flints, utilizes a tool to save herself from complete isolation, and is physically and spiritually transformed by her experience.

Like Crusoe, Jacobs has taken control of her environment rather than the other way around, shaping an identity much different to that of a slave.[13] The crawl space, as Eva Cherniavsky articulates, "becomes a strategic location for the staging of a fictional emancipation—an imagined accession to representable identity—that crucially enables her actual escape from commodity status" (111). Though her readers initially visualize her as a prisoner in an attic and as a slave in hiding, Jacobs does not remain a spectacle to the audience looking in. Jacobs's writing allows the reader to visualize her Middle Passage experience only so far; her enslaved body is open to the outsiders' vision only briefly in two respects. As Michelle Burnham explains, "the loophole, both as hiding-place and as escape route, is that blind spot, and it is in that blind spot that secrets reside and through which bodies may escape"(159). The "blind spot" that Burnham refers to is the "site . . . that elude[s] the gaze" (159). The garret, then, is both Dr. Flint's blind spot and the site of Jacobs's agency (159).[14] Within this blind spot, Jacobs's readers also lose sight of her enslavement. With the help of her Crusoe-like ingenuity, she directs readers' vision outside the hold, outside the garret, to the world around her. From atop her grandmother's shed, she now holds the commanding view, and such a view enables her to write letters that manipulate the system of slavery. On a literal level, she is also redirecting readers to the antics of Flint, the man who once eyed Jacobs's every move. In essence, her castaway heroism has given her the ability, in Burnham's words, to appropriate "the power of surveillance for herself" (154).

Jacobs disrupts the trajectory of the Middle Passage. She escapes captivity by retreating from Flint, slavery, and the objectifying gaze of her audience, by redirecting their eyes away from her body and to the ways in which she is changing her world. Addressing the issue of suffering in Jacobs's narrative, Elizabeth Spelman acknowledges that Jacobs must allow her audience to see her (and in turn, other black women's) suffering so that her audience will feel the "compassion" necessary to abolish slavery. However, Spelman asserts, Jacobs continuously "attempts throughout the text to assert and maintain authority over the meaning of her suffering . . . She insists on her right to have an authoritative—though not unchallengeable—take on the meaning of her suffering" (354). In contradiction to most representations of the suffering female slave, therefore, Jacobs fashions herself as no powerless victim. As Sandra Gunning explains, Jacobs's narrative "calls into question the patterns of representation for blackness" (134). By providing a context for her suffering, says Gunning, Jacobs offers "a critique of the traditional practices of reading blackness as a severed relationship between voice and body, as the epitome of powerless victimization" (334). The recovery of her voice and body is facilitated by her identification with a famous castaway. Such an identification invites readers to see her as a hero rather than a helpless victim, as her passage in the garret results in the orchestration of her own rescue and return to civilization.

Finally, like Prince, who likewise challenges the objectifying gaze of the spectators eyeing her aboard the ship in New Orleans, Jacobs's identification with a heroic castaway illustrates how cultural memories like the Middle Passage coexist with these women's contemporary lives. By mingling Christian (St. Paul) and popular culture (Robinson Crusoe) stories with their experiences as African Americans, Prince and Jacobs create a kind of "cultural syncretism" that "sees the middle passage not as an end or a continuum, but as the beginning of a distinct New World multicultural system" (Pedersen, "Middle Passages" 226–27). Such a blending of identities provides the two writers a way to interpret their lives. Prince and Jacobs transform the Middle Passage, their cultural history, into a sacred and heroic passage memorialized by the rendering of their contemporary experiences.

Both Prince's and Jacobs's representations of their behavior during their experiences and their allusions to their trials at sea contributed to the abolitionist movement. Just as Olaudah Equiano proved himself to be a moral, conscientious, intelligent human being when he serves as the "principal instrument" in his own and others' shipwreck survival,[15] so too do Prince and Jacobs represent intelligent, morally minded black women worthy of being liberated from an institution that assumes them to be uncivilized and valuable only for their reproductive abilities. Even though they were denied full access to the cult of True Womanhood,[16] Jacobs and Prince nevertheless found ways to solicit sympathy for their plight as women.

Like Prince and Jacobs, Anglo-American abolitionists exposed images of women's suffering that recalled the abuse women had experienced during the Middle Passage. However, they typically used these images to construct a different kind of spectacle to provoke a different kind of sympathy than did Prince and Jacobs. White abolitionists recognized the international slave trade had been abolished earlier in the century because of the widespread abuses recounted in accounts of the Middle Passage. Hoping that earlier sentiments of pity would carry over to the present, writers such as Lydia Maria Child, Theodore Weld, the Grimke sisters, and Harriet Beecher Stowe foregrounded the horrors of slavery through portraying women's suffering in a way that recalled shipboard horrors. By presenting images of slave women's suffering within accounts and narratives filled with appeals to the audience's sympathy, these abolitionists hoped that the moral indignation felt toward those who did not put white women and children first would be transferred to those who caused the suffering of black women and children as well.

With the post-1807 abolitionist movement (when the international slave trade was abolished in the United States), images began to shift from suffering men to suffering women, as the appearance of "Am I Not a Woman and a Sister?" in 1830 suggests. Though the image of the male kneeling slave, with the title "Am I Not a Man and a Brother?" appeared in America in 1787, as efforts were brewing for the prohibition of the international slave trade, the companion image of the shackled kneeling woman made its appearance in 1830. Her appearance was widespread (Lapansky 205),[17] suggesting that white abolitionists were interested in disseminating images of suffering black women as a tool of persuasion. The suffering of female slaves in both this popular image and in the examples found in the rest of this chapter attempted to elicit sympathy by connecting women's suffering to the abuses of the Middle Passage.

A closer look at the surroundings found in "Am I Not a Woman and a Sister?" (figure 10) reveals a woman kneeling among palm trees. In 1830, long after the abolition of the international slave trade, the woman appears to be pleading from the shores of Africa before she is about to embark on the Middle Passage. This image was published in America in George Bourne's *Slavery Illustrated in its Effects Upon Woman and Domestic Society* in 1837 and carries a caption written by the famous American abolitionist Lydia Maria Child. The caption states: "By virtue of special contract, shylock demanded a pound of flesh cut nearest the heart. Those who sell mothers separately from their children, likewise claim a legal right to human flesh; and they too cut it nearest to the *heart*" (emphasis in original, frontispiece). Critics have not recognized the connection between the Middle Passage and black women, and Child's caption has been ignored.

As Jacobs's and Prince's narratives reveal, the Middle Passage surfaced between the lines of black women's stories about their experiences as Americans. White abolitionists often alluded to the Middle Passage as well to persuade audiences of the contemporary abuses of slavery. Though historians and literary critics have analyzed the rhetoric of white abolitionists, most notably their use of sentimentality, little energy has been expended in uncovering the often implicit presence of the Middle Passage in antebellum

By virtue of special contract, Shylock demanded a pound of flesh cut nearest to the heart. Those who sell mothers separately from their children, likewise claim a legal right to human flesh; and they too cut it nearest to the *heart*.   L. M. CHILD.

10. "Am I Not a Woman and a Sister?" was a widely circulated image in the antebellum United States and was published in George Bourne's *Slavery Illustrated in its Effects upon Woman and Domestic Society* (Boston: Isaac Knapp, 1837). Special Collections, University of Virginia Library (E449.B774 1837).

abolitionist arguments.[18] More specifically, the disregard for the humanity of slave women, which began with the Middle Passage, came to be integral to abolitionist polemics. After the slave trade was abolished, which in word (not necessarily in practice) prohibited a Middle Passage from ever happening again, abolitionists presented to audiences a spectacle of female slaves' suffering to further their cause. Abolitionists argued that the suffering of mother and child, which began on the slave ships and was unloaded on southern soil, was the epitome of the unnaturalness of slavery. Even though the international slave trade was outlawed, the implicit goal was to extend the most effective images from that abolition campaign—those of the suffering black woman—to the abolition of the internal slave trade and institution of slavery in general.

When the woman in chains questions her status as woman and sister, she asks it as she is about to embark on a voyage that abolitionists in the past had already proved to be dehumanizing and torturous. The question, then, of whether the audience can see her as a woman and a sister is all the more poignant when the audience imagines the answer that she will receive on the upcoming journey. Child's caption in turn connects her suffering during the Middle Passage to the internal slave trade in the United States. Can you, asks Child, outlaw the international slave trade and its dehumanizing passage and still entertain this question of the slave woman's humanity? After the abolition of the international slave trade, Child questions how a slave woman and her child could be traded as if the mother were nothing but a piece of flesh to be divided amongst shylocks (i.e., American slave traders—a racist insult in itself).

Embedded in Child's insinuations is the woman's role as mother, so that the question becomes, "Am I not a woman, a sister, and a mother?" In written and visual abolitionist rhetoric, tales of land-bound slaves with drowned children or children carelessly buried or sold away from mothers mirror the mourning mothers and abused women on slave ships. The practices during the Middle Passage, practices that were part of an international slave trade that had been outlawed for, among other things, its inhumanity, are clearly reproduced in abolitionist writing about the practice of slavery on land. The strategy that had once been successful in abolishing the slave trade was now utilized in arguments intended to rid the country of slavery. The spectacle of the suffering slave woman and child became a shared touchstone of meaning for abolitionists, a reliable image of sentimental appeal, which in turn bonded the abolition movement itself.[19]

The work of four well-known abolitionists makes use of women and the Middle Passage: that of Lydia Maria Child, Theodore Weld, the Grimke sisters, and Harriet Beecher Stowe. Each of their narratives in some way presents a picture of suffering slave women, mothers and children, that had the potential to reshape the symbolic dimensions of female slaves and, in turn, influence the country's sense of its responsibilities toward them. In one of many of Child's abolitionist writings, *An Appeal in Favor of That Class of Americans Called Africans* (1833)—a work that essentially caused her to be blacklisted by her former publishers—much of her opening argument addresses the Middle Passage. One of her most striking anecdotes describes a ten-month-old child flogged to death by a slaver captain who then forces the child's mother to throw her baby overboard (163–64). Such behavior, asserts Child, is "injurious both to nations and individuals" (160), and, apparently, is what struck abolitionists as most "injurious" on land as well. Throughout the collection of narratives from more than twenty thousand Southern newspapers from 1837 to 1839, collected by abolitionists Theodore Dwight Weld, Angelina Grimke Weld, and her sister Sarah Grimke, stories of cruelty to women and their children appear frequently.[20] We hear of a six-year-old slave girl who accidentally drowned the infant she was required to watch while her mother worked in the field (11), a woman who had to clear away brush and uproot bushes while her seven-year-old child was chained to her neck, a slave woman who was whipped for weeping over her child's careless burial (72), and a woman who "became a perfect maniac" when her son was sold to a speculator (97).

These examples exhibit a pattern of spectacle originating in the Middle Passage that proved slavery was "injurious" not just to individuals but to a national identity as well. The pattern of spectacle utilizes one of the more recognizable nineteenth-century visual and emotional motifs—motherhood. Nineteenth-century abolitionists took advantage of the period's reverence for, if not worship of, motherhood.[21] As the previous chapter shows, saving mother and child from danger was an act of heroism that symbolically saved both home and country. Though black women did not hold the same revered position as the middle- and upper-class Anglo-American mother, abolitionists found ways to foreground black women's motherhood in the hope that audiences would transpose their respect for white motherhood on the black mother as well. Visual and visualized acts of abuse against black mothers, it was hoped, would induce a kind of national shame close to that the nation felt when women and children were abandoned during a crisis at sea.

The challenge for abolitionists was to humanize the perception of black females, who were viewed as objects. Female slaves were considered by law and custom as chattel, an especially valued "commodity" during childbearing years (Hartman 40; Hine and Thompson 63). To refashion representations of female slaves so they were portrayed as symbols rather than things, many abolitionists relied on images of the suffering mothers and their children, suffering that recalls the Middle Passage. For some abolitionists, humanizing African American mothers meant rhetorically or pictorially shaping the women into a spectacle of suffering, and, in turn, a symbol of a suffering mother. In the face of white audiences who might have resisted the similitude between black and white motherhood, abolitionists tried to translate slave mothers from objects to signs, from chattel to symbols of maternity. In a culture that increasingly fostered the notion that American women were divinely ordered, and naturally inclined, to foster the spiritual and moral growth of their children within the private sphere, spectacles of mothers suffering as they were torn from their children or forced to surrender their maternal instincts were powerful symbols of the wrongs of slavery.

In order for a spectacle to be an effective tool of persuasion, it must be able to incite a shared, value-laden response from onlookers, the audience. As S. Michael Halloran explains, the audience creates the spectacle. A spectacle is not so much that which is viewed as a "public gathering of people who have come to witness some event and are self-consciously present to each other as well as to whatever it is that has brought them together" (5). He claims that the "spectacle itself is a rhetorical experience quite apart from the speech text because it involves symbolic action that engages the mind, the passions, and the senses, symbolic action that bonds its participants and constitutes them as the 'we' so often invoked in speech texts" (14). Though the spectacle is more pronounced during speech acts in front of a public audience, it is also evoked by written abolitionist texts in which the sights, sounds, and passions of slave women incite a shared reaction from audiences and possibly even mediate the social relationship between members of the audience, a function unique to the spectacle (Debord 12). The spectacle of suffering slave women may be interpreted as most effective when the members of the audience share a reaction among themselves. Abolitionists took advantage of the fact that most white Americans would be appalled by the separation of mothers and children. The aim was to get these same onlookers to see and feel a related outrage when the bodies forced to separate are black.

This isn't to say, however, that white abolitionists were humanizing their African American subjects in any real way. The one-dimensionality of the spectacles within most abolitionist accounts of women's suffering (particularly the rapid-fire portraits listed in Child's, Weld's, and Grimke's accounts) opens up the opportunity for a great deal of projection on the part of the writer and reader. The visual arts, as Karl F. Morrison makes clear, have the potential to produce an "affective fallacy," a term that refers to "the transference of the reader's (or viewer's) emotions to the object of contemplation . . . the object of contemplation becomes a mirror of the contemplator's mind" (272). Empathic transference defines the onlooker's convictions and opinions about slavery. For example, take John Rankin's attempt to humanize a suffering slave through the use of empathy:

My flighty imagination added much to the tumult of passion by persuading me, for the moment, that I myself was a slave, and with my wife and children placed under the reign of terror. I began in reality to feel for myself, my wife, and my children—the thoughts of being whipped at the pleasure of a morose and capricious master, aroused the strongest feelings of resentment; but when I fancied the cruel lash was approaching my wife and children, and my imagination depicted in lively colors, their tears, their shrieks, and bloody stripes, every indignant principle of my bloody nature was excited to the highest degree. (Qtd. in Hartman 18)

As Saidiya Hartman contends, Rankin's attempt at empathy, of replacing, or, rather, displacing other with self perpetuates the "fungibility" of the suffering slave. "In making the slave's suffering his own," explains Hartman, "Rankin begins to feel for himself rather than for those whom this exercise in imagination presumably is designed to reach. . . the humanity extended to the slave inadvertently confirms the expectations and desires definitive of the relations of chattel slavery" (19). As Rankin envisions himself in the position of slave, "the object of identification threatens to disappear" (19).

I agree with Hartman's analysis of the traps such spectacles create. To imagine helping another because, in essence, you have envisioned helping yourself is obviously self-serving. The black body remains subservient to white prerogatives in this type of rhetoric. To build on Hartman's reading, I am proposing that such identification contributed to another transference. White and African American abolitionists were aware that much of the arguments to abolish the international slave trade in 1807 centered on the imprisonment of Africans aboard slave ships after being abducted from their homes, and the subsequent abuse and harsh conditions during the Middle Passage. The violent spectacles of Grimke, Weld, Child, and Rankin are extensions of these abuses on land, and are directed specifically toward slave women. Though Rankin's transposition of his wife and children's suffering threatens the disappearance of the

"object of identification," female slaves, and is yet another violation of slaves' bodies, it nevertheless persuades white audiences to
imagine white women and children's suffering. Transferring that
empathy was likewise a transference of historical abuses deemed
unjust (the Middle Passage) to the suffering of antebellum female
slaves.

Abolitionists worked to make women *and* children come to mind
when audiences imagined slave women. In the accounts above,
and particularly in Rankin's, it is significant that the suffering is
experienced by women and their children. Rankin's "empathy" is
most excited when he imagines the abuse of his wife and children,
which causes "every indignant principle of [his] bloody nature
[to be] excited to the highest degree." This "indignant principle
of his nature" is a loaded representation of his reaction. He is
most emotionally stirred to indignation by the view of a woman
suffering. As I have stressed in the previous chapter, this kind of
indignation felt when a woman was in danger, such as the female
shipwreck victim, contributed to a masculine American ethos
that is the driving force behind the maritime credo of "women
and children first." A national identity was being built out of this
seemingly natural propensity that Anglo-American males had for
saving white women, the symbols of piety and purity. In this respect
Rankin's word choice is significant; he finds his indignation is
not created by outside forces but rather originates in his "bloody
nature." Saving and protecting women seemingly comes naturally
to him, and presumably, to all men, or rather, all white men.

Exhibiting spectacles in print and picture of the suffering of
female slaves appealed not just to a national "manhood" but white
manhood in particular. As Dana D. Nelson explains, antebellum
America came to rely on a sense of a national "white" manhood.
"'White manhood'" as Nelson argues, "was a useful category for
inventing national unity because it abstracted men's interests out
of local issues and identities in an appeal to a nationally shared
'nature'" (*National* 7). Abolitionists recognized that white manhood—man's "nature"—would be threatened if the sanctity of
women and children was not validated nationwide. Recreating suf-

fering through a sentimentalized spectacle designed to inspire empathy for white women appealed to a white manhood increasingly believed to be a part of a national character. Refusing to "save" a suffering black woman meant refusing to save oneself, one's masculine identity. In other words, abolitionist rhetoric insinuated that the mistreatment of black mothers and their children was essentially an exercise in emasculation.

Though there is nearly always mention of female slaves' suffering in most abolitionists' work, few works are like Harriet Beecher Stowe's *Uncle Tom's Cabin* in their impact. The novel Abraham Lincoln suggested was the cause of the Civil War also happens to rely on a string of African American female characters whose behavior and tragedies in the novel echo the behavior and tragedies of women on the Middle Passage. America's first best-selling novel released characters into American culture who have never faded into history. Until recently, critics have followed the lead of Jane Tompkins in pointing to the young girl, Eva, and her interaction with Uncle Tom as the most persuasive of abolitionist characters. These two characters, who have consistently been reproduced in nineteenth-century popular culture artifacts, have been the most visually pervasive characters from *Uncle Tom's Cabin*. A young, white, uncontaminated Christian girl who inspires her friendly black slave to patiently await the kingdom of heaven created "pictures" that helped to constitute "an imagined 'national' community of abolitionists" (Goldner 72). Stowe's description of Uncle Tom as "a large, broad-chested, [and] powerfully-made man" was a useful tool for abolitionists trying to convince people that physically imposing blacks would not be vengeful, violent, or even angry if they were emancipated (27). In fact, as Stowe imagines in her novel, African Americans would look to the abolitionists, as Tom looked to little Eva, as saving angels.[22]

Though Eva and Uncle Tom were important to abolitionist arguments, so too were the pictures recalling the origins of abolitionist arguments: the scenes of desperation and violation during the Middle Passage. Presenting Uncle Tom was only one prong in a many-pronged argument by Stowe. His character addressed white fears of black men. But like the abolitionists before her, Stowe also knew some of the strongest sentimental appeal would come from black women's suffering, as both maidens and mothers. Many of the female African American characters in this novel face the threat or reality of having their womanhood violated, which, for abolitionists, was the most disturbing part of accounts of the Middle Passage. Such abuses are manifested in the separation of mothers and children, insane female suicides, and the violation of women's bodies, all tried and true spectacles of suffering utilized during the movement to abolish the international slave trade. Abolitionists hoped that such images of female suffering, like those presented in the shipwreck narratives of the previous chapter, would prompt the rescue impulse believed to be natural to American men.

The threat of separating a mother and child motivates one of the most famous action scenes in the novel. When Eliza overhears her master, Mr. Shelby, announce to his wife that he was forced to sell Eliza's young son to get out of debt, Eliza feels she has no choice but to run away with her son. Before she leaves, she feels she must say good-bye to the only home she has known. As a house slave, she feels she was well-treated by the kindly Mrs. Shelby, who did not believe in the institution of slavery. The scene recalls accounts of earlier abolitionists who sympathized with Africans being torn from their home country. Stowe writes that Eliza was distraught in "leaving the only home she had ever known, and cutting loose from the protection of a friend whom she loved and revered. Then there was the parting from every familiar object,—the place where she had grown up, the trees under which she had played, the groves where she had walked many an evening in happier days" (54).

What takes her away from the only home she has ever known (like the woman kneeling in Africa in figure 10) is the internal slave trade. Like the transatlantic slave trade, the internal trade has produced a reformed but nevertheless equally transforming passage, which eventually transports Eliza along the underground railroad. The upcoming journey produces in Eliza a "maternal love, wrought into a paroxysm of frenzy by the near approach of a fearful danger"(54), emotions that echo those of her female African ancestors about to depart on their dangerous passage.

11. Eliza's leap across the ice in Harriet Beecher Stowe's *Uncle Tom's Cabin; or, Life among the Lowly*. Clifton Waller Barrett Library of American Literature, Special Collections, University of Virginia Library (PS2954.U5 1853).

The allusions to being torn away from home are then heightened by the body of water she crosses to freedom. In an image that came to be reproduced in worldwide editions of *Uncle Tom's Cabin* and evolved into the highlight of stage performances of the novel for years to come,[23] Eliza runs from the slave trader Mr. Haley with her boy in her arms until she reaches the Ohio River. With the trader on her heels, Eliza gets to the shore, clogged with ice floes, and "vaulted sheer over the turbid current by the shore, on to the raft of ice beyond. It was a desperate leap—impossible to anything but madness and despair" (65). From there, "with wild cries and desperate energy she leaped" from one ice floe to another until she reached the Ohio side of the river, with her shoes gone and blood running from her cut feet (65).

Though Eliza travels from captivity to freedom and her passage takes her over an American river rather than an ocean, it is nevertheless clear that the Middle Passage has been re-imagined as taking place in the United States as a means to elicit sympathy for slave women. Illustrations typically depict Eliza looking back toward what she is escaping. Even with freedom's shore in front of her, she cannot (and the viewer cannot) forget what she is leaving behind—an expanse of water and the slave trade on the other side.

In the illustration, the view is not one of freedom but of the threat of captivity. It is a drama of abduction that recalls events leading up to a forced passage at sea. Eliza's leap of "frenzy" and "madness" likewise brings to mind other slave women who turned into "maniacs" (reported above by the Welds and Sarah Grimke) when they were separated from their children in the slave trade. And if all of these allusions to the Middle Passage did not awaken sympathy in the audience, the image of her walking on water might. As Christians, they would recognize her heroic walk on water as similar to Jesus's walk, and her bleeding feet—a mother's sacrifice for her child—would evoke the image of Christ's bleeding feet as he died for God's children.

The child in Eliza's arms reminds viewers of a second scenario Stowe imagines women to have encountered during the Middle Passage. Stowe uses another character, Lucy, to make a strong parallel between the international and the internal slave trade—the Middle Passage that was outlawed, and the Middle Passage that still existed. Lucy comes aboard a steamer with her child after having been told she was being hired out to someone in Louisville. Once on board however, and as the "bell rung, the steamer whizzed, the engine groaned and coughed, and away swept the boat down the river" (131), Lucy is told she is going to be sold. When she leaves her baby asleep on the deck to peer down the river for a moment, the trader steals her baby and sells him. The loud departure of the vessel punctuates the beginning of a passage that calls to mind the Middle Passage, as does Lucy's reaction to the separation from her child. That evening, after a day of profound distress, Lucy sneaks to the railing and throws herself overboard.

12. Lucy leaps overboard in Stowe's *Uncle Tom's Cabin. With illustrations on wood by George Cruikshank.* Taylor Collection of American Best-Sellers, Special Collections, University of Virginia Library (Taylor 1852 .S86 U5a).

The forced separation of mothers from their children appears in well-known anti–slave trade literature as far back as the 1780s,[24] while the depiction of Lucy's death, with the ship in the background, calls to mind multitudes of Africans who died by suicide or by the hands of slavers who threw them overboard. Ship captains' callous handling of sick or dying slaves aboard their ships was a well-known practice, appearing as the title of J. M. W. Turner's 1840 painting *Slavers Throwing Overboard the Dead and Dying*. Ship captains would rather write off the slaves as losses than take care of them on board their ships. After hearing about Lucy's death, the trader in Stowe's imagined internal slave trade likewise "sat discontentedly down, with his little account book, and put down the missing body and soul under the head of *losses!*" (emphasis in original, 138). In one of the most overt passages that compare the international and internal slave trade, Stowe appeals to the reader with anger and irony: "Who does not know how our great men are outdoing themselves, in declaiming against the *foreign* slave-trade. There are a perfect host of Clarksons and Wilberforces risen up among us on that subject, most edifying to hear and behold. Trading negroes from Africa, dear reader, is so horrid! It is not to be thought of! But trading them from Kentucky,—that's quite another thing!" (139). The Englishmen Clarkson and Wilberforce based much of their late eighteenth-century arguments against the slave trade on the cruelties of the Middle Passage.[25] Stowe's point is that Lucy's desperate leap, like Eliza's, is as "horrid" as the inhumanity of the foreign slave trade.

Long before Stowe highlighted these explicit parallels, other abolitionists were raising objections to the internal slave trade by identifying parallels between the international and internal slave trade. As early as 1817, for instance, Jesse Torrey relates a great many stories of internal slave trading within the United States which invoke images of the kidnapping and slave trading of the international slave trade. Off of the coast of Maryland and Delaware, claims Torrey, the "same drama" as the international slave trade is "performed in miniature"(75), where "Man-Traffickers" sneak ashore for "nightly invasions upon the fleecy flocks" (76). They proceed in "spreading terror and consternation amongst both free-men and slaves throughout the sandy regions" (76). Stowe taps into these well-known scenes of the trafficking of women with her own scenes of kidnapping, transporting, and trading to provoke the audience's transference of their past sympathy for slave women brought from Africa to slave women traded in America.

Stowe represents slavery as the primary threat to slave women's value as human beings; they are mothers, not things. But she also takes one step further into the dark spaces of the slave ship to ex-pose the violation of young black women who were not mothers. The reformed eighteenth-century slave trader John Newton refers to the common occurrence aboard slave ships of the crew raping female slaves.[26] Though it remains decorously unstated, Emmeline likewise experiences the threat of rape in a chapter tellingly entitled "Middle Passage." Aboard the ship, Simon Legree "chuck[s] her under the chin" and tells her to "'keep up [her] spirits'" while she sits chained to another woman (347). When Emmeline responds with a "look of horror, fright and aversion," intimating her sus-picion of what motivates his words, Legree launches into a tirade in front of all of his new slaves. He demands they look at his fist, which has always been strong enough to knock down any slave "'with one crack'" (347). Not only are Legree's violent words evi-dence that young Emmeline will be in physical and sexual danger in the future, but the images within this "Middle Passage" chapter suggest imminent danger as well. The steamer is called The Pirate and the passage to Legree's home is the Red River. The final para-graph is heavy with images that evoke the Middle Passage: "The boat moved on,—freighted with its weight of sorrow—up the red, muddy, turbid current, through the abrupt, tortuous windings of the Red river; and sad eyes gazed wearily on the steep red-clay banks, as they glided by in dreary sameness"(350). The slaves, especially Emmeline, are in for a captivity filled with piratical violence that draws blood as red as the name of the river.

Fifteen-year-old Emmeline is in particular danger since she has been raised as a lady and is most likely a virgin. Stowe comes from a family that found it useful to dramatize such threats to women's virginity. Her brother, the renowned Henry Ward Beecher, utilized this threat during abolition talks in Brooklyn, where he would hold a dramatized "slave auction" during which he would bring to the front of the audience a beautiful African American woman and her daughter. While they stood in front of the audience, he would then speak "eloquently about the dangers that awaited unless they could purchase their freedom . . . At the conclusion of his plea, a basket was passed among the congregation to collect money and jewelry for their aid" (Wolff 23). Apparently, Stowe's illustrators found this kind of scene powerful enough to include. In figure 13, the beautiful Emmeline stands waiting to be purchased by any one of the male spectators, whose designs are no different from Legree's. She is propped in front of two audiences: the onlookers in the illustration who evaluate her usefulness as a slave, and the readers who imagine the dangers awaiting her when purchased. Because Emmeline is a lady, a virgin, and dressed like a white woman, Stowe's book aimed to convince white men that their responsibilities for saving white women should likewise be offered to all respectable women, white or black.

The suffering women of Stowe's novel are put in plain view of two "rows" of spectators, the viewers within and the viewers without. Unlike Prince and Jacobs, who are momentarily spectacles, these women do not talk back or manipulate the reader's gaze in any way. They remain spectacles, one-dimensional representations of suffering. However, their one-dimensionality facilitates Stowe's efforts to prompt a shared sympathy from the audience, creating a correlation between their suffering and white women's suffering. Stowe thereby uses the Middle Passage for very different purposes than Jacobs and Prince. She reads previous abolition efforts as grounded in demands to halt the cruelty of the Middle Passage. She therefore returns to such cruelties that occurred aboard slave ships to draw a connection between slave women's dangers and the dangers faced by white women: mothers losing their children and virgins losing their purity. Eliza's, Lucy's, and Emmeline's emotional dramas as mothers and innocent maidens transform female slaves from chattel aboard a ship to women and sisters.

13. Emmeline for sale in Stowe's *Uncle Tom's Cabin*. *With illustrations on wood by George Cruikshank*. Taylor Collection of American Best-Sellers, Special Collections, University of Virginia Library (Taylor 1852 .S86 U5a).

The Middle Passage was redrawn by abolitionists like Prince, Jacobs, Child, Weld, the Grimkes, and Stowe. For a nation that increasingly looked to "white manhood" as the building material for a virtuous nation, abolitionists (many of whom were white women) saw the opportunity to take advantage of the loyalty and care shown to them by such a national ideology and to clear some space at the altar for female slaves as well. If a black woman is a woman and a sister, as the popular engraving claimed throughout the antebellum years, then she was likewise a mother or a maiden. Therefore, as they would do for white women, the nation's men were called on to defend the suffering female slaves' natural virtues and save them from ruin. As Hawthorne makes explicit in the epigraph to this chapter, the country needed to respond to the consequences of the Middle Passage by "attempt[ing] their rescue." Just as saving white "women and children first" at sea (or failing to do so) meant readjusting and evaluating national priorities, so too did images of slave women and the cruelties of the Middle Passage call for broadening those priorities to include the rescue of slave women and children.

4

Englishwomen and U.S. Shipwreck Narratives

Toward the end of the first decade of the nineteenth century, a curious story of shipwreck and captivity reached the eyes and ears of the American reading public. In 1806 the *History of the Captivity and Sufferings of Mrs. Maria Martin*, a first-person account apparently written by Maria Martin, was published in Boston. In the narrative, Martin conveys the story of her shipwreck off of the coast of North Africa and her subsequent captivity by North Africans, whom she calls "Moors." Martin's story was reprinted another twelve times by 1818. Two years later another tale of shipwreck and captivity was published, this one supposedly written by Eliza Bradley. *An Authentic Narrative of the Shipwreck and Sufferings of Mrs. Eliza Bradley*, first published in 1820 in Boston and Concord, describes disastrous scenes of Bradley's shipwreck and captivity, also at the hands of North Africans. Like Martin's narrative, it was widely popular and was reprinted at least twelve times by 1848. Other tales of women and shipwreck (not all of which involved captivity) appeared during these early years as well, including *Paul and Virginia* (sometimes titled *The Shipwreck*), *Narrative of the Capture, Sufferings and Miraculous Escape of Mrs. Eliza Fraser*, and *Narrative of the Shipwreck and Sufferings of Miss Ann Saunders*. As illustrated in chapter 2, shipwreck narratives involving Anglo-American women were widely read in the first half of the century and often reflected and prescribed national ideals. Given this popularity, the success of the shipwreck tales of Eliza Bradley, Maria Martin, Virginia, and Ann Saunders is unsurprising.

Anglo-American women in distress at sea, as holy as they were human, tested the nation's commitment to its perceived ties to God
and the community. More of such narratives could only make that
test more interesting. However, what is most striking about these
narratives is that they may have drawn interest not because of the
presence of virtuous and loyal American women in them but rather
for the fact that these shipwrecked women were not American.

Placed within the context of early American literary history, this
type of crossover was common; European texts had been published
in the United States since the earliest years of English settlement.
Most revealing about the crossover appeal of several of these texts,
however, are the ways in which the English women in shipwreck narratives could contribute to the construction of an Anglo-American,
middle-class, Protestant community. How could shipwreck narratives offer moral lessons to Americans when English women were
doing the teaching? This chapter examines the curious appeal of
shipwreck narratives purportedly written by Englishwomen. In the
previous chapter, I demonstrated how white abolitionists sought
to minimize the perceived difference between black women and
white women so that Americans would view the suffering of black
women as meaningful. Now, I will discuss another way in which
difference is overlooked: in these shipwreck narratives, the differences between English and American women are elided. Though
abolitionists had to work hard to align black women's moral nature
with white women's in the racist climate of antebellum America,
it was practically effortless to get people to believe in the moral
nature of an Englishwoman, particularly when that woman was
in distress. Shipwrecked Englishwomen who recounted tales of
captivity and cannibalism made room for Americans to conflate
"Englishness" and "Americanness" into an Anglo-American identity.
Such a conflation facilitated a rationalization for Anglo-American
racial superiority within both the United States and abroad.

On a symbolic level, these shipwreck narratives may be likened
to the Atlantic Ocean itself, for they draw on both English and
American traditions. The shipwrecked women are held captive by
North Africans or plead with audiences to empathize with their

desperate situations out of the good of their white, respectable, virtuous, Christian hearts. Such literary traditions are quite similar to the transatlantic traditions of the sentimental novel or captivity narrative, which Michelle Burnham claims were shaped by "transnational and transcultural contexts" (62). These contexts produced texts that fluidly engaged Anglo audiences on either side of the Atlantic. With the shipwreck narrative, the Atlantic continued to serve as an unfixed boundary for literary traditions.[1] Like sea songs, which were of a transatlantic nature from the eighteenth century and into the nineteenth, the shipwreck narrative uses the sea as a site for acting out the social concerns of the dominant social imaginary.[2] Therefore, shipwreck narratives are an "Atlantic" literary tradition with an appeal to both Britons and Americans.[3]

Such fluidity produces, at times, an elision of difference between western cultures, specifically between that of England and the United States. In particular, shipwreck narratives fortify a kind of "fictive ethnicity," to use Etienne Balibar's term, that derives its efficacy from its transatlantic status. Balibar suggests that a fictive ethnicity, within "social formations" that are "ethnicized," is "represented in the past or in the future *as if* they [the social formations] formed a natural community, possessing of itself an identity of origins, culture and interests which transcends individuals and social conditions" (emphasis in original, 96). A fictive ethnicity often existed for Anglo-Americans, who perceived their past as "naturally" tied to the English and who foresaw their future as the advancement of the culture they inherited from their past. Though Anglo-American founders saw their new government as the apotheosis of Enlightenment philosophy, Americans rarely rejected English moral judgments that had existed long before the Constitution. Perhaps Washington Irving characterizes this phenomenon best when he makes explicit the lifeblood that Americans found in English culture: "The manners of [England's] people,—their intellectual activity, their freedom of opinion—their habits of thinking on those subjects which concern the dearest interests and most sacred charities of private life, are all congenial to the American character . . . for it is in the moral feeling of the people that the deep foundations of British prosperity are laid" (86–87). Anglo-American audiences of shipwreck narratives likely emulated or even critiqued the "moral feeling" of Englishwomen in distress, identifying with their fears, desires, and suffering. The "habits of thinking" and "moral feeling" of English women were "all congenial" to the Anglo-American women reading their shipwreck stories, which in turn resulted in an identification that contributed to the production of a United States "ethnicized" as Anglo-American.

The fictive ethnicity of the burgeoning U.S. nation-state in the early nineteenth-century underpinned the nation's perceived mission of carrying forth the torch of European enlightenment and a self-proclaimed moral superiority into the "new" world. Anglo-Americans' historically sanctioned social identification as English allowed them to maintain a sense of mission, particularly when those ethnicized as "Other," such as Native Americans, African Americans, and North Africans, threatened Anglo-American domination. Shipwreck narratives that featured English women acted to reinforce an Anglo-American social imaginary. Americans strengthened their perceived connection to English traditions and values by identifying with Englishwomen's miseries. When Englishwomen were taken into captivity following a shipwreck, Anglo-Americans sided with those traditions and values they perceived as ethnically tied to their own. In so doing, Anglo-Americans were assured that even though they had cut the umbilical cord to England, their perceived superior cultural status, when in conflict with other cultures, remained intact. If Anglo-Americans could rely on their "natural" ties to an English ethnicity (an ethnic group whose "ladies," for example, had a reputation for being mannered, intellectual, and "civilized"), then white Americans could project a hierarchy on those who did not share Anglo-American cultural assumptions. It was a moral identification that determined attitudes toward North Africans, Australian aborigines, and Native Americans, and even became useful to those women who wanted to earn forgiveness for their own uncivilized behavior during shipwreck.

The remainder of this chapter analyzes narratives with a complicated publication history. For instance, the shipwreck narratives of the Englishwomen Maria Martin and Eliza Bradley were published only in the United States, never in England, and appear to be examples of early American popular fiction.[4] The narratives by the Britons Eliza Fraser and Ann Saunders are accounts of authenticated shipwrecks, but the narratives that appeared in the United States differ from their respective published English versions. Using the concept of "fictive ethnicity" as my primary point of reference, I will examine the sources of Martin and Bradley's popularity in the United States, and, secondly, the possible reasons for the changes made to Fraser's and Saunders's stories when their accounts made the voyage from England to the United States. When English women's suffering was conflated with the suffering of shipwrecked Anglo-American women, the threat to English ladies became a threat to the United States as well. Though Anglo-American men could not save English women from shipwreck, they could use English women's experiences to build a case for their own nation's exceptional moral nature.

—▭◠◠▭—

Maria Martin begins her story by informing us that she is English, born "of respectable and wealthy parents," married Captain Henry Martin, a commander of one of the East India Company's ships, in 1797. Since she has always wanted to see the world, Martin convinced her husband to permit her to accompany him on his next voyage to Minorca aboard the *Unicorn*. Nothing noteworthy occurs on the trip until the fifteenth of August, when, after a merciless storm the night before, the *Unicorn* strikes a sandbank near the shore, approximately ninety miles from the city of Algiers. Some escape—including Martin and her husband, his clerk, the first mate, the boatswain, and two sailors—by moving hand over hand along a rope that had been towed from the ship to rocks on shore.[5]

On the first day after the wreck, the party encounters Moors who tell the survivors that they are in Barbary and announce that they are their prisoners. The Moors then herd them "like so many cattle which are to be exposed for sale, to the public market, where were gathered a great number of bidders," including Arab women, who "seemed to exult in [Maria's] miseries" (47). She is separated from her husband and sold to a "Turk,"[6] and as she waits to be led away, she looks around at her "unhappy fellow slaves," some of whom "had large collars about their necks, made much after the form of those worn by the West-India slaves" (48). Martin is led back to her master's house, where she lives with other slaves (only one being English). After giving a short description of life in slavery, she then moves ahead three years to when her master asks her to be his concubine. She refuses his offer, and since laws forbid him from forcing her to agree, he sends her to prison. Though Martin is chained by the neck and waist to the wall, she begins her imprisonment feeling hope and pride: "I glowed with the desire of convincing the world I was capable of suffering what man had never suffered before" (66). A prolonged description of her thirst, hunger, and sickness ensues, finally relieved by the British Consul, who hears of her fate. The narrative comes to a quick end with the information that she is reunited in England with her husband, who has also been liberated with the help of the British Consul.

Eliza Bradley begins her story much like Martin. She tells us she was born in Liverpool, England, "of creditable parents" in 1783 and married Captain James Bradley in 1802. In May of 1818, she consented to accompany him on a trip from Liverpool to Teneriffe, the only female among thirty-two passengers and crew members. Five weeks into the voyage, the ship is tossed about by a storm, springs several leaks, and hits a chain of rocks. Although the crew is hysterical, Eliza claims she maintained her calm: "The reader cannot suppose but that I too in a moment like this, must have shared the terrors of the crew; but my fortitude, by the blessings of Heaven, was much more probably than what would have been exhibited by many females in my situation" (12–13). Eventually, after several pages of description, including an emphasis on the sounds of despair, the "groans and exclamations" of the crew and passengers "amidst the raging of the winds, the roaring of the thunder, and the dashing of the waves," she and her husband and most of the crew make it to shore in a small boat (13–14).

Soon, however, they are captured by Arabs, who plan to hold them for ransom from the British Consul. The Arabs strip Eliza of her gown, bonnet, shoes, and stockings; dressed only in her petticoat and shimmy, she is "claimed" by her "Master" (23). On the long, detailed trip, Eliza eats locusts, camel, snails, and the bones and entrails of a kid goat; rides a camel and shares a trough of water with it; is separated from her husband (but not before he retains and gives her a Bible); and watches her thirsty fellow captives drink their own urine. Over and over, she quotes directly from the Bible. She claims that she savors this book because she is in "a distant heathen clime, a land of darkness, where the enemy reigns triumphant, and where by an idolatrous race the doctrines of a Blessed Redeemer are treated with derision and contempt" (42). After five months of separation from her husband, a messenger brings her a letter from him that tells her he is safe with the British Consul and that she will soon be ransomed. She completes the seven-hundred-mile journey to Mogadore and is reunited with her husband.

Martin's and Bradley's narratives seem as though they are not much different from the typical American captivity narrative, and to some extent they are not. In Richard Slotkin's oft-acknowledged list of the characteristics of captivity narratives, he explains that white women are the most commonly captured. Typically these women go on to exhibit resistance to "the temptation of Indian marriage" and are later redeemed by their family and friends (23). Martin and Bradley characterize themselves as middle-class and respectable, a common gesture of identification in captivity narratives (Castiglia 57). After the women are captured, there comes "an almost incessant mobility," just as in captivity narratives in which the prisoner travels with Indians through rough terrain (Burnham 51).

Also, the implications of these shipwreck narratives are similar to those of captivity narratives. Shipwreck narratives, like captivity narratives, give "symbolic form to the culturally unnameable: confinement in the home, enforced economic dependence, [and] rape," while offering "American women a female picaresque . . . outside the home" (Castiglia 4). As picaresque figures, Martin and

Bradley leave home, go to sea, and traipse around the North African desert. While their suffering subconsciously reminds middle-class women readers of their own restricted private sphere, these characters nevertheless claim pride in their "fortitude" (Bradley) and ability to overcome "suffering what man had never suffered before" (Martin). Another cultural implication of the captivity narrative was that it typically "challenged Anglo America's assertion that racial and gendered identities are innate, unified, and unchanging" (Castiglia 6). Both Martin and Bradley are shocked by their treatment and the changes they must undergo or witness, changes that implicitly question their "natural" ethnic superiority. For instance, some of Martin's European companions have collars around their necks and are being sold as slaves to dark-skinned people, while Bradley is stripped of most of her European clothing and forced to eat the bones and entrails of a goat that the Arabs will not eat.

However, the fact that these are common characteristics of captivity narratives does not mean that shipwreck narratives do not have their own unique features. Captivity narratives are just as much shipwreck narratives as shipwreck narratives are captivity narratives, especially considering that from the sixteenth century onward, shipwreck narratives arose in tandem with captivity narratives. It is perhaps more beneficial to see the boundaries between the two as fluid. I agree with Castiglia that we need to be wary of "patrolling the borders" of the genre of captivity narratives, of standardizing the "'typical' sequence of events in the 'classic' narrative" (23). When we patrol these borders, shipwreck narratives are subsumed by characteristics already assigned to captivity narratives (this is why there are multitudinous studies of captivity narratives and only a couple for shipwreck narratives), and important elements get ignored for the sake of maintaining arbitrary laws of genre. More specifically, when the only captivity narratives studied are those in which white Americans are held captive in America, narratives that include captivity following shipwreck in foreign countries are ignored. Captivity narratives are thereby perceived as taking place only within U.S. boundaries, which is inaccurate and limiting.

In most captivity narratives appearing by 1850, as James R.

Lewis points out, the image of the captive white woman in chains (Martin) and nearly naked (Bradley) became common indicators of the possible horrors of captivity, particularly rape.[7] Yet what makes these narratives so different from typical captivity narratives are the settings of the shipwrecks and the locations of their publication. Unlike typical Indian captivity, which often can be traced to a real historical figure, no female British or American woman was ever held in captivity by any of the Barbary states in the nineteenth century—and yet these fictional accounts were snatched up by the American public as if the fantasy were founded on fact.[8] It is illuminating to question the choice of Barbary as a site for shipwreck, as well as the implications of having English females pose as victims.

The shipwreck's location is of primary importance. Women's shipwreck narratives like Bradley's and Martin's were among the catalysts that awakened the public's outrage over the Barbary states' aggression. For a couple of centuries, these states (Tunis, Algiers, Morocco, and Tripoli) had been capturing Europeans and enslaving them, until the eighteenth century, when North African states received ransoms or tributes in exchange for safe passage through waters patrolled by Barbary natives. Up until the Revolutionary War, the British colony of America was protected from Barbary pirates because Britain paid the high tributes needed for protection. After the war, however, the United States found itself using one-sixth of its annual national budget for tributes to the Barbary states (Kitzen 20). Twenty-one male American citizens were captured and held hostage from July of 1795 to June 1796, during which time more Americans were captured by Barbary corsairs, and nearly one million dollars was paid for their release (20).

The tiresome negotiations and demands of frustrated merchants in the shipping industry led to a resolution to construct a naval force in 1794. Although the hostages were released before the American naval fleet was completed, four frigates were ready for battle in 1797 (Kitzen 19). These naval ships were eventually used for the Tripolitan War (1801–6), which became one of the subjects of the "Marine's Hymn." American victory brought home over three hundred U.S.

captives from the Barbary states (Baepler 25). As Mordecai M. Noah, the U.S. Consul in Tunis and Tripoli, later claimed in 1826, the Barbary conflict was "of vital importance to a nation having an infant navy" (qtd. in Schueller 46). It is therefore appropriate to credit America's desire to save her citizens from captivity as a major impetus for the construction of the U.S. Navy. Martin's and Bradley's narratives contributed to these defense efforts. For the country to continue to finance what was becoming an immense project, the construction of the nation's navy, dangers abroad had to appear as a threat to what was most vulnerable: Christian, middle-class women whose religion, morals, and very nature were threatened by dangerous Arab captors.

Yet it seems odd that women rather than men were imagined as shipwreck victims, since there were no females captured by North Africans in the nineteenth century. Their English origin is even more puzzling, as is the narratives' publication and popularity in America. Yet this is where the transatlantic facets of the shipwreck narrative surface, precisely when issues of gender and ethnicity arise. First of all, the shock value increases when these stories were women's stories rather than men's. The American public had already heard about male captives in the ten years leading up to Martin's 1806 narrative.[9] Though men's stories were frightening, tales of women's captivity were also sensational and carried a kind of modern-day tabloid appeal owing to the unlikely but titillating possibilities they posed. When the captive was an English woman rather than an American woman, the stories likely produced even more voyeuristic pleasure. Both Martin and Bradley emphasize their origins from respectable parents. They are portrayed as captain's wives, upstanding and wellborn women. Audiences would be drawn to these "ladies" and their reactions to lascivious threats and trough-sharing with camels.

Also, an American audience might have felt some level of satisfaction in seeing the wreck of an English ship, even as they identified with the Englishness of its passengers. Trade relations between Britain and the United States were tense at that time. England was at war with France, and British warships were seizing American vessels trading with France and impressing American sailors. In 1806 Britain put into effect "Orders in Council," trade regulations that forbade neutral commerce (American trade with France) and made official the promise that ships would be seized if such commerce continued. The popularity, then, of Martin's and Bradley's stories (Bradley's was published in 1820, less than a decade after the end of the War of 1812, commonly called America's Second War of Independence) may have given American readers the satisfaction of seeing the sinking of British ships.

Whether through resentment or admiration, however, most Anglo-Americans would have identified with English ladies, for Englishness was a source of Anglo-America's fictive ethnicity, an ethnicity Americans could rely on when threatened by a non-Western "Other." The vision of an Englishwoman on a ship full of men and then in a titillating "oriental" environment (Algiers)—far away from home and domestic roles—called to the surface the possibility of an Anglo-American woman in the same circumstance, within, say, a captivity narrative. Like captivity narratives, which may have prompted U.S. readers to wonder what it would be like to exist within a liminal, if not Indian, identity,[10] these shipwreck narratives allowed Anglo readers to wonder what it would be like to be shipwrecked and then live like a Moor.[11] Also, both England and the United States shared the perception that North Africans were the enemy, no less than the sea itself when it destroyed their ships. Victimizing an Englishwoman was like victimizing an Anglo-American woman, particularly when the enemy was mutual, whether that enemy was the sea or the Moors. As both women make clear—especially Bradley, whose story "was used in many Sunday schools as a teaching text" (Baepler 17)—they are Christian women trying to survive in a "heathen" land. Martin and Bradley, though of English origins, were tied to Anglo-Americans because Americans identified with a fictive ethnicity that appeared to naturally tie them to the victim, not the victimizer. Imagining itself through Anglo female victims, the United States had good reason to build its new navy, for to build a national defense, the nation had to imagine that the torchbearers of its moral and Christian heritage, white women, were threatened and must be saved.

In fact, as the nineteenth century wore on, such fictive ethnicity, the seemingly "natural" ties between Englishwomen and American ladies, grew into a firmer fantasy as the United States began to see itself as an imperial force. One of the most famous American novelists of the nineteenth century, James Fenimore Cooper, serves as a useful resource for understanding how an ethnic hybridity was constructed from the Anglo-American and the English lady. Like Bradley's and Martin's narratives, his novel *Homeward Bound* (1838) effectively highlights the imperialistic agenda at work in reading American females as Englishwomen when they became victims of shipwreck off of the coast of Africa. In Cooper's tale, the American Eve Effingham is on a voyage home from England after receiving an English education. Cooper endows Eve with the fictive ethnicity of Englishness even as she remains American in loyalty, so as to demonize the enemy shared by the two transatlantic nations—the "barbarous" North Africans.

In the novel, the American ship *Montauk* is heading to the United States carrying a variety of passengers. The action revolves around Eve; her widowed father, Edward; her Irish nurse, Ann Sidley; and Mademoiselle Viefville, Eve's French tutor; as well as several male admirers. It is made clear throughout the novel that Eve's attractiveness derives from both her American principles and her English refinement. Although Eve was born in America, her father brought her to England to be educated in European arts and languages. According to the men in the novel, Eve displays the best of both worlds in her character. Mr. Blunt, an admirer, speaking bluntly of Eve's attractiveness, claims she is "one so simple and yet so cultivated; with a mind in which nature and knowledge seem to struggle for the possession . . . so little like the cold sophistication and heartlessness of Europe on the one hand, and the unformed girlishness of America, on the other" (114). In other words, Eve displays what is best about English society (she is intellectually cultivated), and American society (she is connected to nature and simplicity).

Eve's description of herself similarly sounds like that of a typical civilized English lady. She sees herself as "single-minded and totally without management; devoted to her duties; religious without cant; a warm friend of liberal institutions, without the slightest approach to the impracticable; in heart and soul a woman" (114). Her words make clear that she is in control of herself, dutiful, religious but not fanatically so, a friend (but not an outspoken activist) to liberal institutions, and always practical. In other words, she is a civilized, respectable young woman, cultivated by English society and re-planted in American soil. And American she is, for she claims she is "as much American in character as in birth" (114). Eve is essentially an American *because* she accommodates an English ethnicity, and as such is worthy of admiration. As we shall see, Eve's fictive ethnic-ity is precisely what the United States needed to believe in when it shared an enemy with England. When North Africans preyed on this English lady, they were abusing an American lady as well.

When a storm destroys the *Montauk*'s main mast and it looks as if the ship will founder and fall into the hands of Moors and Turks, Eve gains an even stronger transatlantic identity in at least two ways. For one, Cooper may be drawing a loose visual parallel between the situation of Eve, her father, her nurse, and her tutor by implicitly referencing a scene from a well-known British shipwreck, the wreck of the *Halsewell*, depicted in famous paintings and nar-ratives that would have been easily recalled by Cooper and recog-nized by his audience. Secondly, it is clear that we are supposed to empathize with Eve because she is English and Anglo-American: a blend of simplicity and cultivation, precisely how respectable Anglo-Americans wanted to see themselves when faced with threatening North Africans.

The story of the wreck of the *Halsewell* in 1786 would have been familiar to the Americans reading Cooper's novel. The *Halsewell* story was published in several popular early nineteenth-century anthologies of shipwreck narratives, notably R. Thomas's *Interesting and Authentic Narratives of the most remarkable shipwrecks*, which ap-peared in 1836, two years before Cooper's novel. Also, at least two paintings dramatically depict the wreck, which killed approximately 165 passengers and crew, among whom were the captain, his two daughters, and five other young women. George Morland's paint-

14. George Morland's *The Wreck of the Halsewell*, circa 1786. Courtesy of the Mariners' Museum, Newport News VA.

ing *The Wreck of the* Halsewell (1786) depicts the females' reaction to the oncoming doom. The captain is seated with his daughters clinging to him while other women huddle around and behind him, having fainted or pleading with God and the heavens.

In *Homeward Bound*, the passengers in the disabled ship await imminent capture by the Turks, and they despair over their hopeless situation. Cooper narrates the scene as if describing Morland's painting: "Mr. Effingham was seated, his daughter's head resting on a knee, for she had thrown herself on the carpet, by his side. . . . Ann Sidley knelt near her young mistress, sometimes praying fervently, though in silence, and at other moments folding her beloved in her arms, as if to protect her from the ruffian grasp of the barbarians" (261). The two women in figure 14 hold a similar pose: one of the women has buried her head in her father's chest, while the woman kneeling next to her wraps an arm around her waist.

Whether or not Cooper intended to create this parallel with Morland's painting, there is certainly an awareness on his part of the appeal of the white woman—English or American—in distress at sea. The hostile ocean and ferocious Turks are collapsed into one threat by the scene's similitude to Morland's painting. The "whiteness" of both females is the source of sympathy. Like the painting of the wreck of the *Halsewell*, which highlights the white women's suffering through the shine of a kind of heavenly light on their plight, Eve Effingham is portrayed as most beautiful when she is left stranded on a wrecked ship and left to the hands of Turks. During the aforementioned scene, when all are awaiting their fate, Eve's face is described as "deadly" pale, and Cooper notes that it "rendered her loveliness of feature and expression bright and angelic. Both of the young men thought she had never seemed so beautiful, and both felt a secret pang, as the conviction forced itself on them, at the same instant, that this surpassing beauty was now likely to prove her most dangerous enemy" (262). The dark sea is about to devour the whiteness of the shipwrecked women of the *Halsewell*, just as the dark "barbarians" are about to enslave the pale, bright, angelic face of Eve. As the nineteenth-century sculpture *The Shipwrecked Mother and Child* demonstrates, it is the whiteness of the distressed woman at sea that makes her most pitiful.[12] Cooper's Eve solidifies an Anglo-American fictive ethnicity. Since Eve is an American woman who identifies with English cultural assumptions about North Africans, her victimization is an affront to all things American and English—to whiteness itself.

Like the wrecks in Bradley's and Martin's narratives, this shipwreck occurs off of the coast of North Africa. Though all three stories allude to the past troubles with Barbary states, they nevertheless are published and consistently reprinted years after the conflicts faded. Some critics believe the stories are captivity narratives that subtly express the United States' tension over the question of slavery. Around the same time Maria Martin's narrative was published, a handful of fictional tales of white captivity in North Africa surfaced as well.[13] Benilde Montgomery concludes that these stories of white captivity on Algerian shores serve as a critique of the American institution of slavery by using the captivity of American men and women "as a mask behind which their abolitionist authors could criticize moral abuses in the political establishment at home" (617). David S. Reynolds also reads North African captivity tales as subversive critiques of American culture. One of the categories of what Reynolds calls "Oriental" tales is made up of stories about captivity and/or spying that "provided a convenient camouflage for satirizing orthodoxy and promoting toleration" for cultures and religions different from Anglo Calvinists (15).

Though Montgomery's and Reynolds's textual examples provide ample evidence for their theories, it is nonetheless problematic to assume that this was the trend for all stories set in North Africa or India, or that these critiques were necessarily reflective of popular opinion. Cooper's Eve attracts attention to her own victimization, not anyone else's, and though Maria Martin alludes to slavery during the auction scene, it is difficult to prove that this is anti-slavery sentiment.[14] Even though Martin is pointing out the indignity of slavery, it is specifically *white* slavery that is depicted as degrading. The mention of the collars on the West Indian slaves may merely have been a way to highlight the revolting reversal of an imposed hierarchy of slave/master, not to gain sympathy for the plight of black slaves.

Eliza Bradley's narrative cannot be notable for its sympathy to abolitionism, or for its satire of religious orthodoxy. She makes the Moors out to be beastly, for they force her to drink camel urine and strip her of her clothing. She emphasizes her reliance on the Bible to sustain her in her miseries, since she has found herself shipwrecked in a "distant heathen clime, a land of darkness, where the enemy reigns triumphant, and where by an idolatrous race the doctrines of a Blessed Redeemer are treated with derision and contempt" (42). The string of racial and religious biases expressed by the tale's heroine does not ring of satire but rather seems more like a reiteration of well-known stereotypes of North Africans that were passed around in the popular culture. At best, her words seem like a diatribe against those believed to embody "moral degeneracy and sensual excess" (Schueller 47). Thus, Martin's and Bradley's narratives complicate Malini Johar Schueller's contention that early North African narratives exemplify how the United States represented its imperialism as a benevolent mission—in opposition to the British, who represented their imperial efforts as part of a civilizing mission (19). Martin implicitly and Bradley explicitly exhibit no benevolence, in either words or actions, toward their captors: their captors are dark, they are heathens, and they are the enemy. The United States, like the British, believed that North Africans needed to be civilized, not for their own good, as would be the goal of a benevolent mission, but because they were an evil, non-Christian presence in the world. This message apparently attracted a large number of readers. Thus, identifying ethnically with England could work to align America's imperialistic goals with that nation as well.

For though some of these tales of Barbary captivity indeed contain antislavery connotations, others do not (Bradley's), or are so ambiguous (like Martin's) that they cannot positively be aligned with abolitionist literature. In comparison with such abolitionist Barbary tales as *Slaves in Algiers*, *The Algerine Captive*, and *The American Captive*, Martin's and Bradley's narratives enjoyed a much longer run of publication and more numerous editions, an indication that they were more popular with American audiences. Martin's narrative, first published in 1806, was reprinted at least twelve more times by 1818, while Bradley's story, first published in 1820, was reprinted at least twelve times by 1848. Thus, it is safe to assume that part of what made these narratives so popular was the fascination with shipwreck and the identification of a perceived ethnic connection between white Americans (especially female) and English women and their imperialistic attitudes toward North Africans. Martin's and Bradley's narratives of victimization by Moors and Turks solidified notions of Anglo racial superiority rather than critiqued it, which seems to have been precisely what American audiences wanted to hear.

The examples of women in shipwreck narratives discussed thus far can be read as moral and political indicators of mainstream cultural desires. These narratives' capacity to reveal cultural attitudes toward ethnic identification, respectable "womanhood," and slavery was multiplied when U.S. publishers altered English shipwreck narratives to suit American tastes. The changes made to a shipwreck narrative that was published first in, say, London, then later in a city such as New York or Boston, often reveal how shipwreck narratives constructed an Anglo-American, middle-class community. Specifically, an examination of the narrative changes illustrates how portrayals of women in shipwreck narratives address particular social problems or trends, like Indian suppression, slavery, and even religious conversion experiences. A look at a couple of examples, the stories of the Englishwomen Eliza Fraser and Ann Saunders, reveals how shipwreck narratives revised the Englishwoman's victimhood for American purposes.

On August 17, 1836, nearly three months after the wreck of the five-hundred-ton British brig *Sterling Castle*, a rescue party finally landed on the shores of the Great Sandy Island off of the coast of Australia. They arrived in order to negotiate the release of a handful of shipwreck victims. The most sensational survivor was the captain's thirty-six-year-old wife, Eliza Fraser, who had survived captivity among Australian aborigines on what is now called Fraser Island. On seeing the condition she was in, the lieutenant leading the rescue party quickly gave Eliza a cloak and a petticoat "to prevent her appearing in a state of nudity before the boat's crew and soldiers" (Curtis 164). Up close, the rescue party saw a woman nearly indistinguishable from her captives, "her head bedizened with feathers and other *ornaments*, after the manner of the natives, so that although partially dressed, her swarthy shrivelled skin presented a figure truly grotesque" (165).

The story of Eliza Fraser's shipwreck and captivity became the subject of ballads and broadsheets, magazine articles, illustrations, woodcuts, and cartoons in England. Like the natives to whom she was compared at the time of her rescue, Fraser's person and experiences were recast through the lens of those who "discovered" her: the rescuers, the newspapers, the illustrators, and the British public.[15] However, the description just given of Fraser's rescue and physical condition comes from the earliest definitive rendition of the shipwreck and rescue of Eliza Fraser, entitled *Shipwreck of the Stirling Castle*, compiled and written by John Curtis. When Fraser returned to London following the rescue and told her story to the Lord Mayor so she could receive monetary aid, her experience was then retold by newspaper reporters, never directly through her own pen, for the public at large. Curtis was a court reporter who recorded Fraser's story during her appearances in front of the Lord Mayor and recounted her story along with other testimony in a 242–page narrative published in 1838. There are several consistent threads in her testimony as it appeared in the *London Times* in 1837 and Curtis's collection of testimony of other *Stirling Castle* firsthand witnesses and shipwreck victims.

Both of the accounts tell how Fraser, her husband, sixteen other passengers, and nine crew members rowed their longboats to the shores of the Great Sandy Island following the shipwreck. All of the survivors were eventually led away by natives. Eliza Fraser is left behind for a short period of time until a group of female natives strip her of her clothing, lead her away, and put her in charge of an invalid woman and her child. Fraser grows to be fond of the woman since she protects Eliza from harsh treatment whenever she can. Fraser witnesses the spearing death of her husband when he refuses to work, though all accounts state that she believes the natives did not intend to kill him, only to wound him. She is forced to climb trees for food and collect firewood. She is rarely allowed to eat and she sees the natives as no different from "the beasts of the forest, except that the savages are ingenious in their cruelty."[16]

It is helpful to keep the bare bones of this narrative in mind as we turn to the American version of the Fraser shipwreck and captivity, published in the United States in 1837. When Fraser's story crossed the Atlantic, her narrative was significantly revised.[17] These changes reveal U.S. attitudes toward the Native American population and the convenient availability of fictive ethnicity. In the U.S. version, no location for the shipwreck is offered, the natives are murderers, the female natives are cruel, and Eliza is nearly raped and forced to marry a native. Entitled *Narrative of the Capture, Sufferings, and Miraculous Escape of Mrs. Eliza Fraser*, the story of the shipwreck of the *Sterling Castle* "on an unknown island, inhabited by savages" (says the long subtitle) is depicted in visual terms on the title page. The illustration portrays the Australian aborigines as North American Indians bearing tomahawks, and wearing headdresses, togas, and high moccasins. In addition to these visual differences, the narrative recasts the Australian aborigines as generic Native American "savages." The native women are cruel "squaws" who approach Fraser on the beach and beat and maim her. No kind invalid woman and her child appear as in the English version; instead, Fraser says she is mistreated by the mother of an infant whom she describes as a "deformed and ugly looking brat" (7). She claims her husband is killed intentionally, and she adds that Mr. Brown, the chief mate, is burned alive at the stake (15–16). This action is followed by a marriage proposal from the chief. When she is about to be raped by him, she is rescued. The narrative is followed by a short account of the wreck of the British ship *Blinderhall*. This brief story tells of the quartermaster's wife, whose baby is nearly eaten by the starving, shipwrecked crew. They are saved before this happens, however, and all, says the anonymous author, is proof of "the remarkable interposition of Divine Providence" (24).

This American version of the Fraser shipwreck follows in the footsteps of dozens of American captivity narratives published throughout early American and U.S. literary history. Kay Schaffer theorizes that Fraser's story was constructed as a captivity narrative because it was published during a time of a resurgence of published (or reprinted) captivity narratives involving women.[18] Schaffer believes the reason for this recurring interest derives from the fact that the United States was embroiled in controversy over the status of Native Americans, specifically, and people of color, generally, following the Supreme Court's decision in *Cherokee Nation v. Georgia* (1831). This court case, which defined indigenous peoples as noncitizens, coincided with the Nat Turner Rebellion in 1831 (a U.S. slave revolt that resulted in slain whites and African

15. Eliza Fraser in captivity. Frontispiece from *Narrative of the Capture, Sufferings and Miraculous Escape of Mrs. Eliza Fraser*, by Eliza Fraser (New York: Charles S. Webb, 1837). Courtesy of the Edward E. Ayer Collection, Newberry Library, Chicago.

Americans), the Seminole wars of the 1830s (58), and, I would add, the heightened tension over the large-scale "removal" policies of President Jackson, which led to the Trail of Tears. It was a decade ripe for a white-authored captivity narrative that portrayed Native Americans as beastly, abusive rapists. As Schaffer makes clear, U.S. accounts of Fraser's rescue represent Eliza "not [as] a woman, but an idea of nation, 'the people',", and thus offer a "celebration of humanitarianism over brutal savagery" (51).

Such notions of "humanitarianism" and "savagery" rely on assumptions of fictive ethnicity. The ease with which a fictive ethnicity is assumed for Anglo-American women and, even more important, tribes indigenous to nations other than the United States, is striking. In the U.S. version of the Fraser shipwreck narrative, Eliza could be any Anglo-American woman, and Australian aborigines are seemingly effortlessly transformed into North American Indians. Most travel and shipwreck narratives at this time attached "ethnographies" that attempted to describe the lifestyles of peoples other than

Americans. Fraser's narrative does not even attempt to portray an indigenous culture different from America's, despite the title's claim that Fraser and her party were shipwrecked on an unknown island on a passage from New South Wales to Liverpool. The title alone assumes that no difference exists between a native tribe in North America and a people indigenous to an island halfway around the world. A kind of homogenized ethnicity is ascribed to the natives and in fact produces the ethnic identification Anglo-Americans would have had with an Englishwoman. A homogenized Other creates a homogenized victimhood that is at once white, American, and English. This process reflects just how convenient it was for Anglo-Americans to call on one kind of fictive ethnicity to create another.

Such efforts to elide differences contributed to Anglo national interests. If Anglo-Americans could believe that the threat of the "savage" "out there" on an unknown island was no different from that posed by those natives (who were already in the process of being defined and contained) within the borders of the United States, then Anglo-Americans could have a kind of global justification for Indian removal policies. By using the stories of Eliza Fraser and others as a source of resistance to Native savagery, American policies of Indian removal could be represented as an act of resistance to brutal aggression directed toward innocent victims (like Eliza Fraser), rather than as an aggressive gesture of removal and land acquisition.

Another subtext of such narratives, however, is the fear of sameness, not difference. At least one captivity narrative published around the time of Fraser's American version depicts a young woman captured by the Seneca Indians; eventually, she chooses to remain among the tribe and twice marry Seneca men.[19] Fraser herself nearly becomes part of the tribe when she almost marries a chief in the U.S. version of her story. The attached short narrative of the wreck of the *Blinderhall*, with its focus on the near cannibalistic acts of the crew members, hints at how easily those of the "civilized" world could enter a savage existence.[20] Anglo readers would be horrified but titillated to see white people becoming the Other.

In such instances, Anglo-Americans' reliable fictive ethnicity is compromised by their own behavior, while their actions as native brides and cannibals call into question the seemingly impenetrable boundaries of an Anglo-English ethnicity.

So far, we have seen how a married, English, middle-class lady could attract an Anglo-American audience to identify with her. Most shipwreck narratives deal with women of this ethnicity and class. But does such readerly identification also occur when the female shipwreck victim is English and working class? Could Americans identify with Englishwomen whose ethnicity connoted respectability but whose class does not? The shipwreck narrative I will discuss next was written by an unmarried, lower-class English woman who published her narrative in the United States after a much different form appeared in a British newspaper account.[21] Ann Saunders's *Narrative of the Shipwreck . . . of Miss Ann Saunders* appeals to audiences' sense of ethnicity because Saunders is an Englishwoman in distress, but her class status complicates this appeal. Her sensational brush with cannibalism likewise distances her from audience identification, and the British version of her wreck reveals degrading assumptions about the lower class. In an attempt to downplay the relevance of her class status to her ethnic identity as a white Englishwoman, the American version of her shipwreck is transformed into a Christian conversion narrative in which Saunders is represented as reformed by her experience and committed to teaching other young ladies the Christian lessons of her tragedy.

Saunders was aboard the *Frances Mary* as an attendant to the captain's wife, Mrs. Kendall. They were the only women out of twenty-one passengers and crew. After the shipwreck, the *Frances Mary* foundered at sea. Stranded for days without food or water, the passengers and crew resorted to cannibalism. Saunders reportedly had to eat her fiancé, Frier, to survive. The reduced party was rescued more than two weeks later, and the London newspapers were the first to tell Saunders's story. The news was published in the *British Traveller* on March 17, 1826. The first, short account reports that survivors of the wreck of the *Frances Mary* had to support themselves by "feeding on the dead bodies of those who died on the wreck" and that after being rescued, they "received the utmost possible sympathy, and everything afforded for their comfort and accommodation." Three days later, the details were much more extensive. The newspaper now offered an account that appears to have been written by a crew member aboard the ship, for it resembles a log of day-to-day activity and refers to the women in third person. He reports that "we . . . got the master's wife and female passenger up [to the maintop while the ship foundered]."[22] In the rambling account, the narrator says that when Saunders "heard of Frier's death, [she] shrieked a loud yell, then snatching a cup from Clerk [mate] cut her late intended husband's throat, and drank his blood, insisting that she had the greatest right to it—a scuffle ensued, and the heroine got the better of her adversary, and then allowed him to drink one cup to her two!" According to this account of Saunders, she had become a kind of expert at preparing the meals: "[S]he performed the duty of cutting up and cleaning the dead bodies, keeping two knives in her monkey jacket; and when the breath was announced to have flown, she would sharpen her knives, bleed the deceased in the neck, drink his blood, and cut him up as usual."

In the first excerpt from this account, the shriek of the woman echoes the shriek of the savage. This account portrays her as a "savage" cannibal as a way to make sense of this British woman's cannibalism. The possibility that a white female might turn to cannibalism was so taboo that Saunders had to be figured as both savage and male, dressed as she was in a monkey jacket and wielding knives. If she were behaving as a savage man, she could not be a respectable woman. Additionally, she ironically takes on the role of cook after eating her fiancé, who was the ship's cook, for she is responsible for cutting and cleaning the bodies and prepares them for eating. Transforming into a man and a cook after ingesting her fiancé, Saunders is an explicit representation of the phrase "You are what you eat." That identity is anything but English, and her behavior is the antithesis of femininity.

Saunders's class is at issue as much as her gender. She is a lower-class woman who, as Mrs. Kendall's female attendant, is under her thumb. At the same time, Saunders is engaged to a man who will make her his property when they marry. Like the natives, who are perceived as propertyless by whites, women in the 1820s rarely owned property under law in either Britain or the United States. The subtle equation between the shrieking lower-class woman and the shrieking native who together consume their "owners" poses a subversive challenge to the established hierarchies of man/woman and colonizer/colonized. After all, Saunders demands a "greater portion of [her fiancé's] blood"; in a sense, she claims property rights. This implicit, illicit challenge to social order by a working-class woman reveals an underlying anxiety in the caricature of Saunders as a fiendish blood-sucker in the British Traveller report.

Perhaps this demeaning caricature was the impetus for Saunders to prepare her own version of the narrative for publication in America. An American audience might be less influenced by the British press, and more inclined to empathize with her sensational tragedy. Plus, the form of her American narrative would be familiar to American audiences: it resembled the conversion narrative and was also an early form of the murder tales that were about to be published throughout the following two decades.[23] The familiarity of these genres (and their often sensational, didactic lessons), as well as the fact that an American audience would possibly be unfamiliar with the British account, helped to create a Saunders more palatable, so to speak, to her reading audience. In particular, Saunders's choice of the conversion narrative genre reveals how lower-class shipwrecked women needed to frame their stories in hopes of gaining the same sympathies offered to middle-class Anglo-American women in distress at sea.

According to Saunders's account, which was published in Providence, Rhode Island, and also represented in a broadside, severe storms staved in the stern of the ship on its return to Liverpool, on February 5, 1826. Because of rough seas, three ships went by without helping. By February 11, the passengers had depleted their food and water provisions, "and hunger and thirst began to select their victims" (12). By February 22, a seaman had died of starvation, and the "calls of hunger had now become too importunate to be resisted" (13). Saunders goes on to explain:

[I]t is a fact, although shocking to relate, that we were reduced to the awful extremity to attempt to support our feeble
bodies a while longer by subsisting on the dead body of the
deceased—it was cut into slices, then washed in salt water,
and after being exposed to and dried a little in the sun, was
apportioned to each of the miserable survivors, who partook
of it as a sweet morsel—from this revolting food I abstained
for 24 hours, when I too was compelled by hunger, to follow
their example! (13)

The passengers go on to consume other dead seamen as well.
Saunders names and lists them by occupation: two cabin boys,
the cook, and four seamen.

By 1827, when this particular version of the narrative was
published, cannibalism would have been familiar to Saunders's
transatlantic audiences. Since the earliest exploration narratives,
transatlantic audiences would have heard stories of cannibalism
among natives. In fact, fascination with cannibalism has led the
anthropologist Gananath Obeyesekere to describe late eighteenth-
century Britons as having a "cannibalistic complex" (641) resulting
from exposure to the stories of explorers' voyages, such as those
of Captain Cook, while U.S. audiences heard their own share of
stories of cannibalism among Native Americans.[24] Less common but
equally persistent were instances of white cannibalism. Audiences
would have been familiar with a few of the most famous stories.[25]
As Saunders tells us in the following passage, white cannibalism
narratives were familiar to her as well: "[H]ow often in my childhood
have I read accounts of sea-faring people, and others, having been
driven to the awful alternative of either starving, or to satisfy the
cravings of nature, subsisting on human flesh . . . accounts which
are pretty generally discredited by those who have not been placed
in a similar situation—but, to such an awful extremity, I can assure
my Christian readers, was I and my wretched companions now
reduced" (13). Yet, beneath this type of recognizable cannibalism
owing to extreme necessity lay the potential for criminality in the
act, a hint of murder born from a twisted class hierarchy. Saunders's

story highlights the understood but unstated hierarchy of the consumer and the consumed in shipwreck narratives involving white cannibalism. As is obvious in the quote just discussed, Saunders wants readers to realize that the people who are consumed were already dead, as is evident in the redundant phrase "subsisting on the dead body of the deceased." That the bodies were both "dead" *and* "deceased" is also emphasized in the title of her narrative. The curious overemphasis of this point may come from the fear of being seen as a murderer, for an audience would probably recognize the likelihood that lots were drawn and someone had to be killed for food and drink. As Obeyesekere explains, stories of cannibalism aboard a ship most often involved the drawing of lots to determine who should die first, and then that person was murdered. Usually a person would be spared only if he were married and had a family (640).

With this in mind, it is possible to read the section of the narrative where Saunders describes the deaths of her companions as double-voiced. She claims that "the heart-piercing lamentations of these poor creatures (dying for the want of sustenance) was distressing beyond conception" (14). We are led to believe the source of their lamentations was the lack of food and water, but they could have been pleading for their lives. Further, Saunders tells about both the seaman Hutchinson, who "had left a numerous family in Europe, [and] talked of his wife and children as well as if they were present," and the ravenous seaman Jones, who spoke of his wife and children to his companions, whom he accused of "being the authors of his extreme sufferings, by depriving him of food, and in refusing him a single drop of water" (14). These two men might have been begging for their lives, since both emphasize that they are family men, with wives and children, and Jones may have been denied provisions so that he would die without having to be overtly murdered.[26]

Nevertheless, murder stays at the fringe of the narrative, close enough to titillate yet not enough to incriminate. The likelihood that Saunders witnessed or even participated in murder serves as the dirty deed often confessed in the conversion narrative. While the hint of murder anticipates the sensational murder confession and "female fiend" character soon to be popular in the antebellum era,[27] Saunders's story most resembles the conversion narrative. In her study of women and conversion narratives in the nineteenth century, Virginia Lieson Brereton identifies the pattern of these narratives: "They typically opened with the convert's early life, went on to describe a period of increasing sense of sinfulness, climaxed with conversion proper, and concluded with . . . zealous conduct of evangelical activity" (3–4). Saunders's odd moment of conversion takes place during her most sinful act. When Saunders's fiancé, James Frier, the cook, dies, she says that her resulting feelings are best judged by "my Christian female readers (for it is you that can best judge)" (15). Saunders explains what happened next: "myself at the same moment so far reduced by hunger and thirst, as to be driven to the horrid alternative to preserve my own life (O! God of Heaven! The lamentable fact is known to thee, and why should I attempt to conceal it from the world?) To plead my claim to the greater portion of his precious blood, as it oozed half congealed from the wound inflicted upon his lifeless body!!!" (15). For Saunders, this "abject moment of despair" was the turning point in her spiritual life, "a chastening rod," as she calls it, which wean[ed] [her] forever from all the vain enjoyments of this frail world; and of fixing [her] hopes and trust in the merits of Jesus" (15–16). Her plea to her "Christian female readers" implies that it is they who will best "judge" this process of conversion, of sin, and then surrender to "the merits of Jesus."

Like a conversion narrative, Saunders's story indicates that she hoped her account would be sermonic in nature. Throughout the narrative and at the end, Saunders earnestly evangelizes, insisting on Christian messages and lessons, particularly one's need to accept God in the present life to achieve salvation. The cover of her narrative reprints a short prayer and informs us that annexed to this shipwreck narrative is a "Solemn Address . . . on the importance of attending to the concerns of [one's] Immortal Soul, and in being prepared for Death." Saunders declares at the end that she was compelled to tell her story because it would be "unpardonable were I to remain silent, and not thus publicly declare to the world what comforts the religion of a blessed Saviour afforded me, during my most severe afflictions" (21). Fashioning herself into a lapsed-then-saved Christian is a plea for the audience to see her as a woman saved from lower-class indecency and to view her as a Christian Englishwoman—the tie that binds a transatlantic fictive ethnicity.

Saunders's narrative works hard to create a sentimentalized Christian conversion narrative. If she is to get respectable Anglo-American readers to identify with her Englishness, or "whiteness," rather than turn away from her lower-class status and uncivilized behavior, Saunders (or her publisher) must attempt to foreground her cannibalism as the moment of her Christian conversion. Saunders's turning point, or moment of conversion, is when she drinks the blood and eats the flesh of her betrothed. This act was both a "chastening rod" and what prompted her to place her "hopes and trust in the merits of Jesus." In the language of Christian ritual, she partakes of the body and blood and is "weaned" from vanity. She represents the consumption of the "sacrificed" body of her fiancé as a reception of saving grace, not an act of savagery.[28] Being that women's nineteenth-century conversion narratives were typically written by those of the middle class, Saunders uses this genre as a rhetorical route to reform herself into the image of a respectable Anglo-American Christian woman.[29] She wants to be like a middle-class convert, and she wants her middle-class female readers to accept her. She pleads specifically with her *female* readers to judge her feelings, since it is the middle-class female readers of sentimental literature she is aiming to persuade of her deserved sympathy.

Even the visual depiction of her tragedy is a plea to the audience to see her as just like them. Unlike the aquatint of the wreck that appeared in England, Saunders's frontispiece clearly foregrounds her suffering. In the British version (figure 16), the survivors are so minute that it is difficult to make out the two women or the presumably dead man hanging from the ship's stern. Saunders's frontispiece, however, reveals her supplication for help, and her trial seems representative of those who can no longer voice their

16. Ann Saunders's wreck is depicted in *The Melancholy Shipwreck of the Frances Mary from St. Johns* (Edward E. Fisher, 1827). Artist unknown. Courtesy of the Mariners' Museum, Newport News VA.

conversion, as is symbolized by the rows of coffins framing the drawing (figure 17). The frontispiece works harder than the aquatint to gain sympathy; Saunders's clasped-hands plead for a physical and spiritual rescue. Though the drawing depicts a ship coming to her rescue, it also suggests Saunders's hope that the audience's sympathy will rescue her from her sins. Also, note that she and the other woman, Mrs. Kendall are indistinguishable from each another. Class cannot be read in the frontispiece. By pleading with her target audience, females, using their own middle-class Christian rhetoric of piety, and aligning herself with Mrs. Kendall in the drawing, Saunders pushes her audience to identify with her. Likely, she hoped the female audience would see themselves in her shoes as the converted Saunders emphasizes her Christian evangelicalism even as she describes a kind of dark fantasy of escape from the realm of domesticity.[30] If Saunders can prove she is like those of the middle class, she might be able to elicit sympathy from those who believe women and children should come first.

17. Ann Saunders appealing for rescue. Frontispiece from *Narrative of the Shipwreck and Sufferings of Miss Ann Saunders* (Providence: Z. S. Crossman, 1827). Courtesy of Department of Special Collections, Stanford University Libraries.

If the printing history of her story is any indication, Saunders's story was not popular in the United States. Perhaps her attempt to appear middle-class was unconvincing. After all, she was a lower-class woman who could be seen as encroaching on a respectable genre to gain forgiveness for an outrageously distasteful act. Unlike Martin and Bradley's narratives, which were reprinted over a dozen times, Eliza Fraser's and Ann Saunders's stories had single runs in 1837 and 1827, respectively. Perhaps these women's behavior was too unseemly for American audiences. Cannibalism and near marriage to an "Indian" from another country may have been too threatening, taking the appeal of "going native" a bit too far. However, another possibility for the poor sales exists on a semantic level, one that takes into account the very term "fictive ethnicity." In a symbolic coincidence, these stories show how fiction could inform Anglo-American fictive ethnicity, specifically fiction that affirmed Americans' notions of themselves as moral, respectable, and superior to nonwhites at home and abroad. The best sellers were not Englishwomen's nonfiction shipwreck accounts, such as Bradley's and Saunders's, but other fictional stories of disaster at sea and captivity abroad. Real stories about real Englishwoman whose femininity and ethnicity were compromised by their ordeals were not as appealing as those of fictional Englishwomen who experienced similar compromises of their femininity and Anglo identity but triumphed over their enemies. Martin, Bradley, and Cooper's Eve all survive with their whiteness intact; they did not eat their fiancés or nearly marry Indian chiefs. They remained on top in the hierarchy of power they assumed existed, a victory Americans wanted to claim for themselves as well. It did not matter if this was fiction, because white Americans relied on a fictional inheritance of their own, a fictive ethnicity that facilitated their growing sense of superiority. Stories like these offer yet more evidence that images of women and the sea helped to construct a larger, national narrative of moral exceptionalism, even if that narrative relied on fiction for its efficacy.

Like Fraser's shipwreck narrative, Saunders's story was revised in its transatlantic crossing, and the revisions to it are a reflection of publishers' assumptions about American tastes and desires. Tales of disaster at sea involving Englishwomen were published in the United States because the nation provided an audience attracted to the vision of an English woman in distress. Furthermore, if Anglo-Americans claimed a fictive ethnicity of Englishness for themselves when their nation was challenged by a mutual enemy, as in Martin's and Bradley's narratives, they could justify the construction of a national defense equal to that of England. Eliza Fraser's narrative, recast as an American captivity narrative yet making clear that the shipwreck was far away and the captors were from another land, reflects the impulse to homogenize the native populations of North America with natives of other nations by defining Others as beastly and uncivilized, regardless of their global location. Through such acts, Anglo-Americans could justify their domestic policy, whether it involved validating the institution of slavery, creating directives for Indian removal, or enforcing aggressive land acquisition.

— 5 —

Cross-Dressed Female Seafarers in Early American Popular Literature

By the end of the War of 1812, the United States renewed its commitment to independence by fighting a second war with England. Yet independence also brought uncertainty. A country composed of people from different cultural backgrounds who were attracted to the land because it promised individual liberty evoked several questions: What kind of community can prosper with so many different people guided by self-interest? Where would loyalties lie? With relatives in other countries? With employers? With business partners? With family? As Philip B. Gould frames the question for post-Revolution writers: "What kinds of personal and civic qualities were necessary to republican life?" (8). Though the "republican life" was typically associated with Anglo-American men, a great deal of early American literature portrayed women's responses to these questions as well. The female "types" in the early nineteenth century, as Linda Kerber and Ann Douglas have shown, respectively, were the "republican mother" and, later, the "true woman."[1] Both types of women were represented as central to the moral virtue of the middle- and upper-class household. However, our understanding of women's role as arbiter of domestic morality needs to be refined.

As Cathy Davidson and others have made clear, interpreting the past as a time when males controlled the public sphere and women controlled the private sphere is too simplistic, particularly when it comes to literature.[2] Though early female authors such as

Susanna Rowson, Hannah Webster Foster, and Lydia Maria Child each had their own vision of women's roles in the new nation, other anonymous or male-authored popular tales of women's adventures in the public sphere tell a story rarely noticed by current literary historians, perhaps because the women in them acted outside of the private sphere traditionally occupied by women. The women in these adventure stories do not spend time reading their Bibles in the parlor or tutoring their sons on how to be good citizens, as a republican mother or true woman should. Rather, they are aboard ships, in drag, and at sea, "principal instruments" in defining a national character. Dressed as men, these female sailors often possess the "personal and civic qualities" necessary to the republican life.

Women disguised as seafaring men appeared long before American writers got ahold of them.[3] It was not until the end of the eighteenth century that the literary American female mariner was invented. The character type appeared in fictional accounts beginning with the female protagonist in *The History of Constantius and Pulchera* at the end of the eighteenth century and surfaced more frequently throughout the first half of the nineteenth century.[4] After the Lucy Brewer character appeared in *The Female Marine* in 1815, more female cross-dressed sailors emerged, such as Almira Paul (1816), Ellen Stephens (1840), Fanny Campbell (1844), Emma Cole (1844), Fanny Templeton Danforth (1849), Eliza Allen (1851), and Marian Moore (1853), as well as several seafaring women in James Fenimore Cooper's sea trilogy.[5]

Nearly all of these stories have one similar purpose: to teach men how to be men, republican citizens who represent America's exceptionally moral, Christian nature. Similar to the women in the sea narratives we have looked at thus far, whose suffering was used to teach men lessons about America's covenant with God and community, the cross-dressed characters discussed in this chapter teach men how they should feel and act. Appearing as men, these women reveal a character that displays the personal and civic qualities necessary for the nation to claim its exceptional nature. Their stories glorified loyalty to family and the origins of the country's founding principles, setting forth an alternative vision of a nation untainted by men's selfishness, greed, or desire to move west. In the works I'll discuss in the first part of this chapter, women's loyalty serves as a model for or indicator of appropriate American personal and civic virtues and demonstrates that these virtues are worthy of love and loyalty. In the second part of the chapter, I will show that cross-dressed female mariners sometimes also served as reminders of the virtues forgotten during westward expansion.

—⁂—

The Female Marine, first published in 1815, was a popular pamphlet-novel about a fictional cross-dressed female marine who fights the British during the War of 1812.[6] Though the marine, Lucy Brewer, became a phenomenon in American publishing, she was not the first American woman to go to war. Soon after the Revolutionary War in the 1790s, Herman Mann, in collaboration with Deborah Sampson, published the true story of Sampson's experience as a cross-dressed Revolutionary War soldier. Following this, the female soldier became a well-recognized figure throughout the first half of the nineteenth century.[7] Revolutionary War–era women were "expected to suffer, to admire the military, and to maintain their innocence" (Kerber 106). Deborah Sampson's narrative disrupted the image of the suffering, admiring, and innocent woman and reimagined her as an adventurous, patriotic freedom fighter. Tapping into Americans' curiosity about the Revolutionary War, publishers saw the second war with England as a prime opportunity to produce another story about a cross-dressed patriot. The fictional story of Lucy Brewer, the female marine, shifts the setting from land to sea and the heroine's disguise from soldier to marine.[8] As such, Brewer models appropriate American virtues by fighting for her country, rescuing females from harm, and remaining loyal to the origins of her country.

Like Deborah Sampson's tale before her, Brewer's cross-dressing story resonated with specific concerns of the time. Brewer's disguise addresses anxieties over the "appearance" of Americans' loyalty.

The opening of The Female Marine is a story of shifting appearances and character revealed. Lucy Brewer (an alias)[9] is duped by a man who appears to be interested in marrying her. His false promises lead to her pregnancy and his desertion. Ashamed and unwilling to hurt her family, Lucy travels by foot to Boston, hoping to find respectable accommodations, but she unknowingly accepts an invitation to stay in what turns out to be a house of prostitution. She remains there until she has the child, who dies at birth. Lucy is forced to work as a prostitute by the madam in order to pay for her care. In the bleak opening pages, the paired themes of disguise and character are established. As a result of a man's duplicitous behavior, Brewer must hide her own condition from her family, leave her home, and survive in an uncharacteristic fashion—through prostitution.

After three years as a prostitute, Lucy decides to dress as a sailor so she will be able to "visit other parts of the country, and to pursue a course of life less immoral and destructive to [her] peace and happiness" (71).[10] She suppresses her curves and breasts with wraps and tight undergarments, dresses as a sailor, and signs on as "George" with the frigate Constitution. With the United States at war with England in the War of 1812, Lucy distinguishes herself in a battle with the British ship the Guierrere by taking up a musket and fighting bravely for her country.[11] Lucy returns home to her parents after three years as a marine, a "prodigal, penitent" daughter (75). The publisher issued two sequels to The Female Marine.[12] In the second installment, Lucy gets restless at home and takes a trip to the South, dressed as a male. Aboard a stagecoach, Lucy gets in a scuffle with a midshipman who is disrespectful to a young lady. Using wit, posturing, and a set of revolvers, she frightens the man into submission. In the third part of Lucy's story, she returns home and is pursued by a suitor, Mr. West. As an admirer of Lucy's deeds as a man who went to sea for her country, Mr. West falls in love. On a visit to Plymouth Rock, Lucy agrees to marry him.

The Female Marine reflects American cultural anxieties of the time. No longer tied to Britain and its social class system, Americans were concerned that the markers of identity, class, and character had become unmoored. Loyalties could no longer be determined through appearance alone. For example, loyalists were hard to detect during the Revolutionary War because they looked just like any other American. During the second war of independence, the War of 1812, in which Brewer fights, American sea merchants not fully committed to the war were difficult to identify. This was especially the case in coastal trading towns like Boston, where the war was unpopular. Published in Boston, Brewer's narrative addresses the relationship between appearances and loyalty. In a study of *The Female Marine*, Daniel Cohen theorizes that Lucy Brewer's story is an "allegory for the ideological inconsistency of mercantile New England between 1812 and 1815," when Boston continued trading with the British in roundabout ways (30). In other words, Bostonians looked like Americans, but their loyalties did not lie with the United States. Brewer's stories about unfortunate beginnings, selfless heroism, and marital bliss, however, assured Bostonians that "past errs could be corrected and forgiven, that a happy marriage could follow an unhappy seduction" (31). Cohen contends that much of the popularity of *The Female Marine* can be ascribed to Bostonians who wanted to celebrate their newfound patriotism and ignore their turncoat past. Thus, Boston readers "purged their collective guilt and anxiety by snapping up copies of *The Female Marine*" (30).

Lucy's experience as a prostitute reveals that although one's surface image can be manipulated, one's essential character remains the same. Lucy makes clear that she was not "born" to be a prostitute; she had to learn how. After she has been forced by the madam to remain and work in the house of prostitution, Lucy explains that she is tutored by the other women. After "receiving the proper lessons from [her] tutoress, [she] became perfected in those fascinating powers which seldom fail to decoy the amorous youth to practice vices" (68). One of those powers is the art of deception. Prostitutes, she says, must disguise their true nature. Brewer describes how prostitutes make themselves look respectable enough to deceive their prey:

Their object is to disguise themselves as much as possible from what they really are! which they effectually do, with the aid of paint, patches, false teeth and hair, that a stranger, to view them by candle light, would suppose some modern Solomon had been collecting beauties from the four corners of the world; but could he but have a peep at these bewitching girls in their dishabille, their awkward gestures, their blotched faces, their crimsoned eyes, their rotten teeth and stenchified breath, would, I think, effectually wean him from every thing like an amorous assault. (69)

Clearly, Lucy had to be tutored to resemble a prostitute. She is being taught that images can be manipulated. But in this passage, Brewer intimates that an image does not reveal one's true character. Looking closely at what appears to be a lady, one sees the prostitute. But Lucy wants us to believe that rotten teeth are as easily disguised as a virtuous heart. When she is able to leave prostitution, she demonstrates that though it is possible to commit one's body to immoral deeds, it is equally possible to recommit it to virtuous ones. Though prostitution provided her with a roof, bed, and bread, Lucy could not continue in a profession that endangered her virtuous, albeit disguised, character. Lucy sends a subtle message to those once traitorous sea merchants or other American men committed more to profit than to their country.[13]

Rather than using her body for personal profit, Lucy insists on playing a part more true to her character—that of a selfless, loyal American. For one, she fights for her country in one of the most famous battles of the War of 1812, that between the American ship the Constitution and the British ship the Guierrere. Like any other virtuous American man on the decks of the Constitution, Lucy wants to "distinguish [herself] at [her] post" during the battle with the Guierrere (72) and does so by firing her "faithful musket with the best success" (73). Though Lucy puts her body on the line for her country, she also puts her body in danger for the sake of helpless young ladies. In the second part of the story, Lucy brandishes her gun and selflessly saves a young lady from the licentious advances of another sailor. The rescue is accomplished merely by explaining to the sailor that any man who "was so unprincipled as to offer insult to old age, or to use a female ill . . . would even betray a want of manly courage by the simple display of a shot bag or powder flask" (86). As these two examples indicate, Lucy is committed to protecting the virtue of her country. First as a marine fighting to defend the Constitution, both literally and figuratively, and next as a gentleman committed to protecting the purity of defenseless young ladies, Lucy models appropriate male virtues: loyalty to the nation and loyalty to the protection of its female population. She embodies the "manly courage" lacking in those who attack the virtue inherent in America's citizens and origins.

One may well wonder where a woman of such difficult circum-stances found the "manly courage" from which to draw the internal resources that show through her disguise. The closing episode of Brewer's story provides the answer. Lucy makes a symbolic return to Plymouth, Massachusetts, a wellspring of her virtuous character, and marries. Resembling many Americans of the time, Lucy is portrayed as considerably mobile, topographically and socially. It was common for Americans to move around, geographically and hierarchically, unlike Britons. According to the historian C. Edward Skeen, after the War of 1812, "no impediment appeared to check a rapid exodus into the areas of the Ohio and Mississippi valleys," which was a "source of both pride and apprehension to most Americans" (18). Lucy's identities take her to various parts of the country, but almost as if to reassure apprehensive Americans, her character returns her to her origins, her disguise gone and her true self intact. Historically, geographical mobility mirrored a kind of social mobility as well, a time when "men were shifting their status and roles as they prospered in maritime commerce and in other enterprises" (Curti 79). Lucy's social status has progressed as well (rather humorously). She has gone from being a disgraced female runaway, to a prostitute, to a marine, to a southern gentle-man—and now, in this final installment of her story, a respectable middle-class wife. Lucy is proof that mobility is no more a threat to virtuous character than a fake name or a disguise, a significant reassurance for Americans.

Though Lucy is mobile on land and in status—and will likely continue to be so (her new surname is West)—the final sequel to her story, *The Awful Beacon*, proves that she will never compromise her virtuous character. She returns home, which is none other than Plymouth, Massachusetts. As Lucy and Mr. West walk on her father's property in Plymouth, Lucy explains that one of her habitual amusements was to travel to the borders of her father's farm "along the broken shores of the briny ocean . . . to a point of the beach where stood a large rock" (107). Lucy shows Mr. West the beloved "rock bordering upon the sea coast" (111). The rock apparently prompts Mr. West's curiosity about another rock, Plymouth Rock, and when Lucy takes Mr. West to see it, he proposes marriage. The visits to both rocks, which symbolize the foundation of Lucy's birth on her father's farm and the foundation of the American character that sprouted from Plymouth Rock, are significant. Despite her travels and disguises, the rocks of Plymouth remain a solid foundation for Lucy's sense of home, identity, and nation. The rocks are both a point of departure, and, more important, a point of return. Her body may be well-traveled, but her heart has always been moored to the spot where the sea found the rocks of her American beginnings. It is a final symbol of commitment to origins, begun when Lucy was a marine named "George" (the namesake of the first president of the United States) fighting for the *Constitution* (the name of the founding document that would sketch the outlines of the ideal American character).

Though Plymouth Rock appears only at the end of *The Female Marine*'s third installment, it has been present all along. This historical site is a metaphor for Lucy herself. During their trip to see the rock, Mr. West expresses surprise on finding Plymouth Rock nondescript and unmarked. Though the rock's "appearance" reveals "nothing very peculiar," Mr. West tells Lucy that it is indeed "the first firm foundation on which the worthy pilgrims set their feet in this now thickly inhabited quarter of the new world" (112). Retelling the tale as cast by the seventeenth-century governor William Bradford's

Of Plimouth Plantation, West describes the "impenetrable forest, abounding with savages and beasts of prey!" which met the "little band of Puritans" who "were not to be disheartened—they landed, and very soon changed the face of New-England . . . the coasts were covered with towns, and the bays with ships—and thus the new world like the old became subject to man" (113).[14] Concluding these remembrances, Mr. West stresses that "these were events worthy of commemoration, and ought to have been perpetuated by a suitable inscription on the rock" (113).[15] West believes that national, virtuous character should be perceptible on the surface.

Lucy's story proves that though the "faces" of the nation may change, virtuous character remains intact. Like Plymouth Rock, Lucy reveals "nothing very peculiar" on the surface, but she does in fact embody the best characteristics of a loyal citizen. Dressed as a man, she reminds American men of how to behave, fighting for the country and women in distress. Dressed as a woman, Lucy reminds men of the loyalty to origins so integral to America's conception of itself as an exceptional nation chosen by God. West sees Plymouth Rock as an unappreciated site that launched America's success. Lucy's experiences show, however, that though the site may appear to be unappreciated, displaying no outer marks of its remarkable American history, it is indeed rich in character. Scratch the surface of the rock or peek into the loyal heart of a disguised marine, and, proves Lucy, you will see what American virtue looks like.

----ᴥᴥᴥ----

While Lucy Brewer returns home and finds comfort in declaring her origins to be in her father's land and the landing of her forefathers, James Fenimore Cooper's female characters make their home at sea out of a similar type of principled loyalty. Just as *The Female Marine* looks to the past through reading Plymouth Rock as a foundation for American character, Cooper's three sea novels, *The Pilot* (1824), *The Red Rover* (1828), and *The Water-Witch* (1830), utilize origin myths as well. Lucy Brewer was a well-known character, and Cooper likely knew her story. Her adventures (and popularity) may have given him the idea to include his own version of cross-dressed female mariners in his novels. While Brewer reminds American men to be virtuous and remember their origins, Cooper uses the motif of the disguised seafaring female to indicate proper behavior. The women in his sea novels point the reader toward men who exhibit appropriate American personal and civic virtues. The men rebel against oppressive governments while professing their belief in the natural rights of man. The cross-dressed women embody these values as they willingly "change colors" out of loyalty to principled men and love of freedom. In their relationships, these women find the virtues and ideals of America, before the country is constituted, in the hearts and minds of men resisting oppression. They plant the seeds of American character by identifying and remaining loyal to those qualities found in a few good men.

Cooper's first sea novel, The Pilot, is set along the coast of Northumberland during the Revolutionary War.[16] The Pilot, the first fictional treatment of the American navy, centers on the pilot John Paul Jones.[17] The plot involves the fate of three females: the Americans Katherine Plowden and Cecilia Howard, and the Briton Alice Dunscombe. If Lucy Brewer is a noble character who reminds American men of their better natures, Katherine of The Pilot sends a message about loyalty in the face of difficulty. Katherine's story is set against the American hero John Paul Jones and Jones's love interest, Alice, who remains loyal to England despite her lover's commitment to the American cause. Alice and Katherine represent two poles of American character, blind obedience and self-determination. Alice cannot see her home in the heart of an American man who rebels against tyranny, while Katherine makes her home by the side of Richard Barnstable, the patriotic American naval officer to whom she commits her life.

The story begins with an American raid of Britain during the Revolutionary War. The American schooner Ariel is accompanied by a frigate of the newly formed naval forces. Orders have been issued to retrieve the pilot, John Paul Jones, from the shores of Northumberland. Jones is supposed to guide the Americans to shore to capture several important Britons. This plan falls by the wayside, however, because two lieutenants of the *Ariel*, Barnstable and Edward Griffith, find out that the women they love, Katherine and Cecilia, are being detained by their loyalist caretaker, Colonel Howard. Once an American, Howard returned to England before the war and now refuses to turn over Katherine, who is his ward, and Cecilia, who is his niece, to the American men. After a series of maneuvers at sea and on land, Barnstable, Griffith, and the pilot succeed in capturing Colonel Howard, liberating the women, and then returning to the United States.

Katherine plays important roles that indicate American qualities worthy of loyalty. Her commitment to the American cause is revealed in her portrayal as the pilot's double and as the antithesis of Alice's blind loyalty to England. First, Katherine's cross-dressing and talents resemble the ambiguous nationality and skills of John Paul Jones, the pilot. Jones is portrayed as a rather mysterious man, and indeed, the real-life story of John Paul Jones was still sketchy for most Americans.[18] When Jones comes aboard the *Ariel*, for instance, he masks his identity by calling himself "Mr. Gray." His pronounced English accent makes the crew doubt whether he is loyal to their mission, but readers quickly become aware of his commitment to the American cause. He serves as a pilot in chapters 3 through 5 of the novel and joins in a battle against a British warship in chapter 33.

As the pilot's double, Katherine likewise disguises her identity and reveals piloting skills that aid the American cause. In the first real action of the novel, Katherine's lover, Lieutenant Barnstable of the *Ariel*, sneaks to the English shore to meet with the pilot, John Paul Jones. When Barnstable arrives at the designated meeting spot, he is deceived into believing he is meeting with the pilot, who is a small figure in a pea jacket. When the figure removes his cap, Barnstable recognizes that it is Katherine, not Jones, and both succumb to "an uncontrollable burst of merriment" (24). Katherine tells Barnstable she has followed the movements of the ships for about a week dressed as a seaman, much as the pilot himself was likely doing, in anticipation of the *Ariel*'s arrival. Jones's sense of national identity and Katherine's gender identity are at first ambiguous but eventually become clear when their loyalty is revealed: he to his country, she to the American man she loves.

This scene casts the mold of Katherine's character as it appears in later episodes in the novel where she appears as a woman with talents traditionally labeled male and female. Beneath her clothes and in her heart, she is a woman, loyal to her lover and country. Whether or not she is dressed as a pilot, Katherine also boasts the skills of this male profession. Later in the novel, for instance, Katherine exhibits her skills at piloting, creating a signal manual she and Barnstable use to communicate with one another from the colonel's mansion. Also, she is an excellent pilot of another sort. When the British apprehend the American sailor Tom Coffin during the American invasion of Colonel Howard's estate, it is Katherine who helps him escape by serving as a "pilot" to lead him back to the ship (265).

Katherine is paired with the pilot rather than Barnstable because her skills and loyalties, like those of the pilot, define her mode of rebellion. Like the pilot, she can use her skills to guide men to safety. The nature of her rebellion is similar to Jones's as well. Jones is described as "a soul not to be limited by the arbitrary boundaries of tyrants and hirelings, but one who has the right as well as the inclination to grapple with oppression, in whose name soever it is exercised" (151). Jones is portrayed as a principled man whose virtuous soul cannot coexist with tyranny, and so he is driven to rebel against the nation of his fathers. Likewise, Katherine chooses not to remain under the roof and rule of those loyal to England. She rebels against Howard's authority by signaling to Barnstable and aiding Coffin in his escape. Like the pilot, Katherine's loyalty drives her to "grapple with oppression."

The cross-dressing scene shows that Katherine chooses to follow her heart rather than tradition. Much as she transgresses the boundaries of traditional dress for women, Katherine's heart defies the traditional notions of loyalty to "home." Her transgression is written between the lines of Alice Dunscombe's conversation with the pilot, Alice's lover. Alice is grateful to be under the care of

Colonel Howard and accuses all Americans like the pilot of turning a "ruthless hand against the land of his fathers" (364). Alice refuses to leave with the pilot and abandon her "homeland," a place she claims is "the dearest of all terms to every woman . . . for it embraces the dearest of all ties!" (364). The pilot's desire for liberty does not inspire Alice's loyalty; she is devoted instead to her ties to father and home. Unlike the pilot—and Katherine—she is "limited by the arbitrary boundaries" of patriarchy and a space she names "home."

Katherine also interprets the term *homeland* differently from Alice. At the end of the novel, we are told what becomes of Katherine and Barnstable after the war: "having no children, [Katherine] eagerly profited by his consent, to share his privations and hardships on the ocean" (420).[19] Katherine reveals that the homeland is only as dear to her as the principles found there and the men who defend them. She is a woman who understands her national and domestic "home," which she believes is not so much a physical space as an ideal. For her, home is in the man; his principle of liberty must exist in his heart and mind before it takes root in a landscape. Alice does not understand this, and the pilot leaves her; conversely, Barnstable does not see home in a land of oppression, and Katherine follows him and his principles to sea. Katherine is willing to become a sailor, first hinted at while she trolls the shores of England in a peacoat in search of her lover, if it means she can show loyalty to the heart and mind of a man like Barnstable. She is an indicator, if not a double of, the American principles worthy of love and loyalty.

Though Katherine's transgressions of gender boundaries and patriarchal traditions could possibly brand her as "unwomanly," Cooper refuses to entertain the prospect. Beneath her masculine skills is a woman who is uniquely American in her loyalties. During the cross-dressing scene, Katherine tells Barnstable, "If I have done more than my sex will warrant, remember it was through a holy motive, and if I have more than a woman's enterprise, it must be . . . [t]o fit me for, and to keep me worthy of being one day your wife" (27). Unlike Alice, Katherine transgresses gender boundaries, to

143

prove a loyalty not to land or to fathers but to a man who liberates her from those boundaries. Katherine characterizes her "motive" for transgressing boundaries as "holy." Like any good American, she perceives her rebellion against England and her loyalty to American men as a holy duty to God. Katherine sees herself as serving both God and the man who is devoted to the nation chosen by God. In effect, Katherine trumps Alice's loyalty to England with her holy motive to serve God and the men who fight for Him.

Though the theme of transgressed identity boundaries is explored throughout the novel in the characters of the pilot and Katherine, Katherine is a cross-dressed mariner only on land and for only a brief scene. In The Red Rover (1827), the sea novel following The Pilot, Cooper again presents a cross-dressed woman, this time in his portrayal of a cabin boy named Roderick, who is, I argue, a woman who follows her lover to sea.[20] If read as a woman, Roderick is more than just an odd character shyly lurking in the fringes of the narrative; she is transformed into an indicator of loyalty, who, not unlike Katherine with her "holy motive," goes to sea to indicate the worthiness of loving a principled American man. While The Pilot takes place during the Revolutionary War, most of The Red Rover takes place in the years leading up to the war. Thus, we can read Roderick as a kind of ancestor to Katherine.

The Rover, the man to whom Roderick is loyal, is known as a notorious pirate throughout the English American colonies. The Rover unwittingly enlists an English naval officer named Harry Wilder, who is disguised as an American seaman. Wilder has been sent to trap the Rover into falling into the hands of the English navy. We never learn the details of the Rover's decision to turn to piracy, but it is clear that he prefers his profession to remaining a British subject. He tells Wilder that he cannot work for representatives of the king in a country so far from England (302). In the past, he has suffered ridicule for being an American, having heard his "commanders dar'd to couple the name of my country with an epithet I will not wound your ear by repeating" (302). Though Wilder is sympathetic to the Rover, he nearly lures him into captivity. The Rover escapes a British attack on his ship and reappears at the end of the Revolutionary War, no longer a fugitive from his homeland.

Though Roderick never reveals herself as a woman, there are quite a few strong indications that she is a female and may have followed her lover or husband to sea. Aboard the ship are several Englishwomen who are unaware that they will become the Rover's prisoners. Two of them suspect the captain to be a pirate and ask Roderick about it; the ensuing conversation leads the two ladies to become very suspicious of Roderick. The women ask about Roderick and her relationship with the Rover, and both her physical appearance and emotional response to the questions nearly expose her identity as a woman. Roderick offers ambiguous answers about her age (she says she is twenty but then revises the number to fifteen); claims she has been at sea for two years on the *Rover* only (306); and is curiously melancholy when asked about the captain, though she claims "never has he said a harsh or unkind word to me" (307). Roderick professes that she has never questioned the motives behind the captain's career choice, and when the women request the opportunity to ask Captain Rover what he intends to do with them, Roderick is startled and claims, "Though her beauty be so rare . . . let her not prize it too highly. Woman cannot tame his temper! (308). Soon thereafter a tear appears "beneath a long and silken lash," and her interrogators take note of "the whole form of the lad, until they reached even the feet that were so delicate that they seemed barely able to uphold him" (310). Roderick is much older than most cabin boys (whether fifteen or twenty), has delicate physical features, is defensive about the Rover, and clearly knows something about the Rover's interaction with women ("woman cannot tame his temper"). The scene ends with Roderick shrinking out of the cabin "before the cold and searching eye" of the female passengers.

When coupled with the chapter's epigraph, words spoken by a cross-dressed woman about her love interest in Shakespeare's *Twelfth Night*, this scene provide strong evidence that Roderick is a young woman. The lines from the play are spoken by Viola, who is cross-dressed as the male character Cesario. In this scene, Viola is realizing that another woman, Olivia, is falling in love with her, believing Viola to be a man: "She made good view of me; indeed so much, / That sure, methought, her eyes had lost her tongue, / For she did speak in starts, distractedly" (2.2.19–21). In Cooper's novel, Roderick represents the cross-dressed woman from Shakespeare's play. Most of the chapter centers on Roderick's women "mak[ing] good view" of her, and only Roderick exhibits ambiguous sexual characteristics. Like Viola/Cesario, whom the audience never sees dressed as a woman, Cooper's Roderick dresses as a boy throughout the novel. As we shall see further on, even at the end of the book, readers can still only surmise that it is Roderick dressed as a woman in the final pages of the novel.

In addition to her delicate appearance, her knowledge about the Rover's relationships with women, and Cooper's telling epigraph as evidence of Roderick's cross-dressing, Roderick also exhibits an intense fidelity to the Rover that suggests they are married. When the *Rover* is attacked by the English, Roderick's pleas and declarations of loyalty suggest that she is the Rover's wife. Wilder, along with reinforcements, demands that the Rover surrender. When the Rover refuses and Wilder is about to return to his British ship to begin an attack on the *Rover*, Roderick speaks up out of fear that the Rover will be killed. Desperately encouraging Wilder to persuade the Rover to surrender, Roderick begs Wilder, "[D]o not yet leave him. Tell him of his high and honorable name, of his youth, ay, and of that gentle and virtuous being that he once so fondly loved, and whose memory, even now, he worships" (401). When the Rover refuses to surrender and the two men try to convince Roderick to board the British ship to save him(her)self, Roderick refuses, claiming "the tie which binds me to thee [the Rover] shall never be broken" (402). Clearly, Roderick knows personal details about the Rover's family name and his youth and that he once loved someone that he now worships. That lost love appears to be Roderick, for she claims that "the tie that binds," a phrase recalling the bonds of marriage, exists between herself and the Rover.

The Rover and the cabin boy escape Wilder and the British attack. At the end of the novel, the Rover returns to America after the

Revolutionary War and is accompanied by a woman whose history is not explained. It seems highly likely that this woman is Roderick, no longer cross-dressed. Though the woman is never named, her role is wifely in nature. She helps the dying Rover fulfill his final wish to once more see Wilder, with whom he had developed a bond before being attacked by the British. Unlike a hired nurse, the Rover's companion appears emotionally attached to him, carrying a "tremulous" tone (437) of "grief and resignation" (435) while making travel arrangements to Wilder's home. When the two arrive at Wilder's, she sobs "long and bitterly" before being able to explain their presence. Rover's female companion says, "You may deem this visit an intrusion . . . but one whose will is my law, would be brought hither," at which point she is interrupted by the Rover, who claims he has come to die. These are the last words we hear from her, and this is the last time we see her in the final pages of the novel. Her emotional attachment to the Rover as well as her claim that his "will" is her "law" indicate that she is his wife, the same cabin "boy" who once claimed the tie binding her to the Rover could never be broken (402).

Though there is no explicit cross-dressed female mariner in The Red Rover, Cooper's portrayal of the sexually ambiguous cabin boy once again summons the portrait of a woman's loyalty for a man dedicated to America's liberty. Roderick's fidelity to the tie that binds them leads her to dress like a man, to disguise her gender for the sake of her loyalty. Her behavior indicates the virtue of the Rover, a nascent American patriot whose dedication to his own pursuit of independence from the British leads him to appear as a pirate. Like the Rover, who has shed the identity of a pirate and now lives in his skin as an American, Roderick can now live as a woman. Appropriately, their identities become authentic at the point in the novel when America has revealed its true nature as a land of liberty. Though Roderick may have been looked on disapprovingly, with a "cold eye" by others, she is the one proven right in her loyalty.

Though paired with John Paul Jones's talents throughout The Pilot, Katherine only briefly dresses as a sailor, and then on land.

The Red Rover is ambiguous throughout as to whether Roderick is a woman or man. The female character that completes the trilogy of cross-dressed women arrives in Cooper's third novel, *The Water-Witch* (1830). Through Eudora, Cooper offers his first portrayal of a cross-dressed woman who is disguised (as a pirate) throughout the novel. Before there was a Katherine who devoted herself to an American husband, and before there was a Roderick who stood by her rebellious British subject turned pirate, there was a Eudora who, years before the war of independence, fell in love with the principles of her lover. Her loyalty to her lover, even at the expense of her father, is an indicator of the virtues worthy of hardship and devotion.

The Water-Witch recedes further in time than the Revolutionary era or the prewar period, taking place in the early Dutch settlements, specifically the colony of New Netherland in the first decade of the 1700s. The wealthy bachelor burgher Alderman Van Beverout is in the process of engaging his niece, Alida, to either Captain Ludlow, a British seaman, or a wealthy landowner, Olaff Van Staats. Unbeknownst to the other characters, Van Beverout has for many years been conducting trade with a man named Seadrift, who commands the pirate ship the *Water-Witch*. Believing the *Water-Witch* to be a threat to the English, the British Captain Ludlow attempts on several occasions to capture it. He fails each time, often because the ship's masthead, a water witch, displays a seemingly supernatural power. The water witch is a sorceress draped in seaweed; by magically changing colors from green to blue, she confuses any attempt to determine whether she is a ship or an apparition.

Eventually we learn that the pirate Seadrift does not act alone: there is a woman aboard the ship who disguises herself as Seadrift when the ship is being chased by the English. When Ludlow eventually catches Seadrift, he discovers that he does not have the real pirate in his custody; rather, it is a woman named Eudora disguised as Seadrift. In the final scenes of the book, we learn why Eudora was on board the *Water-Witch*. In a meeting with Van Beverout, Seadrift tells him that Eudora is the long-lost offspring of a past affair. Seadrift knew Eudora's mother well and vowed to bring

Eudora to her father when her mother died. But when the pirate returns Eudora to her father and tries to board his ship to leave, Eudora refuses to stay with her new family, choosing instead to go to sea with Seadrift, for whom she declares her love. They depart, Ludlow and Alida marry, and the *Water-Witch* is never seen again.

Like the pilot and the Rover before him, Seadrift believes in the principles that would one day inform the U.S. Constitution. Early on, Seadrift explains that he will be a pirate until "governments shall lay their foundations in natural justice . . . [and] when bodies of men shall feel and acknowledge the responsibilities of individuals" (23, 24). The woman who remains by his side, Eudora, is the natural and supernatural ancestor of Roderick from *Red Rover* and Katherine of *The Pilot*. Like her literary ancestors, she is committed to the man dedicated to the revolutionary ideals of natural justice and individual responsibility. She indicates an American character worthy of loyalty.

Eudora's identification with her lover and his ship is so complete that her identity is collapsed into both the man and his ship. Eudora is captured because she is dressed like Seadrift, and her skill at changing her appearance mirrors the ship itself. Acknowledging both the likely prospect of having a female masthead and mariners' belief in the supernatural, Cooper creates a water-witch masthead that symbolizes Eudora. The masthead's tendency to change colors, or "change dress," as it is described in the novel, parallels not only Eudora's change of dress from woman to pirate but her decision to deny one identity as Van Beverout's daughter to take up another, as Seadrift's lover. Her loyalty to Seadrift as her lover and her close identification with him are indicated by her proclamation "Thy world is my world!—thy home my home" (443). When they leave together, her conflation with the ship is solidified, for the last line of the novel explains that no one ever "again heard of the renowned SKIMMER OF THE SEAS, or of his matchless WATER-WITCH" (444).[21] Eudora, then, is not only "reject[ing] wealth, respectability [and] stability . . . in favor of a life of adventure, beauty, and imagination," as George Dekker suggests (122), but the supernatural link between her and the water witch suggests that her lover and his *Water-Witch* could not leave without her. Eudora not only takes on the dress of her lover, she is the ship that carries him.

In effect, Eudora's devotion to his virtues is the buoy that keeps American principles afloat so that one day, they will take root. All three women from Cooper's sea novels do similar work. If, as Thomas Philbrick proposes in his foundational study of Cooper's sea fiction, the trilogy "depict[s] the growth of the separation between America and England and the slow awakening of an American national consciousness" (58), it is not only a product of male characters like the pilot, Red Rover, or Seadrift. Rather, the corresponding female seafarers—Katherine, Roderick, and Eudora—clarify an American consciousness by indicating the national virtues most worthy of loyalty. In essence, the object of these female characters' loyalty is to define the ideals of American manhood. These women indicate and at times embody the virtues of American character by suggesting the value of responsibility in the pursuit of natural justice.

Coming on the heels of the popularity of The Female Marine, Cooper's trilogy finds its richest resources in the potential of the disguised woman of the sea. Cooper asserts, often in melodramatic ways, that women are willing to change colors—to be female pirates if necessary—and join in their outlaw husbands' noble pursuit of independence and personal liberty.[22] As if working to delineate the family tree of a woman like Lucy Brewer, Cooper sets each novel further back in the annals of American history before the nation was independent. In this way, he recreates a nation that emerges as much from the loyalty of women as from the noble virtues found in the hearts of their men. Cooper's three novels make the Revolutionary War seem inevitable, destined long before the colonies were well-established, and the United States seem as old as the mythical, magical tales of water witches.

My reading of Cooper's novels is not intended to suggest that Cooper was proposing a feminist reading of the past. As feminist critics have noted, his female characters often display the submissive, innocent characteristics so common to early nineteenth-century sentimental novels (Schriber, "Toward" 238). After all, these women take on the identity of a male in order to support their lovers and husbands. They disguise themselves to fulfill their role as dutiful wives, not to engage in some sort of swashbuckling adventure of their own. These women appear to submit to the will of their men. However, they do so through their own reason and courage to disguise themselves. Their decision to act is based on their desire to leave behind an Old World identity in favor of a newly developing world found, for the moment, only in the hearts and minds of their principled lovers and husbands. As Mary Suzanne Schriber has noted, Cooper "must be credited with using the conditions of American life to expand the potential of his heroines in areas of practical abilities that did not violate the culture's notions of female virtue" (*Gender* 30). By conserving women's roles while setting them to the task dressed as men, Cooper kept women's motives pure so that their judgment of their rebellious husbands would appear trustworthy to his readers.

Cooper constructs a story of origins, a project critics have seen again and again in his work. Through writing what Paul Downes describes as "historically reverential national literature" (165), Cooper hoped to remind Jacksonian Americans of their male and female forebears who first and foremost stuck to their principles. As Heinz Ickstadt explains, Cooper even went so far as to provide "models of right conduct" and dramatize the "'simple dignity of moral truths'" (17). He wanted American readers to understand and revere their past as something to preserve, and he helps them to do so by making American virtues the object of loyalty and love. Though these models of right conduct are embodied in pre-Revolution and Revolutionary War idealists and patriots like Barnstable, the pilot, the Red Rover, and Seadrift, it is the women characters who dramatize the dignity of moral truths. Their loyalty clarifies the purity of the cause, and in turn the purity of the nation's origins. As Mark R. Patterson explains, Cooper recognized that "[b]ecause of its association with disruption and revolution, United States history, ratified in the Constitution, promised only divergence from its origin" (84). Cooper's novels resist this divergence by singling out the founding principles and noble workings of the early rebels who remind readers of their duty to honor their past. Though these women seemed to have diverged from the roles assigned to their sex, they in fact stayed solidly rooted in their "holy motives," as Katherine puts it. Should the men around them diverge from the right conduct of their forefathers, these women indicate the right path to the virtues of the past.

The differences between Lucy Brewer fighting for the *Constitution* and Cooper's heroines who follow their men to sea are worthy of further consideration. While Cooper's female mariners were loyal to the men committed to republican principles, Lucy Brewer is the man who models American virtues. Cooper does not go that far in his depiction of cross-dressed female mariners. Given his resistance to portraying "strong, independent women," as Joyce W. Warren contends (105), it is likely that Cooper simply could not imagine a woman patriot tearing up the seas with philosophies about personal responsibilities and natural rights, and instructing others about the origins of the nation. But Lucy Brewer is imagined as just such a man; situated within the historical context of *The Female Marine*'s publication, we see her disguise as a tool that assuages the guilt felt by Americans who traded with the British during wartime and teaches them to read character rather than appearances in the people and landscapes of America. While Cooper imagined women who could discern noble philosophies in the conduct of men, thereby serving as indicators of American virtues deserving loyalty, numerous other cross-dressed female characters were like the female marine, Lucy Brewer. They embodied the men who should be doing the sailing, the fighting, or the rescuing but were incapable of fulfilling their duties.

As the majority of my book has shown, America relied on the notion that men must save women first. Women portrayed as pure innocence or as mothers of innocence represented America's covenant with God and commitment to the community. The urgency of the directive was driven by the possibility that men might choose to ignore it in favor of securing their own protection and advancement, thereby tainting the nation's self-proclaimed image as morally exceptional. Rather than envisioning principled men saving women, the stories of cross-dressed female mariners that I will now discuss exhibit anxiety over whether men *would* or even *could* preserve the life of anyone.

Though the sea remained a stage on which national ideals were tested, by the 1830s and 1840s that setting was expanded to include another wild, unpredictable location—the frontier. As Lucy Brewer's marriage to Mr. West suggests, as early as the second decade of the nineteenth century, women were marrying men with the west practically written in their name. Posing a new challenge to national character, the west (like the sea) took men away from home and steered the country toward an aggressive expansionist ideology, potentially threatening the integrity believed to be inherent in American men and women. Two contrasting visions of westward expansion surface in the following cross-dressed female mariner stories. Both reflect anxieties over the changing character of men and women, and call into question men's ability to save women when men's and women's character faced new challenges.

In her study of transvestism in a variety of cultures, Marjorie Garber contends that transvestism indicates a crisis of category when divisions like race, class, and gender are transgressed (32). Anxieties arising from the transgression of boundaries and concerns with the character of both men and women became even more pronounced in the decades following Cooper's *Water-Witch*. The bounds of the nation by land and sea were being transgressed by westward expansion in the 1840s. Women either followed men—became a "Mrs. West"—or remained in the east, worrying about whether their men would remain loyal when plunged into lawlessness and adventure. The fear was that greedy and adventure-seeking men would shed their sensibilities and responsibilities toward their families and their nation. Equally unsettling was the possibility that women who headed west would lose their femininity—and the pious virtue that accompanied feminine behavior. The famous (and infamous in America) English writer Frances Trollope played on these fears when she gave a less than flattering account of western women in *Domestic Manners of the Americans* (1832) as being run-down, over-worked, prematurely aged, and uncultured.[23]

In fact, throughout the antebellum era, Americans consistently maintained an interest in the fate of women of the west. The physical danger that western migration posed for women was often the appeal of popular captivity narratives, which, tellingly, featured far more female than male captives. As June Namias explains in *White Captives*, the west in general, and captivity narratives in particular, produced multiple anxieties, including the fear that "the limits of Anglo-American male prowess" to protect vulnerable women would be revealed and that as a result, women might then be required to transgress gender boundaries and perform "Amazonian feats" of their own (272). And the kinds of Amazonian feats that seemed to worry Americans the most were very similar to those exhibited by cross-dressed women at sea. The anxiety over whether women at sea could retain their femininity and whether men had the ability or desire to save them from that fate was expressed in numerous stories of fictional cross-dressed female mariners in the 1840s, including Ellen Stephens's *The Cabin Boy Wife* (1840), Almira Paul's *The Adventures of Almira Paul* (1840, though first published in 1816), Emma Cole's *The Life and Sufferings of Miss Emma Cole* (1844), Maturin Ballou's *Fanny Campbell, the Female Pirate Captain* (1844), Cooper's serial installments of *Jack Tier* in *Graham's Magazine* (1846–48), and Marianne Moore's *The Touching and Melancholy Narrative of Marian Moore, the Shipwrecked Female Sailor* (1853). These narratives tend to present either women in search of men who abandoned them, or women who are in trouble and in need of rescuing. Nearly all the women head west in their adventures, such as Stephens, who chases her recalcitrant husband up and down the Mississippi River. In most of these narratives, the image of the cross-dressed female evokes expectations and fears surrounding national expansion and the move west.

Responding to the fear that frontier men would leave their homes and rebel against the moral and Christian sensibilities so important to the American self-image, writers often figured women as men's virtuous and Christian conscience in these stories. Rather than acting as indicators of the virtues existing in the men they love, as do Cooper's women characters, these women travel as men to remind men how to be American. The cross-dressed mariner characters Fanny Campbell and "Jack" Tier intimate anxiety over the limitations of men and the altered role of western women. Each character exhibits what women could do on the frontier and what the frontier could do to women, while at the same time serving as a mirror to the fears and faults of greedy men.

Written by a male writer, Maturin Murray Ballou, and reprinted several times throughout the 1840s, *Fanny Campbell, the Female Pirate Captain* takes place during the Revolutionary War era.[24] Before the war, Fanny hears that her fiancé is being held as a prisoner in Cuba. Determined to rescue him, Campbell dresses as a sailor and enlists aboard a ship tellingly named *Constance*. During the voyage, the Revolutionary War begins, and the British captain plans to force his sailors to fight for the British. Fanny (a.k.a. Mr. Channing) helps the crew to mutiny and then becomes the captain herself. She and her fellow seamen retrieve her lover, William, from a Cuban jail, and after the Revolution, she and William marry and live a life at sea together. Though the adventure takes place on the high seas, the story is also about westward expansion and the women and men involved in it.

The frontier is very much a part of the lessons to be learned from Ballou's narrative. The lover Fanny Campbell is rescuing is being held in Cuba. By the 1840s Cuba and the United States had mutual interests in annexation. John Quincy Adams's interest in Cuba was followed by an annexation plan drawn up by Nicholas Trist in 1833, then the private secretary to President Andrew Jackson.[25] When Spain threatened to outlaw slavery in Cuba, Cuban planters and U.S. Southern slaveholders pushed for the annexation of Cuba to preserve the slave trade. Within three years of the publication of *Fanny Campbell*, John L. O'Sullivan, the man who coined the term "Manifest Destiny," which would repeatedly be used to describe white America's god-given right to take the west, carried out a rousing campaign advocating the annexation of Cuba (Thomas

211). When Fanny sails to Cuba, she is traveling to a new frontier—a target for U.S. expansionist desires—to rescue a man held captive in a kind of frontier prison.

Unlike the captivity narratives that Namias described, however, the focus of Fanny Campbell is not a female captive, but Fanny, the cross-dressing rescuer. Dressing as a sailor, Fanny's mutiny, advancement to captain of the ship, and her rescue of a man all hint at the anxieties over the gender boundaries women crossed when they chose to live on a lawless frontier. Without men willing or able to protect them, women might behave like men, and even come to look like them. On their own, women are pushed into the "crisis of category" that Garber claims cross-dressing reflects. If westward expansion resulted in the loss of men and produced women who looked and acted like men to survive, then expansionism could pose a threat to the nation and American virtue.

Fanny is capable of looking and acting like a man as she leads her party to a new frontier, but Ballou is careful to balance her masculine talents with traditional feminine skills. Numerous examples prove she is a skilled sailor. Nevertheless, Ballou is at pains to attribute these skills to her fisherman father and a family pastor. After rescuing William from jail, Fanny explains that her father habitually tutored her from nautical books and on sailing trips, while her local pastor (a former seaman) taught her navigation (55). These skills made it possible for Fanny to take over the British ship Constance, symbolic of her constancy as a lover and American patriot. Necessarily, she is sexually pure as well. When propositioned by an officer, she fights off his advances. She is also forgiving, as illustrated by her absolution of the officer's sins later in the story.

Fanny's various feminine attributes include physical beauty. Though Fanny is dressed as a captain of a sailing ship, her beauty cannot be hidden. Her figure is described as "voluptuous," and "unlike your modern belles, delicate and ready to faint," she "could row a boat, shoot a panther . . . [and] write poetry too" (12). Though she may dress like a man, her feminine curves cannot be hidden. Sanctioned by the skills she learned from family and church, she is an all-purpose athlete on both American frontiers, and aided by her own strength and skills, she is a good rower and an accurate shot. Apparently, shooting panthers, animals commonly associated with the frontier, does not diminish her beauty. Though she has physical talents resembling those of a man, she still has the sensitivity to pen poetry. Ballou spares no opportunity to remind the reader of her artistic, feminine side and that her voluptuous figure remains intact beneath her rough sailors' clothing. For "modern belles" of the time, Fanny Campbell was a model frontier woman.

Though women and men might have feared the frontier woman's loss of femininity, Fanny assures us that women's moral character will remain intact. Campbell is depicted, according to Barbara Cutter, "as an angel in the world . . . She moves in a 'man's' world, but her character is that of a woman" (148). Campbell cuts an attractive figure of an American woman of the west: she stays committed to the patriarchal secular and nonsecular roots of her girlhood, fearlessly works to keep her husband by her side, holds tight to her virtue, and adapts physically to new landscapes/seascapes without losing the cultural value her femininity brings to the rough-and-tumble man's world of the American frontier.

Thus, in some part, Fanny is a model of "redemptive womanhood," a term Cutter uses to describe characters like Fanny who exhibit a particular "religious, moral, and nurturing nature" (8). Such a nature, argues Cutter, "gave women an obligation to promote morality and religion and to selflessly nurture others"—to redeem others when they are unable to do so themselves (8). Indeed Fanny redeems her husband, rescuing him from both prison and the vices of the frontier.[26] However, as much as Campbell is the embodiment of the redemptive woman, she is also a model for men. As such, her character is a challenge to them. Just as the men of the story take her for a man, men of the frontier must see themselves when looking at her—literally in male clothing, and figuratively in her efforts to remain loyal to family, religion, and moral standards. She challenges men to keep their virtue snug and safe beneath their clothing, secure from the temptations and troubles of life in the west.

Two years after the publication of *Fanny Campbell*, another author expressed interest in the challenge cross-dressed women offered to men involved in U.S. expansionism. Not surprisingly, James Fenimore Cooper once again could not resist presenting the reader with a cross-dressed female sailor in another sea novel. Unlike Fanny's story, however, Cooper's vision of frontier women and expansionist-minded men is very skeptical. The main male character in *Jack Tier* is a portrait of the corrupting effects of expansionism when men ignore God and their ties to their community. The female protagonist and the namesake of the novel, Jack Tier, is a cross-dressed sailor who embraces these ties but has lost her femininity to her harsh environment. Gone are the lovely water witches from Cooper's previous novels who served as indicators of the male virtues worthy of women's loyalty. In their place stands a woman who loses herself when forced to be the virtuous man that men were supposed to be.

Jack Tier, originally published serially under the title *Rose Budd* in *Graham's Magazine* from 1846 to 1848, takes place mostly off of the coast of Florida aboard Captain Stephen Spike's *Molly Swash* during the U.S.-Mexican War. On board the *Molly* are Rose Budd, whom the traitorous Captain Spike and his honest mate Harry Mulford hope to marry, and Rose's aunt Mrs. Budd. The captain has convinced Mrs. Budd to bring her niece aboard to improve her health. What the women do not know is that the purpose of the journey is to clandestinely trade gunpowder to the Mexican government for gold. During the voyage, Rose becomes attached to Jack Tier, a short, stout, graying steward's assistant of middle age. Tier is torn between an intense attraction to Captain Spike and a revulsion for Spike's treasonous acts and aggressive pursuit of Rose Budd. Rose and Harry Mulford fall in love and escape the ship to report Captain Spike to U.S. authorities. Later, a U.S. naval vessel finds and seriously injures Captain Spike.

In the final scenes of the novel, Jack Tier, whose female gender has been revealed to Rose earlier in the novel, appears at the Captain's deathbed dressed as a woman. Jack reveals to Captain Spike that she is the wife whom he deserted for another woman nearly twenty years earlier, and for whom he named the ship Molly Swash. After Spike deserted her, Molly/Jack spent her entire life at sea, earning a living as a sailor and searching for her husband. She now offers the captain forgiveness if he will turn to God in his final hours and pray. After the captain's death, Jack Tier, "still known by that name" (511), lives the rest of her days with the married Rose and Henry.

Cynicism now pervades the characterization of types that Cooper portrayed as noble and heroic in his earlier sea trilogy, in particular the ship captains and cross-dressed women. Captain Spike, the outlaw who might be expected to parallel the exemplary outlaw patriots from Cooper's earlier novels, is instead a traitor and a sexual predator. He has been disloyal to God, country, and woman for the sake of gold. Jack, the cross-dressed sailor, is in some ways unlike her predecessors as well. Unlike Katherine in The Pilot, Eudora in Water-Witch, and even Roderick in Red Rover, Jack is a middle-aged woman hardened by seafaring life: "Her skin had acquired the tanning of the sea; the expression of her face had become hard and worldly," she "smoked and chewed," and "her walk was between a waddle and a seaman's roll" (484). There are no coils of luxuriant long hair exposed when she reveals herself as a woman but rather "short, gray bristles" (482). Though Jack "is dropping gradually into the feelings and habits of her sex" at the end of the novel when she takes up residence with the Mulfords, it is understood that "she never can become what she once was" (511). Unlike Katherine and Eudora, who are physically beautiful, Jack is unattractive. Unlike Roderick, who returns at the end of the novel looking and acting like a woman, Jack can never truly return to what she once was.

Those critics who have commented on the character of Jack Tier yet again believe Cooper is revealing his disapproval of independent women. Joyce W. Warren contends that Cooper portrays Jack/Molly's cross-dressing as "a crime against her sex" (92) because he refuses to characterize women as "strong [and] independent" (105). Cooper's vision of "American individualism," Warren argues, includes only "male self-exploration," not women's (105). Robert K. Martin believes Cooper's presentation of cross-dressing women changed from the women in the earlier sea trilogy as women began to make "real claims of political and social equality" in the 1840s. (288). The cabin boy in The Red Rover, argues Martin, "is described in terms of sexual ambiguity that are enticing, not freakish . . . [whereas] twenty years later Jack Tier arouses repugnance" (290). Similar to Warren's assertion that Cooper could not imagine an independent woman, Martin's interpretation of Jack Tier is that Cooper feared "the dangerous aggression of the independent woman" (290).

I agree with Martin's judgment that Cooper represents Jack Tier as "repugnant" and Warren's claim that Cooper was more interested in "male self-exploration" than women's. Jack does not have a voluptuous figure to be hidden like a Fanny: even when Jack returns to dressing like a woman, she is grizzled and gray, and her mannerisms mirror her looks, as she walks, talks, smokes, and chews like a sailor. Her appearance throughout the novel would likely be considered "repugnant" by readers put off by the sight of a woman looking like a well-weathered sailor. Contrary to Martin and Warren, however, I don't believe Cooper's portrayal of Jack as hopelessly manly is a way of condemning her for a "crime against her sex" or that her aggressive behavior as a sailor should be interpreted as the acts of a dangerously independent woman. As Warren states, Cooper is interested in "male self-exploration," not women's. In this novel, he explores the ways in which Spike's greed and moral faults have in essence "unsexed" his wife, a term Cooper uses to describe Jack Tier.[27] Jack Tier is to be empathized with because she represents the consequences of a man's crime against his sex—Spike's failure to be a virtuous man. Captain Spike is disloyal to God, his country, and his wife during the U.S-Mexican War. If anything, it is Spike who stands as a portrait of the danger of aggressive individualism, of self-interest, and of desire for profit. He is tempted by unlawful opportunities presented by American expansionist endeavors like the U.S.-Mexican War, and he fails to resist immoral temptations. His greedy behavior has created Jack, the hardened steward's assistant, out of Molly, the deserted frontier wife.[28]

As Mary Suzanne Schriber points out about Cooper's westerns,

"Cooper's fiction suggests that just as the peculiar conditions of frontier life contributed to the formation of a distinctively American male, so these conditions inevitably impinged on the development of females as well" (Gender 30). Since Cooper sees frontier women as in danger of losing the appearance and mannerisms of a proper woman, he appears to be worried, as Martin contends, "that a change of dress . . . would amount to a change of nature" (286). Jack Tier follows the traditional role of women, even to a heroic level. She spends years of her life as a sailor in pursuit of her husband, she does everything she can to convince the Captain to make moral choices, and she urges him to behave like a Christian on his deathbed. However, Jack has suffered irreparable damage to her femininity. At the close of the novel, Jack has grown back her hair and dons women's clothing, but "she never can become what she once was" (511). Men's selfish and immoral choices have produced a woman who may never find herself again.

In fact, Jack Tier is as much a man as she is a woman. Contrary to Julie Wheelwright's assertion that women disguised as men simply traded roles with men and adopted male values (12), female sailors challenged audiences to see them as both male and female. Dressed as a man, Jack Tier models the man that Spike should be. Dressed as a woman, she embodies the woman Spike should be saving. Jack is a brave sailor who puts the lives of others ahead of her own. Jack continuously steers Spike away from making immoral decisions when she can, exhibiting loyalty to her captain. When dressed as Molly, she proves to be a woman whose heart holds the virtues of the nation. While Spike lies on his deathbed, Jack, dressed as Molly, reveals herself to Spike as his wife. He pleads forgiveness from her, and she grants his wish. Though Molly forgives him "from the bottom of my heart," she does not believe her forgiveness is enough, however, for "'my sayin' that I forget and forgive cannot help a man on his death-bed'" (504). Rather, she turns her energies to prayer, explaining that "I shall pray to God that he will pardon your sins as freely and more marcifully than I now pardon all" (504). Her wish that he be forgiven by God prompts Spike to pray himself (504). Molly is portrayed as a loyal, pious wife who appreciates God's role in the lives of her and her husband. Her virtue is so appealing that even Spike returns to God to ask for forgiveness.

Molly forgives Spike from "the bottom of [her] heart," a cliché that actually holds significance in this context. Molly's loyalty to God and her community suggests that although her appearance has changed her outward identity, her heart remains virtuous. It is not women's nature Cooper doubts, for their hearts are tightly tied to their commitment to God, family, and the community. Rather, Cooper questions the integrity of money-hungry American men who are forgetting the moral, historically grounded ideals that promise to make the United States an exceptional nation. Jack Tier essentially warns men about the dangers of pursuing individualistic goals while ignoring ties to God, country, and family.[29] When westbound men abandon females so they can pursue money, Cooper's novel argues, the female body and the body politic are damaged. The essential nature of the state may remain, but, as with the visage of women, so too the image of the nation is tarnished.

Nearly all of the cross-dressed mariner stories discussed thus far imagine women who indicate the virtues worthy of loyalty in American men or model those virtues themselves. Though these women indicate and embody national virtues, however, the fact remains that women dressed as men sailing the high seas do not resemble the traditional female snug in her parlor or drawing room and performing her feminine, middle-class duties. We might draw the conclusion, therefore, that audiences may simply have been drawn to these tales for the titillating appeal offered by the cross-dressed woman and the adventurous predicaments young ladies found themselves facing when they departed from their domestic sphere.[30] The stories, however, take great pains to be pedagogical, offering many lessons about loyalty, particularly to God and American men. What keeps these female characters from appearing to be dangerously independent—of men and gender and class boundaries—are the holy motives for their actions. Lucy Brewer ends her narrative pleading the case for a sexual and spiritual "virtue" that she believes "makes God our friend, assimilates and unites our minds to him, and engages his almighty power in our defence" (127). Katherine Plowdon equates her holy motive with being a good wife in one breath: "'If I have done more than my sex will warrant, remember it was through a holy motive, and if I have more than a woman's enterprise, it must be . . . [t]o fit me for, and to keep me worthy of being one day your wife'" (27). Jack Tier convinces her husband to pray for God's forgiveness so that he will be awarded her forgiveness (a not uncommon equivocation of God and woman). Fanny Campbell makes it clear that her skills as a mariner came from her pastor and her father, providing implicit Christian, patriarchal approval for her actions.

These women's Christian and moral ideals served as complements or challenges to the men with whom they went to sea. Just as nineteenth-century men were judged for their selfish or selfless responses to shipwrecked women, male characters in cross-dressed mariner stories were judged for their capacity to live up to the women modeling men's clothing and appropriate virtues. It is no coincidence that in Cooper's story of the cross-dressing Jack Tier, the most condemnatory example of Captain Spike's missing masculine virtue comes after his ship is wrecked. The crew and passengers, including two women and Jack Tier, escape the sinking ship aboard a small craft that is judged as too low in the water to withstand the breakers. Captain Spike orders his crew to toss overboard several sailors and the two female passengers. His cruelty is so profound that when one of the women clings to the boatswain's hand as he tosses her overboard, Spike orders him to "'cast off her hand'" (474). Though somewhat affected by the second woman's plea to be allowed to pray, Spike orders her into the sea as well. He even orders Jack, his own wife (unbeknownst to him), to follow the fate of the others, but not before Jack asks God to "pardon the sins" of Captain Spike (477).

Spike's cruel behavior during and after the shipwreck is not just criminal, it is akin to an act of treason. These women at sea are embodiments of virtue, maintaining their commitment to God even when their lives are in danger. They pray to God, they ask for God's forgiveness, and they are sacrificed for the good of the community. When Spike orders that his victim's hand be removed, he is severing his ties with *both* women and God. Jack Tier, who is also a woman, likewise appeals to God for forgiveness. Looking and acting like a man, she is also the image of men's best nature. When Spike orders Jack Tier, the image of the virtuous American male, overboard, he is tossing overboard not just his family but his own best self. Spike's selfishness, his desire to save himself instead of preserving the virtue expected of American men and women, is an act of disloyalty to God, family, and community. Spike's violent disloyalty betrays the nation's exceptional virtues and as such is not just a crime, it is treason.

The anxiety over whether men could or would exhibit the virtuous character expected of them when women were in distress at sea underlies the adventures of Lucy, Katherine, Roderick, Eudora, Fanny, and Jack. The unsettling truth of their stories is that women are the heroes here, and though their motives are everything they are supposed to be, there lies a disquieting subtext. Women are doing the saving, while men are missing. Adventures like these envision women who, as Cutter puts it, "save people when men cannot or will not" (150). Cross-dressed seafarers who become stand-ins for men reveal the antebellum anxiety that America may not have had a national manhood worthy of the nation's exceptional origins and ideals, not just because American men wouldn't save endangered women and children, and by extension their community, but because men's own selfish desires would render them irrelevant as men, replaceable and interchangeable with more able-bodied women. Thus, most of these stories share a common anxiety, one that has appeared again and again in this book. When women are constructed as embodiments of middle-class values, of commitment to God, family, and community, and men are incapable of saving them, what or who can "save" Anglo-America's identity?

These cross-dressed women were imagined as mariners rather than as railroad or factory workers because the sea was the pre–Civil War life force driving the myth of American identity. The sea launched non-native Americans' history as Americans, whether they were male or female, rich or poor, black or white, Irish, English, or European. Writers reported real-life disasters and fictionalized struggles at sea because the stories were part of a communally shared past of immigration, of trade, of war. How men aboard a ship behaved in a microcosm of the larger national community either mirrored or questioned the character of its citizens. When women set foot aboard a ship, the vessel was often transformed into a symbolic ship of state, because women's behavior and men's behavior were interpreted as indices of a kind of national moral nature perceived as exceptional. As real people or as figures of imagination, women were assumed to have brought with them a set of moral and Christian codes. If these morals and codes were to be ignored, abandoned, or abused, the new nation questioned whether it truly was an exceptional nation chosen by God.

The capacity for women to influence these reflections was so boundless that some female characters came to embody the model American man *and* woman. These characters act bravely on behalf of others, while underneath the male clothing, female mariners reveal the character of the model woman: committed to God, family, and, when called, the nation. She is the amalgam of the perfect American man and woman whose adventures pull them to the frontier either at sea or on land. When her life is threatened, when she is in distress, the priorities and ideals—in essence, the life—of the nation are imperiled.

—✐· Notes ✐—

Preface

1. Other sea narrative films within the past ten years include *Amistad* (1997); *The Endurance: Shackleton's Legendary Antarctic Expedition* (2000); *Ghost Ship* (2002); and *Master and Commander: The Far Side of the World* (2003).

2. In the last decade, both mainstream and academic presses have published a glut of books about shipwrecks and storms: a sampling of recent titles includes *The Lost Shipwreck of Paul*, by Robert Cornuke (2005); *Pride of the Sea: Courage, Disaster, and a Fight for Survival*, by Tom Waldron (2004); *Lifeboat*, by John R. Stilgoe (2003); *The Sea Hunters: True Adventures with Famous Shipwrecks*, by Clive Cussler (1996); *In Harm's Way: The Sinking of the USS Indianapolis and the Extraordinary Story of Its Survivors*, by Doug Stanton (2001); *The Ship and the Storm: Hurricane Mitch and the Loss of the Fantome*, by Jim Carrier (2002); *Until the Sea Shall Free Them*, by Robert Frump (2002); and *The Hungry Ocean: A Swordboat Captain's Journey*, by Linda Greenlaw (1999). The 2003 novel *Life of Pi*, by Yann Martel, a story of a boy castaway at sea, has been on most best-seller lists since its publication.

3. Though Robert Foulke's comprehensive *The Sea Voyage Narrative* (1997) uses gender-neutral pronouns in describing the common characteristics of sea narratives, he nevertheless gives very little indication in his study that women contributed to the construction of the sea narrative as a genre.

4. I have been most influenced by Nelson's *National Manhood* and *The Word in Black and White*.

5. See for instance John Carlos Rowe's chapters on Melville and Poe in *Literary Culture and U.S. Imperialism*; the collection of essays in *America and the Sea*, edited by Haskell Springer; and Thomas Philbrick's *James Fenimore Cooper and the Development of American Sea Fiction*.

6. Several historians have examined the increasing popularity of women

at sea, including those included in *Iron Men, Wooden Women*, a collection of essays edited by Creighton and Norling. See also Creighton's "American Mariners and the Rites of Manhood, 1830–1870"; and Norling's "The Sentimentalization of American Seafaring." Druett has studied instances of women at sea in *Hen Frigates* and *She Captains*. For a more general history of women at sea, see Linda Grant DePauw's *Seafaring Women*. For a study of manuscripts of diaries and letters written by captain's wives at sea, most of them written after 1850, see Haskell Springer's "The Captain's Wife at Sea" in Creighton and Norling.

7. A helpful overview of most of these political and social trends is Stephen J. Hartnett's *Democratic Dissent and the Cultural Fictions of Antebellum America*. For an analysis that specifically focuses on how slavery influenced pre–Civil War politics and economics, see John Ashworth's *Slavery, Capitalism, and Politics in the Antebellum Republic*.

8. The print culture of the early nineteenth century exploded because of better printing technologies and increased access to both urban and rural populations resulting from more organized routes and systems of transportation. A helpful recent review of the proliferation of various forms of print can be found in Isabelle Leuu's *Carnival on the Page*. The ways in which economic trends influenced the book trade in particular are addressed in Ronald J. Zboray's *A Fictive People*.

9. As Shelley Streeby's recent study of the U.S.-Mexican War has shown, the United States relied on the "exceptionalist premise that U.S. expansion was uniquely good or benign" (107) because it was bringing the democratic principles of truth and justice to the rest of the country and the world. The various children that this concept of exceptionalism bore are numerous and include the notion that abundant opportunities existed in America for economic advancement because of its inherent appreciation for truth and justice. See for instance Jonathan A. Glickstein's *American Exceptionalism, American Anxiety*.

10. See Sacvan Bercovitch's foundational work on this topic in *The American Jeremiad* and *The Puritan Origins of the American Self*.

11. In a discussion of the War of 1812, Hugh Egan points out that when President Madison highlighted five reasons for war with Britain, four "involved illegal acts at sea" (64).

12. For a helpful study of U.S. relations with North African rulers, see

Michael L. S. Kitzen's *Tripoli and the United States at War*; and James Field Jr.'s *America and the Mediterranean World, 1776–1882.*

13. See Wharton's "The Colonial Era" in *America and the Sea*, ed. Springer; and Stephen Fender's *Sea Changes.*

14. See Paul Baepler's introduction to *White Slaves, African Masters*; my article, "Transatlantic Touchstone"; and James R. Lewis's "Images of Captive Rape in the Nineteenth Century" and "Savages of the Seas."

1. Shipwreck Narratives in Early American Literature

1. See chapter 1, "The Ritual of Consensus," of Sacvan Bercovitch's *Rites of Assent* for a useful summary of his own work with Puritan rhetoric, interpretations that have served as the foundation for many scholars of early American literature and culture.

2. All references to Bradford's *Of Plimouth Plantation* rely on the 1966 edition edited by Samuel Eliot Morison. In his detailed account of the publication history of *Of Plimouth Plantation*, Morison points out that although Bradford's history was never published in his own day, it was often used as a resource for New England chroniclers of the seventeenth and eighteenth centuries, and was already a well-traveled chronicle by the time of its first publication in 1856, by Little, Brown and Company.

3. Like Bradford's text, The Mayflower Compact became a celebrated document by the end of the eighteenth century, well on its way to a consistent presence in most history textbooks. See Mark L. Sargent's "The Conservative Covenant."

4. Relying on the foundational descriptions of the Puritans' covenant vision, Roger G. Betsworth describes the "logic of the covenant" as God's promise to be the Puritans' God as long as they kept their promise to serve him by being "bound" to others in their community (26).

5. For a more specific consideration of whether Winthrop read his speech before or during the crossing of the Atlantic, see Hugh J. Dawson's two studies "John Winthrop's Rite of Passage," which proposes the discourse was not written in midcrossing, and "'Christian Charitie' as Colonial Discourse," which reads the speech as if it were given at the Puritans' departure.

6. For more thorough discussions of Winthrop's reliance on contract law

in his speech, see Scott Michaelsen's "John Winthrop's 'Modell' Covenant and the Company Way"; and pages 119–20 of Dawson's "'Christian Charitie' as Colonial Discourse."

7. Although Caldwell acknowledges the effect of migration on many Puritan narratives, in that it serves "as a keystone in the structure of deliverance" (27), she gives limited consideration to the sea and shipwreck as primary factors in that deliverance. In particular, see Caldwell's introduction and part 2 of The Puritan Conversion Narrative.

8. Mather's use of this family's desire to die together as proof of Americans' commitment to their covenant with God and one another enlarges the relevance of their experience. As Andrew Wiget points out in his essay on American "origin stories," professions of faith (as in this case, during and after shipwreck) are ironic in that the "public profession of faith in any story signals that the structure of events it represents is no longer taken for granted but requires the energy of deliberate commitment to sustain it" (215). Mather's way of sustaining the import of the lesson is to tell this individual story as if it were the colony's story.

9. Carla Mulford uses the term social imaginary as a definition of a nation, rather than Benedict Anderson's term imagined community. Mulford's concept is sensitive to the fact that labeling a nation as an "imagined community," as Anderson does, may "erase . . . inequities in the social formation which the term 'community' mystifies" (19). Replacing imagined community with social imaginary makes room for the realities of social stratification—often based on class, gender, race, and sexual preference—that a finite-sounding imagined (singular) community does not.

10. Thomas Philbrick catalogues these dramas and more in James Fenimore Cooper and the Development of American Sea Fiction, particularly chapter 1.

11. Keith Huntress has complied a list of shipwreck narratives and their publication history in his invaluable A Checklist of Narratives of Shipwrecks and Disasters at Sea to 1860, with Summaries, Notes, and Comments and provided these titles and dates.

12. Many of these narratives were made available by the publication of an anthology of shipwreck narratives, edited by Archibald Duncan. See Huntress's Checklist for a helpful summary of individual publication dates and content summaries.

13. *The Portfolio and New York Monthly Magazine* 1.3 (March 1822): 250–52.

14. Information pertaining to the *Turtle* was gathered from the Shipwreck! exhibit at the Vancouver Maritime Museum, Vancouver, British Columbia, July 11, 1997, through May 2, 1999.

15. See for instance Eric Wertheimer's article, which shows how this poem portrays Columbus as "the historical symbol of cosmic possibility and renovation and the contemporary symbol of an opportunity for the nation to restore the legacy of New World civilization" (45). For a discussion of how this poem constructs the myth of America as a pastoral ideal, see Annette Kolodny's seminal *The Lay of the Land* (31–33).

16. Biographical information about Freneau is taken from Harry Hayden Clark's introduction to *Poems of Freneau*.

17. Freneau often represents the ships in his poems as American "ships of state." See Gilbert L. Gigliotti's analysis of Freneau's oft-anthologized poem "The Hurricane."

18. As Jerry Phillips explains, cultural forces in general "do not obey singular transcendent laws of nationhood . . . rather they collide and lock and 'leak' into each other (to use Salmon Rushdie's evocative phrase) to produce a distinctive sound with no one origin, no one logic of progress, no ultimate (metaphysical) goal" (58). Likewise, the shipwreck as a national narrative does not undermine or detract from other national narratives' significance, nor does it replace considerations of individual social imaginaries as integral to conceptions of nationhood. For, as Patricia Wald points out in *Constituting Americans*, "national narratives . . . do not supply missing conceptions of personhood; rather, they forge one conception out of another to constitute an individual as a national subject with a new cultural identity."

19. Disturbed by contemporary critics' assumption that Equiano's *Narrative* was as well received in the United States as it was in Britain when first published in 1791, Akiyo Ito focuses on the reasons behind the first U.S. publication of Equiano's *Interesting Narrative* by researching Equiano's list of subscribers. In trying to understand why the narrative took so long to be reprinted, Ito found that the first publication was appreciated more for its religious content than antislavery messages. Ito acknowledges,

however, that by the 1820s and throughout the 1840s, Equiano's narrative was popular in the United States, particularly among abolitionists.

20. Prompted by Vincent Carretta's research, literary historians are still wrestling with the possibility that Equiano was actually born in South Carolina, which casts doubt on Equiano's account of the Middle Passage. Even if Equiano created his story of the Middle Passage or cribbed it from other sources, however, the author makes clear how important captivity at sea was in the trajectory of Equiano's life. For more information on Carretta's findings, see his articles "Olaudah Equiano or Gustavus Vassa?" and "Three West Indian Writers of the 1780s."

21. By the early nineteenth century, notes W. Jeffrey Bolster, "black men . . . filled about one-fifth of sailors' berths" for the American shipping industry (2).

22. See Carolyn A. Haynes, who interprets Equiano's contradiction between repentant sinner and powerful hero as a consequence of the teaching of George Whitefield, who greatly influenced Equiano. Haynes believes Equiano was enacting "self-denigration and self-enlargement" to attain "an acceptable masculine selfhood and thus a certain self-empowerment" modeled after Whitefield (Divine 3).

23. One of the most comprehensive investigations of Anglo perceptions of the nature of blacks from the sixteenth through the early nineteenth centuries is Winthrop D. Jordan's White over Black. Also, Londa Schiebinger studies how early natural historians, anthropologists, and anatomists molded "scientific" knowledge of gender and race in Nature's Body. Chapters 4 and 5 of Schiebinger's work focus most specifically on racial theories. For a study concerning the increasing popularity of scientific racialism in the United States, see Reginald Horsman's Race and Manifest Destiny, particularly chapters 6 and 7.

24. Emmanuel Chukwudi Eze's Race and the Enlightenment is a collection of excerpts from the works of a variety of Enlightenment philosophers who concerned themselves with race, particularly the "nature" of blacks. My quotation from Kant is from his essay "On the Different Races of Man" (1775), while the second example is from Carl von Linne's The System of Nature (1735).

25. The long-term political effectiveness of the representation of Equiano's time at sea is apparent in the fact that the sea and the possibili-

ties it held for other selves and identities in the lives of other blacks would reappear in future antislavery writings of Americans such as Frederick Douglass, who escaped slavery disguised as a sailor, and Harriet Jacobs, who disguised herself as a sailor during one of her steps toward eventual freedom.

26. *The Portfolio* 2.1 (July 1822): 15.

27. *New York Monthly Magazine* (January 1, 1824): 53.

2. Women and Children First

1. Though Donald P. Wharton interprets shipwreck narratives from the seventeenth through the nineteenth centuries as evolving in genre from the "providential sea-deliverance" in the seventeenth century to "the romantic fiction of the nineteenth century" (Introduction 24), he and other critics of American sea narratives have not addressed the influence of women on these transformations.

2. In his extensive annotated bibliography of shipwreck narratives, Keith Huntress lists Sarah Allen's account but offers no proof that her shipwreck occurred.

3. See John Seelye's *Memory's Nation*, which analyzes sermons and plays that highlight the significance of the historical moment of the landing and the role of Plymouth Rock.

4. Although Bradford's *History of Plimouth Plantation* wasn't recovered from the library of the bishop of Oxford until 1855, its contents were well known thanks to the efforts of his son-in-law in 1669 to retell the account in *New England's Memorial* (Seelye 32, 78).

5. For information about the origins and popularity of emblems and emblem books in early modern Europe, see pages 79–90 of David D. Hall's chapter "The World of Print and Collective Mentality in Seventeenth-Century New England," in *Cultures of Print*. See also the collection of essays in *The English Emblem and the Continental Tradition*, edited by Peter M. Daly.

6. The emblems in figures 2 and 3 are copied from William Holmes and John W. Barber's 1855 edition of *Religious Emblems*. This text, filled with emblems, poems, and explanations, was quite popular in the 1840s and 1850s. First published in 1846 in Cincinnati, Ohio, it was reprinted at least twenty times by 1860 in such cities as Boston, Cincinnati, New Haven,

New York, Philadelphia, Providence, and even Greenville, Tennessee. The same emblem of Hope leaning on an anchor appeared in *Choice Emblems, Natural, Historical, Fabulous, Moral, and Divine* (emblem 7, 46), published in New York in 1818. Though there is no author listed for my edition of *Choice Emblems*, an emblem book with the same title, authored by John Huddlestone Wynne, was consistently in print at the end of the eighteenth century and the beginning of the nineteenth. Based on the publication records of these two emblem books, it is likely that this particular emblem of Hope was widely circulated.

7. Like other writers of the time, Edgar Allan Poe believed "the death, then, of a beautiful woman is, unquestionably, the most poetical topic in the world" ("Philosophy of Composition" 486).

8. Sprague is probably referring to the Englishwoman Mary Lundie Duncan, whose biography/memoir was published and reprinted in the United States throughout the 1840s and beyond. Duncan died young, and her piety as a mother and wife nearly martyred her, as is evinced by the following epitaph on her tombstone, which also sums up the lessons contained in the memoir itself: "To the Memory of Mary . . . In the morning of life, the sweet affections of her heart, and every energy of a powerful and highly refined intellect, were consecrated, by the Holy Spirit, to the service of JESUS CHRIST. Lovely, alike in person and in character, she discharged with fidelity the duties of a wife and of a mother, and prayerfully sought to improve every opportunity of usefulness among the people of this parish; till, unexpectedly, but not unprepared, she fell asleep in Jesus, on the 5th day of Jan. AD 1840. AGED 25" (283).

9. The captain of the doomed *Pulaski* labeled Miss Rebecca Lamar "our preserving angel" because she rallied the passengers' "sinking and despairing spirits" (*American* 246).

10. Two helpful sources that explore the importance of motherhood in the nineteenth century are E. Ann Kaplan's *Motherhood and Representation* and Eva Cherniavsky's *That Pale Mother Rising*, which argues that the "social affect" caused by sympathy is derived from "the maternal body," which holds a central "nationalist resonance" in nineteenth-century culture (12).

11. According to Roger B. Stein, the sculpture was "exhibited at the Boston Athenaeum first in 1852 and yearly thereafter until 1866," and was later "placed in Mount Auburn Cemetery" (153).

12. In *Manhood in America*, Kimmel quotes a letter written by John Adams to Thomas Jefferson that asks, "Will you tell me how to prevent riches from producing luxury? Will you tell me how to prevent luxury from producing effeminacy, intoxication, extravagance, vice and folly?" (19).

13. See also Anne S. Lombard's *Making Manhood*, which traces seventeenth- and eighteenth-century American notions of manhood. Her study shows how "the source of manhood . . . was not inside the individual but without, in the attribution of virtues that signified a community's agreement that a man had fulfilled its expectations for the male role" (9).

14. As E. Anthony Rotundo explains, the idea that the "best man wins" came about in the early 1800s. Owing to the "reassessment of self-interest and individual initiative . . . the notion that free competition would reward the best man" became a popular belief (19).

15. These prints were apparently engraved and published by John C. McRae in New York, ca. 1855. Thank you to Jan Grenci, the reference specialist at the Prints and Photographs Division of the Library of Congress, for this information.

16. The fear that human effort is also useless is illustrated in William B. Tappan's poem "To the President Steamship," published alongside a narrative of the wreck of the *President*. The persona emphasizes that though God is "trusted," the "noble frame of steel and oak; / Strong as thy mates" was "trusted too," as well as "science, and the perfect skill / Which could a trackless way pursue, / And make a distant port at will. / We trusted man, well-tried of old" (Howland 184).

17. The notion that women and children should be saved first was not written into maritime code in the antebellum era. It was an expectation increasingly pressing as more and more women went to sea to travel with husbands or family. Most commentators on shipwrecks identify the wreck of the *Arctic* as the point when the "women and children first" credo became a more explicit mandate in American maritime procedures, though it was consistently assumed to be policy throughout the antebellum years. See E. Merton Coulter's "The Loss of the Steamship *Central America*, in 1857," and Alexander Brown's *Women and Children Last*.

18. See *Sea of Glory*, Nathaniel Philbrick's account of U.S. expeditions to the Arctic in the antebellum era.

19. The information about the sources for Longfellow's poem mostly

comes from his *Letters*, to which I will be referring as such. I was occasionally pointed to specific segments of Longfellow's letters by Eugene Hollahan's "Intertextual Bondings between 'The Wreck of the Hesperus' and *The Wreck of the Deutschland*."

20. See Genesis 19.1–29 and Ezekiel 16.49–51. In this story in the book of Genesis, Lot and his family are reluctantly led from the cities of Sodom and Gomorrah before God destroys them for their sexual vices as well as in punishment for a people who were arrogant, overfed, and apathetic.

21. The woman was a passenger on the schooner *Favorite*, which wrecked on Norman's Woe. See Henry Wadsworth Longfellow Dana's 1939 *Boston Herald* article, "Centenary of Hesperus Wreck on Norman's Woe" (3).

22. Women still associate their physical appearance with the girl in this shipwreck story. A colleague of mine told me that she and other girls grew up labeling themselves "the wreck of the Hesperus" when they didn't like what they saw in the mirror, and most women are familiar with the pronouncement "I'm a wreck" when they are feeling unattractive or stressed.

23. See Longfellow's *Letters* (2: 206–9) for the original poem in full. In Henry Wadsworth Longfellow Dana's (Longfellow's grandson) 1939 article in *The Boston Herald* commemorating the centenary of the wreck of the *Hesperus*, he says, "It was only just before the poem was printed that this defiant reply of the skipper was crossed out" (3).

24. The potential influence females could have on national values was a consistent concern in Longfellow's work throughout the late 1830s and 1840s. As Eric L. Haralson explains in "Mars in Petticoats," works such as Longfellow's "Defense of Poetry" and *Evangeline* "announced the poet's plan to foster a process . . . in which the arena of civic virtue slowly shifted from male preserves of power . . . to female spheres of influence" in the case of the former (336), and also "mourned a loss of innocence in both the culture and the individual life," as is the case with the main female character in *Evangeline* (339).

3. Women and the Middle Passage

1. See *Women at Sea*, a collection of essays edited by Lizabeth Paravisini-Gebert and Ivette Romero-Cesareo.

2. See for instance three recent studies that address African American

interpretations of the Middle Passage: *The Black Columbiad*, edited by Werner Sollors and Maria Diedrich; *Black Imagination and the Middle Passage*, edited by Maria Diedrich, Henry Louis Gates, Jr., and Carl Pedersen; and *Radical Narratives of the Black Atlantic*, by Alan Rice.

3. There is some debate among historians about whether that number should be even higher. A summary of the debate can be found in John Hope Franklin and Alfred A. Moss Jr.'s *From Slavery to Freedom* (41).

4. Prince recounts the stories of her stepfather and other members of her family as a matter of form as well. As Cheryl Fish explains, the "opening pages detailing her familial origins also ground Prince's identity as a rational, Enlightenment subject," not unlike other autobiographers at the time. Her "ancestry and position establish her as a reliable narrator" ("Journeys" 227).

5. Prince alternates between calling her stepfather "father" and "stepfather."

6. Though impossible to define psychically for all slaves, common Middle Passage experiences appear to fall into general stages. In the most general terms, as Werner Sollors and Maria Diedrich have explained, slavery's origins are defined by "departure, "passage," and "arrival." These words, however, gain a "different meaning, a tragic quality in reference to an analysis of [the Middle Passage]" (11). Departure is kidnapping, passage is confinement and abuse, and arrival is equivocated with enslavement, though all three could be experienced simultaneously.

7. Though Susan A. Glenn is referring to the practice of the "theatrical producers" in late nineteenth and early twentieth-century American theater, her characterization of the expected passivity of the spectacle applies to Prince's situation as well.

8. In an article about William "Box" Brown and the parallels between his escape and the Middle Passage, Wolff contends that the Middle Passage is the "*beginning* of every 'slave narrative'" (emphasis in original 27), thus suggesting that a kind of cultural unconscious memory existed for all African American slaves.

9. As the Flints' house slave, Jacobs is sexually harassed by Dr. Flint, who wants to make the teenager his mistress. Jacobs escapes from the Flints and takes refuge in a small attic above her grandmother's shed where she hides for seven years.

10. In her fascinating analysis of the literary, philosophical, and legal implications of the term *loophole* in Jacobs's chapter title, Michelle Burnham explains that even though "Jacobs' loophole of retreat is the most confining space imaginable, it is finally a space of escape" (155).

11. A sample of one of these drawings can be found in Thomas Clarkson's *The History of the Rise, Progress and Accomplishment of the Abolition of the African Slave Trade by the British Parliament* (1808).

12. An artful coincidence is the parallel between the names and means of survival in both stories. Defoe's Crusoe was based on the real experiences of Alexander Selkirk. Just as Selkirk is renamed as Crusoe, so too does Jacobs use a fictional name, "Linda Brent," in place of her own. Crusoe's survival relied on Friday, much as Linda Brent's survival relies on the help of an extended network within the African American community.

13. In a rare mention of Jacobs's use of the Crusoe comparison, Harryette Mullen makes the important point that Jacobs is identifying with Friday when she compares herself to Crusoe. Though Mullen does not expound on the connection at length, she does claim Jacobs's identification with the Crusoe story is an example of her "notable capacity for the imaginative transformation and reconstruction of metaphorical and ideological material (249–50).

14. Burnham explains that the term *blind spot* refers to Teresa de Lauretis's description of one type of female agency as "the blind spots, or the space-off, of its representations[,] . . . spaces in the margins of hegemonic discourses, social spaces carved in the interstices of institutions and in the chinks and cracks of the power/knowledge apparati" (159).

15. See chapter 1, pages 15–21.

16. For more on black women's complex relationship with the ideology behind the concept of True Womanhood, see Dorothy Sterling's introduction to *We Are Your Sisters* and Valerie Smith's *Self Discovery and Authority in Afro-American Narrative*, particularly pages 9–43.

17. Lapansky also points out that the images of the kneeling man and woman "were also replicated on handicraft goods and even manufactured items such as chinaware, tokens, linen, and silk goods sold by the antislavery women at their annual fund-raising fairs" (206)

18. Marianne Noble's *The Masochistic Pleasures of Sentimental Literature*, particularly the chapter on Stowe's *Uncle Tom's Cabin*; Karen Sánchez-Eppler's

Touching Liberty; and Saidiya Hartman's *Scenes of Subjection* are each excellent studies of white abolitionists' rhetoric in the nineteenth century.

19. See Carolyn Sorisio's study of the abolitionists' use of sentimentality when representing slave women's pain, particularly her helpful review of scholars who have theorized about this type of rhetoric (54–59). Sorisio explains that a kind of "sentimental empathy" seems to be at the core of many abolitionists' attempts to represent the body in pain. Such an empathy is defined as "the idea that the reader should be guided into a physical reaction to scenes of cruelty to be spurred to social action" (56).

20. Though published anonymously in 1839, *American Slavery As It Is* was known to be compiled by the Welds and Sarah Grimke, according to William Loren Katz, general editor of the Arno Press edition.

21. Early groundbreakers in the study of white motherhood include Barbara Welter's seminal article, "The Cult of True Womanhood, 1820–1860," and Ann Douglas's *The Feminization of American Culture*.

22. As Thomas F. Gossett points out, Tom wasn't the only type of black man Stowe envisions. There is also George Harris, the angry slave who escapes to Canada and later emigrates to Africa. Gossett explains that "for readers who might not be able to accept the idea that most blacks would be like Uncle Tom, Stowe apparently has in reserve the idea of colonization. If the blacks are troublesome in society, the reader might legitimately conclude, they would be troublesome in Africa and not in the United States" (161). I agree that Stowe also provides this option, but it is telling that the most lasting character from this novel is Uncle Tom, who, as Gossett himself observes, is anything but "a source of disruption in society" and would continue to be so even "if he had been freed" (161).

23. See chapters 14 and 19 in Gossett's *Uncle Tom's Cabin and American Culture*. Chapter 14 recounts the dramatization of the novel on stage during the 1850s and chapter 19 does the same for the years following the Civil War. Gossett's study also includes several contemporary illustrations of Eliza's crossing.

24. In 1788, John Newton, a self-described "reformed slave trader," relates a story about a shipmate, who, frustrated with a slave woman's crying infant, threw the baby overboard. Though the women's "lamentations" disturbed him, she "was too valuable to be thrown overboard" (86). He urges white mothers to see their own motherhood as threatened when he

comments further, "I am persuaded that every tender mother, who feasts her eyes and her mind when she contemplates the infant in her arms, will commiserate the poor Africans" (86).

25. Thomas Clarkson published *The History of the Rise, Progress and Accomplishment of the Abolition of the African Slave Trade* in 1808 and Parliament member William Wilberforce presented motions and gave abolition speeches in Parliament for eighteen years. Both Englishmen were seen as powerful rhetoricians who were largely responsible for the abolition of the slave trade.

26. Newton writes, "When the women and girls are taken on board a ship, naked, trembling, terrified, perhaps almost exhausted with cold, fatigue, and hunger, they are often exposed to the wanton rudeness of white savages . . . In imagination, the prey is divided, on the spot, and only reserved till opportunity offers. Where resistance or refusal, would be utterly in vain, even the solicitation of consent is seldom thought of" (87).

4. Englishwomen and U.S. Shipwreck Narratives

1. According to Burnham's version of early American literary history, "National literary traditions can be imagined as coherent . . . only by imagining the border between them to be fixed and uncrossed." Rather, literary traditions, like the Atlantic, have "porous borders" allowing for the "movement and exchange of texts" (62).

2. For the origins of American sea songs, hymns, and chanteys, and their transatlantic influences, see Robert D. Madison's "Hymns, Chanteys, and Sea Songs."

3. I compare several other shipwreck narratives published in England with U.S. narratives in my article "Transatlantic Touchstone." For an analysis of the relationship between British culture and shipwreck narratives, see Margarette Lincoln's "Shipwreck Narratives of the Eighteenth and Early Nineteenth Century."

4. No evidence exists of either shipwreck, according to Keith Huntress (Introduction) and Paul Baepler (11). Both stories were published exclusively in the United States and were likely an attempt by American publishers to write books destined for good sales.

5. Although it is impossible to determine for sure, this means of escape

may be an allusion to the influential stories of the wreck of the *Grosvenor*, a version of which had been published in the United States in Archibald Duncan's popular anthology *The Mariner's Chronicle; or, authentic and complete history of popular shipwrecks*. This type of escape was often the subject of prints depicting the *Grosvenor* wreck. The writer of Martin's narrative may have been capitalizing on the appeal of the *Grosvenor* wreck to U.S. audiences, readers who may have been fascinated by the mythos surrounding the *Grosvenor*'s wrecked women, who were captured by Africans and subsequently disappeared. For more information about the wreck of the *Grosvenor*, see Percival R. Kirby's *A Source Book on the Wreck of the* Grosvenor East Indiaman and *The True Story of the* Grosvenor East Indiaman.

6. The use of the term *Turk* by Martin suggests she is bought by a pirate, or corsair. See Baepler (6).

7. See "Images of Captive Rape in the Nineteenth Century" for Lewis's discussion of the connections to sexual assault found in captivity narratives, and see "Savages of the Seas" for a more specific study of Barbary captivity narratives, which he divides into four categories: historical, propagandistic, sensationalistic, and romantic-heroic (77). Lewis briefly mentions Maria Martin's narratives as an example of the sensationalistic tales published around the time of the Barbary difficulties; it is sensational, he claims, because of the "sexualized violence" found therein (78).

8. According to Baepler, there were female captives, perhaps as many as two thousand. However, these women were held in the 1630s (3), and no narratives exist of their captivity.

9. See Baepler's informative introduction to his anthology of Barbary captivity narratives.

10. See Burnham, who proposes that Americans were partly intrigued by pre–Revolutionary War captivity narratives because they were drawn to imagining what it would be like for an Englishwoman to have "a liminal or hybrid, if not an Indian, cultural identity" (46).

11. Within Bradley's narrative and attached to Martin's are appendices, apparently cribbed from one of the various anthropological source books circulating at the time that offer seemingly objective ethnographic details about the everyday life and customs of the Moors and Turks. The narrative voice of the ethnography sounds as if it is coming from an objective perspective, much different from the sentimental language used in the

plotting of the women's stories. However, this was not unusual. In *The Story of the Voyage*, Philip Edwards characterizes male-authored sea-voyage narratives as "schizophrenic" in that they alternate between voices aimed at the scientist and the general reader (8), while many male- and female-authored travel narratives likewise gave similar types of information. Whatever the case, the presence of the anthropological information is indicative of the need to satisfy Anglo-Americans' desire for knowledge about the lifestyles of the "mysterious" North Africans they perceived as so threatening to the captured women.

12. See figure 5 in chapter 2.

13. Some examples include Susannna Rowson's *Slaves in Algiers* (1794), Royall Tyler's novel *The Algerine Captive* (1797), James Ellison's *The American Captive* (1812), and David Everett's *Slaves in Barbary* (1817).

14. Martin claims she and the other captives were herded "like so many cattle . . . to the public market" (47), and when she looks around at her fellow "slaves," she notes that some "had large collars about their necks, made much after the form of those worn by the West-India slaves" (48).

15. For an analysis of the various versions of Fraser's story, from the nineteenth century to its present-day manifestations in Australian art and literature, see Kay Schaffer's excellent *In the Wake of First Contact* as well as a collection of essays, edited by Ian J. McNiven, Lynette Russell, and Schaffer, entitled *Constructions of Colonialism*. In *Constructions*, there is an oral account of Fraser's shipwreck given by Olga Miller, an elder of the Badtjala people of Fraser island: it is the first Aboriginal account of Fraser's story.

16. Spoken by Eliza Fraser in a hearing with the Lord Mayor and reported in the London *Times*, Thursday, August 24, 1837.

17. There is really no way of telling if Fraser actually penned the story published in the United States, though its sensational and false details lead me to suspect it was written by the New York publisher C. S. Webb, who may have heard of her story from an English source.

18. Schaffer points out that in 1838 alone (the year after the publication of the U.S. version of Fraser's shipwreck), "six separate, new captivity narratives were published" (57).

19. The title of this captivity narrative is *A Narrative of the Life of Mrs. Mary Jemison*; it was first published in 1824. Kathryn Zabelle Derounian-Stodola

identifies Jemison's story as a "best-seller" that was "regularly reprinted and reedited" throughout the nineteenth century (121).

20. I have been unable to find any narrative of the wreck of the Blinderhall. It is not listed in Keith Huntress's comprehensive Checklist, though it could have been reported in the newspapers.

21. Ann Saunders's account seems to be authentic, but it would likely have been recorded by someone else, because she may not have been able to write. She tells us in her narrative that her father died young and her mother had to care for five children on her own. She admits to having "an education sufficient to enable me to peruse the sacred Scriptures" (7). On the first page of the book, her story is authenticated with an official letter from the District Clerk's Office of Massachusetts recording the reception of this narrative from Ebenezer Frier. The letter is followed by a "Recommendation" to confirm "the truth of the facts" by Ebenezer Wakefield of Liverpool on July 7, 1826, who calls the narrative "a work of great merit."

22. In an anthology that summarizes a variety of shipwreck narratives, one of which is Saunders's story, Edward E. Leslie says that this newspaper account was written by Captain Kendall (229). The quote, however, clearly indicates that the tale is told by someone else on the ship, probably a crew member, since the narrator says he got the master's (captain's) wife and female passenger up to the maintop during the wreck.

23. See the first chapter of Daniel A. Cohen's Pillars of Salt, Monuments of Grace, which offers an overview of the succession of genres from 1674 to 1860.

24. Robert F. Berkhofer Jr. contends that the supposition that Native Americans were cannibals is what led Columbus to justify the selling of natives into slavery (119). By the eighteenth century, as James Axtell shows, captivity narratives had contributed to the Anglo assumption that the Iroquois were cannibals (263). Richard Vanderbeets believes this assumption was widespread, arguing that "from the seventeenth to the nineteenth centuries . . . a geographical span of tribes ranging from New England forest Indians to tribes of the Great Lakes to the Plains and Southwest Indians: Mohawks, Delawares, Chippewas, Miamis, Ottawas, Shawnees, Chickasaws, and Comanches," were believed by whites to be cannibals, a perception derived mostly from captivity narratives (550).

25. Examples include the wreck of the *George* (1822); the wreck of the *Essex* (1820), one of the sources for Herman Melville's *Moby Dick*; the wreck of the *Medusa* (1816), memorialized by Gericault's famous painting; and the wreck of the *Peggy* (1765). Descriptions of these wrecks and the cannibalism among the survivors can be found in Brian A. W. Simpson's *Cannibalism and the Common Law*. Also, the short summaries in Huntress's *Checklist* indicate whether and when passengers and crews participated in cannibalistic practices.

26. Those so unfortunate as to be young, unmarried, black, or poor shared none of the privileges of the married man. Through fixing the drawing of lots, or by sheer force, black cooks, common seamen, or slaves were usually chosen to be sacrificed, as were young men or boys without family or dependents, while the captain or his officers were rarely victims (Simpson 128). This explains why in most nineteenth-century shipwreck narratives there is usually no mention of what the cabin boys had to say about their death. It may have been because they were the most "valid" choice of victims: they were perceived as lacking family ties, and as cabin boys, they were the lowest rung of the ship's hierarchy. That Saunders lists the occupations of the dead is important because it makes obvious the fact that all of the victims who died were common seamen; none were officers or passengers.

27. Cohen studies the evolution of the early American conversion narrative into murder confessionals in *Pillars of Salt, Monuments of Grace*. Dawn Keetley labels the women characters in these stories "female fiends." Keetley's description of the female fiend—someone who is "white, of ambiguous class status (although not desperately poor)," and whose adventure involves the possible murder of her lover (344)—sounds an awful lot like Saunders.

28. In an uncanny way, her beloved is incorporated into herself. Within a Judeo-Christian tradition, this is an act of goodness, as Maggie Kilgour points out, and in fact "becomes identified with a return to home and proper identity from a state of alienation" (11). Thus, by calling on the symbology of communion, the narrative makes Saunders's act appear to be as holy as it is horrifying.

29. According to Brereton, the female-authored conversion narrative

NOTES TO PAGES 128–132

of the nineteenth century occasionally "penetrated class boundaries, but it was largely a middle-class luxury—or necessity" (4).

30. See Christopher Looby, who describes how sensational literature involving women often "restores sentimental domestic ideology even as it provides a fantasy of escape from it" (655).

5. Cross-Dressed Female Seafarers

1. Foundational historical studies include Ann Douglas's *The Feminization of American Culture* and numerous books by Linda K. Kerber. Kerber's notion that the "model republican woman was to be self-reliant (within limits), literate, untempted by the frivolities of fashion . . . [with] responsibility to the political scene, though not to act on it" and that the model Republican Mother was to be "dedicated to the service of civic virtue" within her domestic sphere has been relatively uncontested by other critics ("The Republican Mother," in *Toward an Intellectual History of Women*, a collection of Kerber's essays from 1973 to 1993, 58). Also, see the work of Shirley Samuels, whose *Romance of the Republic* shows how post-Revolutionary narratives consistently worked to put women in a separate domestic sphere as a kind of "backlash" to the growing "political viability of women" (13, 15).

2. In 2003 Davidson edited a collection of essays entitled *No More Separate Spheres*, which was originally published as a 1998 special edition of *American Literature*. In her article in that collection, Davidson claims, "Much of the criticism of nineteenth-century American literature written during the last quarter century has structured itself by the binary of the 'separate spheres,' a retrospective construction that has had the effect of recreating a binaric gender division among contemporary critics that influences what books we write, read, teach, and cite in our own work" (443).

3. The most famous female sailors, Anne Bonny and Mary Read, were eighteenth-century pirates. Their legacy is explored in Marcus Rediker's "Liberty beneath the Jolly Roger." Dianne Dugaw's studies of the British female warrior in "Female Sailors Bold," "'Wild Beasts' and 'Excellent Friends,'" and *Warrior Women and Popular Balladry, 1650–1850*, are also extremely informative for those interested in the tradition of British female soldiers and sailors.

4. The first edition of *The History of Constantius and Pulchera* was published

in 1794 and reprinted at least a dozen times by 1831. A shipwreck divides the American lovers Constantius and Pulchera. Pulchera is rescued by an American privateer, the captain of which advises her to dress as a naval lieutenant in case the ship is captured. She remains a cross-dressed seaman throughout several adventures until she is reunited with Constantius.

5. The titles are The Pilot (1824), The Red Rover (1827), and The Water-Witch (1830).

6. The series of pamphlets that make up the stories of Lucy Brewer were most likely authored by either Nathaniel Coverly Jr. or a ghostwriter in his employ. See Daniel A. Cohen's introduction to The Female Marine (2–5).

7. Deborah Sampson was a real cross-dressed soldier who later petitioned George Washington for veteran benefits. Her definitive biography was published by the historian Alfred F. Young in 2004. Also, see Linda Kerber's Women of the Republic (107). Sampson is mentioned as an inspiration in The Female Marine, Ellen Stephens's The Cabin Boy Wife (1840), and Eliza Allen's Female Volunteer (1851). Her story was published as a memoir by Herman Mann in 1797, The Female Review; or, Memoirs of an American Young Lady; whose life and character are peculiarly distinguished—being a continental soldier, for nearly three years, in the late war, and was reissued throughout the first half of the nineteenth century.

8. In 1966 Da Capo Press published the first twentieth-century edition of The Female Marine, the first since the nineteen editions issued between 1815 and 1818 in the United States. Few scholars have sorted out the cultural significance of The Female Marine and female sailor narratives in general. A brief analysis of The Female Marine was published in 1966 by Alexander Medlicott Jr. In 1997 Daniel A. Cohen edited an edition of The Female Marine that included the sequels; Cohen introduced the stories with an excellent historical essay about Lucy Brewer's story. Cohen's edition of the novel was followed by a short analysis in Joseph Fichtelberg's Critical Fictions (112–16).

9. Lucy Brewer is an alias for her "real" name, Louisa Baker, later to become Mrs. Lucy West. For clarity's sake, I will refer to her as Lucy Brewer.

10. The page number refers to Cohen's edition of the collected works, The Female Marine and Related Works. Hereafter, I will be quoting from this

edition. Cohen's collection reprints the three installments of pamphlet novels about Lucy Brewer that were published between 1815 and 1816.

11. Neither Medlicott's nor Cohen's searches of town records and muster rolls have turned up any evidence that Lucy Brewer existed. See Cohen, Introduction (7).

12. Their titles are *The Adventures of Lucy Brewer* (1815) and *The Awful Beacon* (1816). Based on his research, Cohen concludes that all three pamphlets "were almost certainly issued by Nathaniel Coverly Jr." and written by "a hack author in his employ" (3).

13. In his recent study of how sentiment reflected market changes in pre–Civil War America, Fichtelberg views this theme of Lucy's alterability as a source of her virtue. Fichtelberg explains that, according to the sentimental tradition preceding her, "virtue" is Lucy's primary characteristic, but now that quality encompasses the desires of a market economy. He writes, "Lucy's virtue is as subtle and pliable as that of any English competitor. She is both corrupt and saved, passive and active, an abused innocent and an aggressive materialist, who has left behind the profit motive but has absorbed the lessons that profit has to teach. In this way she can manage to be *both* an aggressive international competitor *and* one who upholds the superior virtues of modest retirement" (116).

14. In Bradford's *Of Plimouth Plantation*, he describes the trials he perceived the *Mayflower* encountered, saying "[W]hat could they see but a hideous and desolate wilderness, full of wild beasts and wild men" (62).

15. Mr. West does not show any signs of checking pride in his nation's origins when he refers to the "savages," who, as Americans were well aware, had been dispersed and/or decimated by the growth of New England settlements. As Scott Bradfield explains in his study of transgression in the burgeoning tradition of antebellum American romance, "American colonists and revolutionaries always bury their originating moment of violence underneath monuments to their fathers" (36) such as that of Lucy's father's rock and the Pilgrim fathers' Plymouth Rock.

16. According to James D. Wallace, Cooper's sea tales were so popular that they became well-loved stage dramas as well. *The Pilot* was produced at the Chatham Theatre in New York in 1828, while *The Red Rover* "was dramatized in four different separate versions between 1828 and 1831" (180).

17. Hugh Egan identifies this novel as the first fictional treatment of the American navy (69).

18. At the time Cooper wrote and published *The Pilot*, according to Kay Seymour House, there was no biography of John Paul Jones available to him, only stories circulating about Jones's assistance to American troops. Cooper utilized the few documents describing his naval feats to create a more human Jones. As a result, *The Pilot* "reawakened an interest in Jones as a naval hero, brought to light documents Jones had left in the United States, and resulted in the first attempt at a biography a year later" (xxi).

19. Alice claims a wife's duty is "to partake of his joys, or to share in his sorrows, whose life is a continual scene of dangers and calamities, of disappointments and mishaps" (361). Ironically, Katherine fulfills Alice's definition of a good wife while also making Alice appear hypocritical.

20. I have not found any studies of Roderick, and only a mild assertion that she is a woman. In his article on Cooper's *Jack Tier*, Robert K. Martin merely mentions the cabin boy in *The Red Rover*, who is, he claims, "described in terms of sexual ambiguity that are enticing, not freakish" (290). Most critics are more concerned with the relationship between the male characters Wilder and the Rover. See Charles H. Adams's "Cooper's Sea Fiction and *The Red Rover*" for an analysis of Wilder's role as "double," particularly pages 161–65. For an exploration of Wilder as the Red Rover's disciple, see Thomas and Marianne Philbrick's historical introduction to *The Red Rover*, particularly page xxxiv. The Rover's involvement in the slave trade is examined in Gesa Mackenthun's "Postcolonial Masquerade."

21. Eudora's loyalty and taste for saltwater also may have influenced the other woman in the novel. For instance, the possibility remains that Alida will follow in her cousin's footsteps, for she has married a captain; is a blood relative to Eudora, who already has a connection to the sea; and is strongly attracted to the ocean, ships, and seamen. Once, when Alida is looking out of the window at the sea, the narrator explains that she is fascinated by the seaman's devotion to those ashore, their "broken and interrupted connection with the rest of the human family, and finally to those weakened domestic ties," which indicates her desire to have a connection with the sea (80–81). Also, in naming her Alida, it is highly probable that Cooper was alluding to Alwilda, a French female pirate whose story had been recounted in tales of pirates circulating at the time. At the very

least, Cooper was intimating Alida's interest in pirates by having her claim to have read *The History of American Buccaneers* (93), perhaps the truncated rewording of Samuel B. H. Judah's *The Buccaneers* (1827).

22. Cooper recognized Americans' potential to form a connection with the ideals of the pirate. Contemporary historians have explored this often subtle connection between the belief system of pirates and American democratic principles. For instance, see Marcus Rediker's *Between the Devil and the Deep Blue Sea*, particularly chapter 6. Another related study is Jesse Lemisch's "Jack Tar in the Streets," which explores the seaman's influence on revolutionary rhetoric in the colonies. Both resources contribute to an understanding of Cooper's choice of occupation for his early American seafaring heroes and heroines in *Red Rover* and *Water-Witch*.

23. On the other side of the issue, American writers such as Margaret Fuller expressed concern for the unhappy frontier woman who continued to allow themselves to be "ornaments of society" rather than learn to "tread the wildwood paths" (39).

24. According to Madeline B. Stern's *Publishers for Mass Entertainment in Nineteenth Century America*, Ballou saw a market in "stories about naval warfare and piracy" in the antebellum era. Under the pseudonym "Lieutenant Murray," he published several works with nautical themes, with *Fanny Campbell* among the most successful, selling "80,000 copies within the first few months" (28).

25. Adams did not feel the United States was prepared to annex Cuba at that time, but he saw it as inevitable. See Hugh Thomas, *Cuba* (101).

26. See Cutter's excellent analysis of Fanny's redemptive womanhood in *Domestic Devils, Battlefield Angels* (147–53).

27. When Jack, dressed as a woman, reveals herself as Molly to her husband on his deathbed, Cooper describes her as "unsexed" and "changed by years and suffering" (495).

28. In no way, however, is Cooper criticizing expansionism itself. In a preface to a revised edition of the novel, he explains that it was deigned by "Providence" that Mexico become part of the United States (vi). He believes that "war, however ruthless and much to be deplored, may yet confer on her [Mexico] the inestimable blessings of real liberty, and a religion released from 'feux d'artifice,' as well as all other artifices" (vi–vii).

29. Published around the same time as Cooper's novel, *The Cabin Boy*

Wife, supposedly written by Ellen Stephens, is a cross-dressed female drama that likewise enacts the drama of the abandoned female (so common in all cross-dressed female stories). In the narrative, Stephens is forced into a marriage to a rich man who deserts her and runs away with her child. Dressed as a cabin boy, she pursues him up and down the Mississippi, but she never finds them. The moral of her story is essentially not to marry for money, only honesty and industry. A woman's lifelong "desire," says Stephens, is "to cheer [her husband] through the pilgrimage of life . . . [even if] his earthly possessions should be ever so small" (11). For every vision of failure provided by Cooper, however, there were cross-dressed women representing success in the western expansionist project. More optimistic views of men and women's virtue appear in a later narrative of a cross-dressed female. Published in 1851, *The Female Volunteer*, purported to have been authored by Miss Eliza Allen, has a wonderful subtitle that summarizes her story: "Being a truthful and well-authenticated narrative of her parentage, birth and early life—her love for one whom her parents disapproved—his departure for Mexico—her determination to follow him at all hazards—her flight in men's attire—enlistment—terrific battles of Mexico—her wounds—voyage to California—the shipwreck and loss of her companions—her miraculous escape—return to her native land—meeting of the lovers—reconciliation of her parents—marriage, and happy termination of her trials and sorrows." To cap off the fantasy, the couple returns home rich with a treasure of gold they have successfully mined in California after the war. Their story is the success story that Cooper's was not: Eliza's husband William willfully serves his country; she follows him to share his life; they return home (Eastport, Maine); and they settle down in marital bliss, wealthy and surrounded by her beloved family.

30. When reading about cross-dressed mariners, audiences may have enjoyed the game of "decoding," a concept Marjorie Garber identifies as one of the sources of the "erotics" of cross-dressing. Garber explains, "Vestimentary codes, clothing as a system of signification, speak in a number of registers: class, gender, sexuality, erotic style. Part of the problem—and part of the pleasure and danger of decoding—is in determining which set of referents is in play in each scenario" (161). Many of the women in the narratives I discuss, from Lucy Brewer to Fanny Campbell to Almira Paul, are at some point in the story threatened by licentious male characters.

Keeping their gender hidden from view produced suspense about what was underneath the surface and whether the inevitable revelation (by accident or intentionally) would result in a violation of the revealed body. In his study of American sensational fiction, Christopher Looby rightly claims that much of it should be named "urban porno-gothic" (652), partly for its "countless forms of violence" and "the unveiling of an ugly truth hidden by sham surfaces" that calls on the reader to act as voyeur (653).

⟞⟞ Bibliography ⟝⟝

Adams, Charles H. "Cooper's Sea Fiction and *The Red Rover*." *Studies in American Fiction* 16.2 (Autumn 1988): 155–68.

Allen, Miss Eliza. *The Female Volunteer; or the Life and Wonderful Adventures of Miss Eliza Allen, a young lady of Eastport, Maine*. Cincinnati: H. M. Rulison, 1851.

Allen, Sarah. *A Narrative of the Shipwreck and Unparalleled Sufferings of Mrs. Sarah Allen, (late of Boston) on her passage in May last from New York to New Orleans. Being the substance of a letter from the unfortunate Mrs. Allen to her sister in Boston*. 2nd ed. Boston: Benjamin Marston, 1816.

American Adventure by Land and Sea, being remarkable instances of enterprise and fortitude among Americans: shipwrecks, adventures at home and abroad, Indian captivities, etc. Vol. 2. New York: Harper & Brothers, 1855. 2 vols.

American Slavery as It Is: Testimony of a Thousand Witnesses. New York: Arno Press, 1968.

Andrews, William L., and Nellie Y. McKay. Introduction to *Toni Morrison's Beloved: A Casebook*. Eds. Andrews and McKay. New York: Oxford University Press, 1999. 3–19.

Ashworth, John. *Slavery, Capitalism, and Politics in the Antebellum Republic*. New York: Cambridge University Press, 1995.

Auden, W. H. *The Enchafed Flood; or, The Romantic Iconography of the Sea*. New York: Random House, 1967.

Axtell, James. *The Invasion Within: The Contest of Cultures in Colonial North America*. New York: Oxford University Press, 1985.

Baepler, Paul. Introduction to *White Slaves, African Masters: An Anthology of American Barbary Captivity Narratives*. Ed. Baepler. Chicago: University of Chicago Press, 1999. 1–58.

Balibar, Etienne, and Immanuel Wallerstein. *Race, Nation, Class: Ambiguous Identities*. New York: Verso, 1991.

Ballou, Maturin Murray. *Fanny Campbell, the Female Pirate Captain. A Tale of the Revolution*. New York: E. D. Long & Co., 1844.

Bercovitch, Sacvan. *The American Jeremiad*. Madison: University of Wisconsin Press, 1978.

———. *The Puritan Origins of the American Self*. New Haven: Yale University Press, 1975.

———. *The Rites of Assent: Transformations in the Symbolic Constructions of America*. New York: Routledge, 1993.

Berkhofer, Jr., Robert F. *The White Man's Indian: Images of the American Indian from Columbus to the Present*. New York: Vintage Books, 1978.

Betsworth, Roger G. *Social Ethics: An Examination of American Moral Traditions*. Louisville: Westminster/John Knox Press, 1990.

Bolster, W. Jeffrey. *Black Jacks: African American Seamen in the Age of Sail*. Cambridge: Harvard University Press, 1997.

Bourne, George. *Slavery Illustrated in Its Effects upon Women and Domestic Society*. Boston: Isaac Knapp, 1837.

Bradfield, Scott. *Dreaming Revolution: Transgression in the Development of American Romance*. Iowa City: University of Iowa Press, 1993.

Bradford, William. *Of Plimoth Plantation, 1620–1647*. Ed. Samuel Eliot Morison. New York: Alfred A. Knopf, 1966.

Bradley, Eliza. *An Authentic Narrative of the Shipwreck and Sufferings of Mrs. Eliza Bradley*. 1820. Boston: J. Walden, 1821; Fairfield: Ye Galleon Press, 1985.

Brereton, Virginia Lieson. *From Sin to Salvation: Stories of Women's Conversions, 1800 to the Present*. Bloomington: Indiana University Press, 1991.

Brewer, Lucy. *The Female Marine, or the Adventures of Miss Lucy Brewer*. 10th ed. 1816. Ed. Daniel A. Cohen. *The Female Marine and Related Works: Narratives of Cross-Dressing and Urban Vice in America's Early Republic*. Amherst: University of Massachusetts Press, 1997.

Brown, Alexander. *Women and Children Last*. New York: Putman, 1961.

Burnham, Michelle. *Captivity and Sentiment: Cultural Exchange in American Literature, 1682–1861*. Hanover: University Press of New England, 1997.

The Burning of the Ocean Monarch with a full account of Frederick Jerome, the noble hearted sailor. Richmond: Barclay & Co., 1850.

Burstein, Andrew. *Sentimental Democracy: The Evolution of America's Self-Image.* New York: Hill and Wang, 1999.

Caldwell, Patricia. *The Puritan Conversion Narrative: The Beginnings of American Expressionism.* Cambridge: Cambridge University Press, 1983.

Carretta, Vincent. "Olaudah Equiano or Gustavus Vassa? New Light on an Eighteenth-Century Question of Identity." *Slavery and Abolition* 20.3 (December 1999): 96–105.

———. "Three West Indian Writers of the 1780s Revisited and Revised." *Research in African Literatures* 29.4 (Winter 1998): 73–86.

Castiglia, Christopher. *Bound and Determined: Captivity, Culture-Crossing, and White Womanhood from Mary Rowlandson to Patty Hearst.* Chicago: Chicago University Press, 1996.

Cherniavsky, Eva. *That Pale Mother Rising: Sentimental Discourses and the Imitation of Motherhood in 19th-Century America.* Bloomington: Indiana University Press, 1995.

Child, Lydia Maria. *An Appeal in Favor of That class of Americans Called Africans.* 1833. *Against Slavery: An Abolitionist Reader.* Ed. Mason Lowance. New York: Penguin, 2000. 160–75.

Choice Emblems, National, Historical, Fabulous, Moral, and Divine, for the instruction and amusement of youth; displaying the beauties and morals of the ancient fabulists. New York: Samuel Wood and Sons, 1818.

Clark, Harry Hayden. Introduction to *Poems of Freneau.* By Philip Freneau. New York: Harcourt, Brace and Co., 1929. xiii–lx.

Clarkson, Thomas. *The History of the Rise, Progress, and Accomplishment of the Abolition of the African Slave Trade by the British Parliament.* Vol. 2. London: n.p., 1808.

Cohen, Daniel A. Introduction to *The Female Marine and Related Works: Narratives of Cross-Dressing and Urban Vice in America's Early Republic.* Ed. Cohen. Amherst: University of Massachusetts Press, 1997. 1–45.

———. *Pillars of Salt, Monuments of Grace: New England Crime Literature and the Origins of American Popular Culture.* New York: Oxford University Press, 1993.

Cole, Emma. *The Life and Sufferings of Miss Emma Cole, being a faithful narrative of her life. Written by herself.* Boston: M. Aurelius, 1844.

Cooper, James Fenimore. *Homeward Bound; or, the Chase*. Chicago: Belford, Clarke & Co., 1838.

———. *Jack Tier; or, The Florida Reef*. New York: Burgess, Stringer, 1848. Rpt. in *Works of J. Fenimore Cooper*. Vol. 7. New York: P. F. Collier: 1892. 436–679.

———. *The Pilot: A Tale of the Sea*. New York: Wiley, 1824. Ed. Kay Seymour House. Albany: State University of New York Press, 1986.

———. *The Red Rover, A Tale*. Ed. Thomas and Marianne Philbrick. Albany: State University of New York Press, 1991.

———. *The Water-Witch; or, The Skimmer of the Seas: A Tale*. Philadelphia: Carey and Lea, 1830. St. Clair Shores, Michigan: Scholarly Press, n.d.

Coulter, E. Merton. "The Loss of the Steamship *Central America*, in 1857." *Georgia Historical Society* 54.4 (Winter 1975): 453–92.

Creighton, Margaret S. "American Mariners and the Rites of Manhood, 1830–1870." *Jack Tar in History: Essays in the History of Maritime Life and Labour*. Ed. Colin Howell and Richard Twomey. Fredericton, New Brunswick: Acadiensis Press, 1991. 143–63.

———. "Davy Jones' Locker Room: Gender and the American Whalemen." Creighton and Norling 118–37.

———. *Rites and Passages: The Experience of American Whaling, 1830–1870*. Cambridge: Cambridge University Press, 1995.

Creighton, Margaret S., and Lisa Norling, eds. *Iron Men, Wooden Women: Gender and Seafaring in the Atlantic World, 1700–1920*. Baltimore: Johns Hopkins University Press, 1996.

Curti, Merle. *Human Nature in American Thought: A History*. Madison: University of Wisconsin Press, 1980.

Curtis, John. *Shipwreck of the Stirling Castle*. London: George Virtue, 1838.

Cutter, Barbara. *Domestic Devils, Battlefield Angels: The Radicalism of American Womanhood, 1830–1865*. DeKalb: Northern Illinois University Press, 2003.

Daly, Peter M., ed. *The English Emblem and the Continental Tradition*. New York: AMS Press, 1988.

Dana, Henry Wadsworth Longfellow. "Centenary of Hesperus Wreck on Norman's Woe." *The Boston Herald* December 17, 1939: D3.

Danforth, Fanny Templeton. *The Startling, Thrilling, and Interesting Narrative of the Life, Sufferings, Singular and Surprising Adventures of Fanny Templeton Danforth*. Philadelphia: E. E. Barclay, 1849.

Davidson, Cathy N. "Preface: No More Separate Spheres!" *American Literature* 70.3 (September 1998): 443–64.

Dawson, Hugh J. "'Christian Charitie' as Colonial Discourse: Rereading Winthrop's Sermon in Its English Context." *Early American Literature* 33.2 (1998): 117–48.

———. "John Winthrop's Rite of Passage: The Origins of the 'Christian Charitie' Discourse." *Early American Literature* 26.3 (1991): 219–31.

Debord, Guy. *The Society of the Spectacle*. Trans. Donald Nicholson-Smith. New York: Zone Books, 1995.

DePauw, Linda Grant. *Seafaring Women*. Boston: Houghton, 1982.

Derounian-Stodola, Kathryn Zabelle, ed. *Women's Indian Captivity Narratives*. New York: Penguin, 1998.

de St. Pierre, Bernardin. *Paul and Virginia*. Philadelphia: Porter and Coates, n.d.

Diedrich, Maria, Henry Louis Gates, Jr., and Carl Pedersen, eds. *Black Imagination and the Middle Passage*. New York: Oxford University Press, 1999.

Dimock, Wai-chee. *Empire for Liberty: Melville and the Poetics of Individualism*. Princeton: Princeton University Press, 1989.

Douglas, Ann. *The Feminization of American Culture*. New York: Anchor, 1977.

Downes, Paul. *Democracy, Revolution, and Monarchism in Early American Literature*. Cambridge: Cambridge University Press, 2002.

Druett, Joan. *Hen Frigates: Passion and Peril, Nineteenth-Century Women at Sea*. New York: Touchstone, 1998.

———. *She Captains: Heroines and Hellions of the Sea*. New York: Simon and Schuster, 2000.

Dugaw, Dianne. "Female Sailors Bold: Transvestite Heroines and the Markers of Gender and Class." Creighton and Norling 34–54.

———. *Warrior Women and Popular Balladry, 1650–1850*. Cambridge: Cambridge University Press, 1989.

———. "'Wild Beasts' and 'Excellent Friends': Gender, Class and the Female Warrior, 1750–1830." *Jack Tar in History: Essays in the History of Maritime Life and Labour*. Ed. Colin Howell and Richard Twomey. Fredericton, New Brunswick: Acadiensis Press, 1991. 132–42.

Duncan, Archibald. *The Mariner's Chronicle; or authentic and complete history of popular shipwrecks*. Philadelphia: n.p., 1806.

Duncan, Mrs. Robert. *Memoir of Mrs. Mary Lundie Duncan, being recollections of a daughter*. New York: Robert Carter, 1846.

Edwards, Philip. *The Story of the Voyage: Sea-Narratives in Eighteenth-Century England*. Cambridge: Cambridge University Press, 1994.

Egan, Hugh. "Cooper and His Contemporaries." Springer, *America and the Sea* 64–82.

Ellison, James. *The American Captive, or, Siege of Tripoli*. Boston: Joshua Belcher, 1812.

Emerson, Ralph Waldo. "Self-Reliance." *The Portable Emerson*. Ed. Carl Bode and Malcolm Cowley. New York: Penguin, 1981. 138–64.

Equiano, Olaudah. *The Interesting Narrative of the Life of Olaudah Equiano, or Gustavus Vassa, The African, Written by Himself*. Ed. Werner Sollors. New York: Norton, 2001.

Everett, David. *Slaves in Barbary*. Boston: C. Bingham, 1817.

Eze, Emmanuel Chukwudi, ed. *Race and the Enlightenment: A Reader*. Cambridge: Blackwell Publishers, 1997.

Fender, Stephen. *Sea Changes: British Emigration and American Literature*. Cambridge: Cambridge University Press, 1992.

Fichtelberg, Joseph. *Critical Fictions: Sentiment and the American Market, 1780–1870*. Athens: University of Georgia Press, 2003.

Field, Jr. James. *America and the Mediterranean World, 1776–1882*. Princeton: Princeton University Press, 1969.

Fish, Cheryl. "Journeys and Warnings: Nancy Prince's Travels as Cautionary Tales for African American Readers." *Women at Sea: Travel Writing and the Margins of Caribbean Discourse*. Ed. Lizabeth Paravisini-Gebert and Ivette Romero-Cesareo. New York: Palgrave, 2001. 203–24.

———. "Voices of Restless (Dis)continuity: The Significance of Travel for Free Black Women in the Antebellum Americas." *Women's Studies* 26 (1997): 475–95.

Foulke, Robert. *The Sea Voyage Narrative*. New York: Twayne Publishers, 1997.

Franklin, John Hope, and Alfred A. Moss, Jr. *From Slavery to Freedom: A History of African Americans.* 7th ed. New York: McGraw-Hill, 1994.

Fraser, Eliza. *Narrative of the Capture, Sufferings and Miraculous Escape of Mrs. Eliza Fraser.* New York: Charles S. Webb, 1837.

Freneau, Philip. *Poems of Freneau.* Ed. Harry Hayden Clark. New York: Harcourt, Brace and Co., 1929.

Fuller, Margaret. *Summer on the Lakes, in 1843.* 1844. Urbana: University of Chicago Press, 1991.

Garber, Marjorie. *Vested Interests: Cross-Dressing and Cultural Anxiety.* New York: Routledge, 1992.

Gates, Henry Louis, Jr. Introduction. *The Classic Slave Narratives.* Ed. Gates, Jr. New York: Mentor, 1987. ix–xviii.

Gerzina, Gretchen Holbrook. "Mobility in Chains: Freedom of Movement in the Early Black Atlantic." *South Atlantic Quarterly* 100.1 (2001): 41–59.

Gigliotti, Gilbert L. "Off a 'Strange, Uncoasted Strand': Navigating the Ship of State through Freneau's *Hurricane.*" *Classical and Modern Literature* 15.4 (1995): 357–66.

Gilroy, Paul. *The Black Atlantic: Modernity and Double Consciousness.* Cambridge: Harvard University Press, 1993.

Glenn, Susan A. *Female Spectacle: The Theatrical Roots of Modern Feminism.* Cambridge: Harvard University Press, 2000.

Glickstein, Jonathan A. *American Exceptionalism, American Anxiety: Wages, Competition, and Degraded Labor in the Antebellum United States.* Charlottesville: University of Virginia Press, 2002.

Goldner, Ellen J. "Arguing with Pictures: Race, Class and the Formulation of Popular Abolitionism through *Uncle Tom's Cabin.*" *Journal of American and Comparative Cultures.* 24:1,2 (Spring/Summer 2001): 71–84.

Gossett, Thomas F. *Uncle Tom's Cabin and American Culture.* Dallas: Southern Methodist University Press, 1985.

Gould, Phillip B. *Covenant and Republic: Historical Romance and the Politics of Puritanism.* Cambridge: Cambridge University Press, 1996.

Gunning, Sandra. "Reading and Redemption in *Incidents in the Life of a Slave Girl. Incidents in the Life of a Slave Girl: A Norton Critical Edition.* Eds. Nellie Y. McKay and Frances Smith Foster. New York: W. W. Norton, 2001. 330–53.

Gutfeld, Arnon. *American Exceptionalism: The Effects of Plenty on the American Experience*. Portland: Sussex Academic Press, 2002.

Hall, David D. *Cultures of Print: Essays in the History of the Book*. Amherst: University of Massachusetts Press, 1996.

Halloran, S. Michael. "Text and Experience in a Historical Pageant: Toward a Rhetoric of Spectacle." *Rhetoric Society Quarterly* 31.4 (Fall 2001): 5–17.

Haralson, Eric L. "Mars in Petticoats: Longfellow and Sentimental Masculinity." *Nineteenth-Century Literature* 51.3 (December 1996): 327–55.

Harris, Sharon M. "Early American Slave Narratives and the Reconfiguration of Place." *Journal of American Studies Association of Texas* 21 (October 1990): 15–23.

Hartman, Saidiya. *Scenes of Subjection: Terror, Slavery, and Self-making in Nineteenth-Century America*. New York: Oxford University Press, 1997.

Hartnett, Stephen J. *Democratic Dissent and the Cultural Fictions of Antebellum America*. Urbana: University of Illinois Press, 2002.

Hawthorne, Nathaniel. "Chiefly About War Matters." *The Atlantic Monthly* 10.57 (July 1862): 43–61.

Haynes, Carolyn A. *Divine Destiny: Gender and Race in Nineteenth-Century Protestantism*. Jackson: University Press of Mississippi, 1998.

———. "Women and Protestantism in Nineteenth-Century America." *Perspectives on American Religion and Culture*. Ed. Peter W. Williams. Malden MA: Blackwell, 1999. 300–318.

Hedges, William L. "The Myth of the Republic and the Theory of American Literature." *Prospects* 4 (1979): 101–20.

Hine, Darlene Clark, and Kathleen Thompson. *A Shining Thread of Hope: The History of Black Women in America*. New York: Broadway, 1998.

The History of Constantius and Pulchera, or Constancy Rewarded. New York: John Tiebout, 1801.

Hobsbawm, E. J. *Nations and Nationalism since 1780: Programme, Myth, Reality*. Cambridge: Cambridge University Press, 1990.

Hollahan, Eugene. "Intertextual Bondings between 'The Wreck of the Hesperus' and *The Wreck of the Deutschland*." *Texas Studies in Literature and Language* 33.1 (Spring 1991): 40–63.

Holmes, William, and John W. Barber. *Religious Emblems: Being a Series of*

Emblematic Engravings, with written explanations, miscellaneous observations, and religious reflections, designed to illustrate divine truth, in accordance with the cardinal principles of Christianity. Cincinnati: Henry Howe, 1855.

Horsman, Reginald. *Race and Manifest Destiny: The Origins of American Racial Anglo-Saxonism.* Cambridge: Harvard University Press, 1981.

House, Kay Seymour. Introduction to *The Pilot; A Tale of the Sea.* By James Fenimore Cooper. Ed. Seymour. Albany: State University of New York Press, 1986. xvii–xlvii.

Howe, Henry. "Destruction of the Ocean Steamer 'Arctic.'" *Life and Death on the Ocean: A Collection of Extraordinary Adventures.* New York: n.p., 1860. 323–40.

Howland, S. A. *Steamboat Disasters and Railroad Accidents in the United States, to which are appended accounts of recent shipwrecks, fires at sea, thrilling incidents, etc.* Worcester: Warren Lazell, 1846.

Huntress, Keith. *A Checklist of Narratives of Shipwrecks and Disasters at Sea to 1860, with Summaries, Notes, and Comments.* Ames: Iowa State University Press, 1979.

————. Introduction to *An authentic narrative of the shipwreck and sufferings of Mrs. Eliza Bradley.* By Eliza Bradley. Boston: J. Walden, 1821. Fairfield: Ye Galleon Press, 1985. 5–10.

Ickstadt, Heinsz. "Instructing the American Democrat: Cooper and the Concept of Popular Fiction in Jacksonian America." *James Fenimore Cooper: New Critical Essays.* Ed. Robert Clark. London: Vision Press, 1985. 15–37.

Irving, Washington. "English Writers on America." *The Sketch-Book of Geoffrey Crayon, Gent.* New York: G. P. Putnam's Sons, 1868. 75–87.

Isenberg, Nancy, and Andrew Burstein. Introduction to *Mortal Remains: Death in Early America.* Eds. Isenberg and Burstein. Philadelphia: University of Pennsylvania Press, 2003. 1–13.

Ito, Akiyo. "Olaudah Equiano and the New York Artisans: The First American Edition of *The Interesting Narrative of the Life of Olaudah Equiano, or Gustavus Vassa, the African.*" *Early American Literature.* 32.1 (1997): 82–101.

Jacobs, Harriet. *Incidents in the Life of a Slave Girl.* Ed. Nellie Y. McKay and Frances Smith Foster. New York: Norton, 2001.

Jordan, Winthrop D. *White over Black: American Attitudes toward the Negro, 1550–1812.* Chapel Hill: University of North Carolina Press, 1968.

Judah, Samuel B. H. *The Buccaneers: a romance of our own country in ancient days.* Boston: Munroe & Francis, 1827.

Kadir, Djelal. *Columbus and the Ends of the Earth: Europe's Prophetic Rhetoric as Conquering Ideology.* Berkeley: University of California Press, 1992.

Kaplan, Amy. *The Anarchy of Empire in the Making of U.S. Culture.* Cambridge: Harvard University Press, 2002.

Kaplan, E. Ann. *Motherhood and Representation: The Mother in Popular Culture and Melodrama.* New York: Routledge, 1992.

Kasson, Joy S. *Marble Queens and Captives: Women in Nineteenth-Century Sculpture.* New Haven: Yale University Press, 1990.

Keetley, Dawn. "Victim and Victimizer: Female Fiends and Unease over Marriage in Antebellum Sensational Fiction." *American Quarterly* 51.2 (1999): 344–84.

Kerber, Linda K. *Toward an Intellectual History of Women: Essays.* Chapel Hill: University of North Carolina Press, 1997.

———. *Women of the Republic: Intellect and Ideology in Revolutionary America.* New York: W. W. Norton, 1986.

Kilgour, Maggie. *From Communion to Cannibalism: An Anatomy of Metaphors of Incorporation.* Princeton: Princeton University Press, 1990.

Kimmel, Michael. *Manhood in America: A Cultural History.* New York: Free Press, 1996.

Kirby, Percival R. *A Source Book on the Wreck of the Grosvenor East Indiaman.* Cape Town: Van Riebeeck Society, 1953.

———. *The True Story of the Grosvenor East Indiaman.* Cape Town: Oxford University Press, 1960.

Kitzen, Michael L. S. *Tripoli and the United States at War: A History of American Relations with the Barbary States.* Jefferson NC: McFarland, n.d.

Koch, Tom. *The Wreck of the William Brown: A True Tale of Overcrowded Lifeboats and Murder at Sea.* Camden ME: International Marine/McGraw-Hill, 2004.

Kolodny, Annette. *The Lay of the Land: Metaphor as Experience and History in American Life and Letters.* Chapel Hill: University of North Carolina Press, 1975.

Lapansky, Philip. "Graphic Discord: Abolitionist and Antiabolitionist Images." *The Abolitionist Sisterhood: Women's Political Culture in Antebellum America.* Ithaca: Cornell University Press, 1994. 201–30.

Lemisch, Jesse. "Jack Tar in the Streets: Merchant Seaman in the Politics of Revolutionary America." *William and Mary Quarterly* 25 (July 1968): 371–407.

Leslie, Edward E. *Desperate Journeys, Abandoned Souls: True Stories of Castaways and Other Survivors*. Boston: Houghton Mifflin, 1988.

Leuu, Isabelle. Carnival on the Page: Popular Print Media in Antebellum America. Chapel Hill: University of North Carolina Press, 2000.

Lewis, James R. "Images of Captive Rape in the Nineteenth Century." *Journal of American Culture* 15.2 (Summer 1992): 69–77.

———. "Savages of the Seas: Barbary Captivity Tales and Images of Muslims in the Early Republic." *Journal of American Culture* 13.2 (Summer 1990): 75–84.

Lincoln, Marguerite. "Shipwreck Narratives of the Eighteenth and Early Nineteenth Century: Indicators of Culture and Identity." *British Journal for Eighteenth-Century Studies* 20.2 (1997): 155–72.

Lombard, Anne S. *Making Manhood: Growing Up Male in Colonial New England*. Cambridge: Harvard University Press, 2003.

Longfellow, Henry Wadsworth. *The Letters of Henry Wadsworth Longfellow*. Ed. Andrew Hilen. Vol. 2. Cambridge: Belknap-Harvard, 1966.

———. "The Wreck of the Hesperus." *The Works of Henry Wadsworth Longfellow*. Ware, Hertfordshire: Wordsworth Editions, 1994. 48–49.

Looby, Christopher. "George Thompson's 'Romance of the Real': Transgression and Taboo in American Sensation Fiction." *American Literature* 65.4 (December 1993): 651–72.

Mackenthun, Gesa. "Postcolonial Masquerade: Antebellum Sea Fiction and the Transatlantic Slave Trade." *Early America Re-Explored: New Readings in Colonial, Early National, and Antebellum Culture*. Ed. Klaus H. Schmidt and Fritz Fleischmann. New York: Peter Lang, 2000. 537–68.

Madison, Robert D. "Hymns, Chanteys, and Sea Songs." Springer, *America and the Sea* 99–108.

Mann, Herman. *The Female Review; or, Memoirs of an American Young Lady; whose life and character are peculiarly distinguished—being a continental soldier, for nearly three years, in the late war*. Dedham MA: Nathaniel and Benjamin Heaton, 1797.

Mannix, Daniel P. *Black Cargoes: A History of the Atlantic Slave Trade, 1518–1865*. New York: Viking Press, 1962.

Martin, Maria. *History of the Captivity and Sufferings of Mrs. Maria Martin.* 1806. Boston: W. Crary, 1807.

Martin, Robert K. "'No Longer Revolting': Cross-Dressing in Cooper's *Jack Tier.*" *English Studies in Canada* 23.3 (September 1997): 285–95.

Mather, Increase. *Remarkable Providences Illustrative of the Earlier Days of American Colonisation.* London: John Russell Smith, 1856. Rpt. New York: Arno Times, 1977.

McLoughlin, William G. *Revivals, Awakenings, and Reform.* Chicago: University of Chicago Press, 1978.

McNiven, Ian J., Lynette Russell, and Kay Schaffer, eds. *Constructions of Colonialism: Perspectives on Eliza Fraser's Shipwreck.* London: Leicester University Press, 1998.

Medlicott, Alexander, Jr. "The Legend of Lucy Brewer: An Early American Novel." *The New England Quarterly: A Historical Review of New England Life and Letters* 39 (1966): 461–73.

Michaelsen, Scott. "John Winthrop's 'Modell' Covenant and the Company Way." *Early American Literature* 27.2 (1992): 85–100.

Miskolcze, Robin. "Transatlantic Touchstone: The Shipwrecked Woman in British and Early American Literature." *Prose Studies* 22.3 (December 1999): 41–56.

Montgomery, Benilde. "White Captives, African Slaves: A Drama of Abolition." *Eighteenth-Century Studies* 27.4 (Summer 1994): 615–30.

Moore, Marian. *The Touching and Melancholy Narrative of the Shipwrecked Female Sailor.* New York: J. Merone, 1853.

Morison, Samuel Eliot. Introduction to *Of Plimouth Plantation 1620–1647.* By William Bradford. New York: Alfred A. Knopf, 1966. xxiii–xliii.

Morrison, Karl F. *'I Am You': The Hermeneutics of Empathy in Western Literature, Theology, and Art.* Princeton: Princeton University Press, 1988.

Morrison, Toni. *Playing in the Dark: Whiteness and the Literary Imagination.* New York: Vintage, 1992.

Mulford, Carla. "Benjamin Franklin and the Myths of Nationhood." *Making America/Making American Literature: Franklin to Cooper.* Ed. A. Robert Lee and W. M. Verhoeven. Amsterdam: Rodopi, 1996. 15–58.

Mullen, Harryette. "Runaway Tongue: Resistant Orality in *Uncle Tom's Cabin, Our Nig,* and *Incidents in the Life of a Slave Girl.*" Samuels, *Culture* 244–64.

Mulvey, Christopher. "The Fugitive Self and the New World of the North: William Wells Brown's Discovery of America." Sollors and Diedrich 99–111.

Murphy, Geraldine. "Olaudah Equiano, Accidental Tourist." *Eighteenth-Century Studies* 27.4 (Summer 1994): 551–68.

Namias, June. *White Captives: Gender and Ethnicity on the American Frontier.* Chapel Hill: University of North Carolina Press, 1995.

Narrative of the Loss of the Steam-packet Pulaski, which burst her boiler and sunk on the coast of North-Carolina, June 14, 1838. Providence: n.p., 1838.

Nelson, Dana D. *National Manhood: Capitalist Citizenship and the Imagined Fraternity of White Men.* Durham: Duke University Press, 1998.

———. *The Word in Black and White: Reading "Race" in American Literature, 1638–1967.* New York: Oxford University Press, 1992.

Newton, John. *Thoughts upon the African Slave Trade.* London, n.p. 1788. Excerpt rpt. in *The Atlantic Slave Trade.* Ed. David Northrup. Lexington MA: Heath, 1994. 80–89.

Noble, Marianne. *The Masochistic Pleasures of Sentimental Literature.* Princeton: Princeton University Press, 2000.

Norling, Lisa. "Ahab's Wife: Women and the American Whaling Industry, 1820–1870." Creighton and Norling 70–91.

———. "The Sentimentalization of American Seafaring: The Case of the New England Whalefishery, 1790–1870." *Jack Tar in History: Essays in the History of Maritime Life and Labour.* Ed. Colin Howell and Richard Twomey. Fredericton, New Brunswick: Acadiensis Press, 1991. 164–78.

Obeyesekere, Gananath. "'British Cannibals': Contemplation of an Event in the Death and Resurrection of James Cook, Explorer." *Critical Inquiry* 18.4 (Summer 1992): 630–54.

O'Connell, Catharine E. "'The Magic of the Real Presence of Distress': Sentimentality and Competing Rhetorics of Authority." *The Stowe Debate: Rhetorical Strategies in Uncle Tom's Cabin.* Ed. Mason I. Lowance, Jr., et al. Amherst: University of Massachusetts Press, 1994. 13–36.

Paravisini-Gebert, Lizabeth, and Ivette Romero-Cesareo, eds. *Women at Sea: Travel Writing and the Margins of Caribbean Discourse.* New York: Palgrave, 2001

Patterson, Mark R. *Authority, Autonomy, and Representation in American Literature, 1776–1865.* Princeton: Princeton University Press, 1988.

Paul, Almira. *The Surprising Adventures of Almira Paul*. New York: C. E. Daniels, 1840.

Pedersen, Carl. "Middle Passages: Representations of the Slave Trade in Caribbean and African-American Literature." *Massachusetts Review* 34.2 (Summer 1993): 225–59.

———. "Sea Change: The Middle Passage and the Transatlantic Imagination." *The Black Columbiad: Defining Moments in African American Literature and Culture*. Sollors and Diedrich 42–51.

Philbrick, Nathaniel. *Sea of Glory: America's Voyage of Discovery*. New York: Viking, 2003.

Philbrick, Thomas. *James Fenimore Cooper and the Development of American Sea Fiction*. Cambridge: Harvard University Press, 1961.

Philbrick, Thomas, and Marianne Philbrick. Introduction to *The Red Rover, A Tale*. By James Fenimore Cooper. Eds. Philbrick and Philbrick. Albany: State University of New York Press, 1991. xvii–xl.

Phillips, Jerry. "Apocalypse or Utopia? Christopher Columbus and the Contest of Cultural Values." *The Journal of Commonwealth Literature* 27.1 (1992): 56–79.

Poe, Edgar Allan. "The Philosophy of Composition." *The Fall of the House of Usher and Other Writings*. Ed. David Galloway. New York: Penguin, 1986. 480–92.

Potkay, Adam. "Olaudah Equiano and the Art of Spiritual Autobiography." *Eighteenth-Century Studies* 27.4 (Summer 1994): 677–692.

Prince, Nancy. *A Black Woman's Odyssey through Russia and Jamaica: The Narrative of Nancy Prince*. New York: Marcus Wiener Publishing, 1990. Rpt. of *A Narrative of the Life and Travels of Mrs. Nancy Prince*. Boston: N. Prince, 1850.

Rediker, Marcus. *Between the Devil and the Deep Blue Sea: Merchant Seamen, Pirates, and the Anglo-American Maritime World, 1700–1750*. Cambridge: Cambridge University Press, 1987.

———. "Liberty beneath the Jolly Roger: The Lives of Ann Bonny and Mary Read, Pirates." Creighton and Norling 1–33.

Reynolds, David S. *Faith in Fiction: The Emergence of Religious Literature in America*. Cambridge: Harvard University Press, 1981.

Rice, Alan. *Radical Narratives of the Black Atlantic*. London: Continuum, 2003.

Rogers, E. P. "The Sovereignty of God in Calamity: a discourse delivered in the North Dutch Church, in Albany, September 20th, 1857, being the sabbath after the intelligence was received of the loss of the Central America." Albany: Sprague & Co., 1857

Rotundo, E. Anthony. *American Manhood: Transformations in Masculinity from the Revolution to the Modern Era*. New York: Basic Books, 1993.

Rowe, John Carlos. *Literary Culture and U.S. Imperialism: From the Revolution to World War II*. New York: Oxford University Press, 2000.

Rowson, Susanna. *Slaves in Algiers, or A Struggle for Freedom*. Philadelphia: Wrigley & Berriman, 1794.

Saint-Pierre, Bernardin de. *Paul and Virginia*. Philadelphia: Henry Altemus Co., 1800.

Samuels, Shirley S., ed. *The Culture of Sentiment: Race, Gender, and Sentimentality in Nineteenth-Century America*. New York: Oxford University Press, 1992.

————. *Romances of the Republic: Women, the Family, and Violence in the Literature of the Early American Nation*. New York: Oxford University Press, 1996.

Sánchez-Eppler, Karen. "Bodily Bonds: The Intersecting Rhetorics of Feminism and Abolition." Samuels, *Culture* 92–114.

————. *Touching Liberty: Abolition, Feminism, and the Politics of the Body*. Berkeley: University of California Press, 1993.

Sargent, Mark L. "The Conservative Covenant: The Rise of the Mayflower Compact in American Myth." *New England Quarterly* 61.2 (1988): 233–51.

Saunders, Ann. *Narrative of the Shipwreck and Sufferings of Miss Ann Saunders*. Providence: Z. S. Crossman, 1827.

Schaffer, Kay. *In the Wake of First Contact: The Eliza Fraser Stories*. Cambridge: Cambridge University Press, 1995.

Schiebinger, Londa. *Nature's Body: Gender in the Making of Modern Science*. Boston: Beacon Press, 1993.

Schriber, Mary Suzanne. *Gender and the Writer's Imagination: From Cooper to Wharton*. Lexington KY: University Press of Kentucky, 1987.

————. "Toward Daisy Miller: Cooper's Idea of 'The American Girl.'" *Studies in the Novel* 13.3 (Fall 1981): 237–50.

Schueller, Malini Johar. *U.S. Orientalisms: Race, Nation, and Gender in Literature, 1790–1890*. Ann Arbor: University of Michigan Press, 1998.

Seelye, John. *Memory's Nation: The Place of Plymouth Rock*. Chapel Hill: University of North Carolina Press, 1998.

Shaw, Thomas. *Melancholy Shipwreck*. Portland ME: n.p., 1807.

Simpson, Brian A. W. *Cannibalism and the Common Law: The Story of the Tragic Last Voyages of the Mignonette and the Strange Legal Proceedings to Which It Gave Rise*. Chicago: University of Chicago Press, 1984.

Skeen, C. Edward. *1816: America Rising*. Lexington KY: University Press of Kentucky, 2003.

Slotkin, Richard. *Regeneration through Violence: The Mythology of the American Frontier, 1600–1860*. Middletown CT: Wesleyan University Press, 1973.

Smalley, Elam. "A Sermon Occasioned by the Loss of the Arctic: preached in the Second Presbyterian Church, Troy, Oct. 15, 1854. Troy: A. W. Scribner and Co., 1854.

Smith, Valerie. *Self-Discovery and Authority in Afro-American Narrative*. Cambridge: Harvard University Press, 1987.

Sollors, Werner. Introduction to *The Interesting Narrative of the Life of Olaudah Equiano, or Gustavus Vassa, the African, Written by Himself*. By Olaudah Equiano. Ed. Sollors. New York: W. W. Norton, 2001. ix–xxxi.

Sollors, Werner, and Maria Diedrich, eds. *The Black Columbiad: Defining Moments in African American Literature and Culture*. Cambridge: Harvard University Press, 1994.

Sorisio, Carolyn. *Fleshing Out America: Race, Gender, and the Politics of the Body in American Literature, 1833–1879*. Athens: University of Georgia Press, 2002.

Spelman, Elizabeth V. "The Heady Political Life of Compassion." *Incidents in the Life of a Slave Girl: A Norton Critical Edition*. Eds. Nellie Y. McKay and Frances Smith Foster. New York: W. W. Norton, 2001. 353–64.

Sprague, William B. "An Address Delivered April 11, 1845, in the Second Presbyterian Church, Albany, on occasion of the interment of Mr. William Davis, Misses Lucinda and Anna Wood, and Miss Mary Anne Torrey, who perished in the wreck of the steamboat Swallow, on the evening of the 7th." Albany: Erastus H. Pease, 1845.

Springer, Haskell, ed. *America and the Sea: A Literary History*. Athens: University of Georgia Press, 1995.

———. Introduction to *America and the Sea: A Literary History*. Ed. Springer. Athens: University of Georgia Press, 1995. 1–31.

————. "The Captain's Wife at Sea." *Iron Men, Wooden Women: Gender and Seafaring in the Atlantic World, 1700–1920.* Creighton and Norling 92–117.

Stein, Roger B. "American Seascape Art." Springer, *America and the Sea* 146–89.

Stephens, Ellen. *The Cabin Boy Wife; or, Singular and Surprising Adventures of Mrs. Ellen Stephens.* New York: C. E. Daniels, 1840.

Sterling, Dorothy, ed. *We Are Your Sisters: Black Women in the Nineteenth Century.* New York: W. W. Norton, 1984.

Stern, Madeleine B. *Publishers for Mass Entertainment in Nineteenth Century America.* Boston: G. K. Hall, 1980.

Stowe, Harriet Beecher. *Uncle Tom's Cabin.* Oxford: Oxford University Press, 1998.

Streeby, Shelley. *American Sensations: Class, Empire, and the Production of Popular Culture.* Berkeley: University of California Press, 2002.

Thomas, Hugh. *Cuba, or The Pursuit of Freedom.* New York: Da Capo Press, 1998.

Thomas, R. *Interesting and Authentic Narratives of the most remarkable shipwrecks, fires, famines, calamities, providential deliverances, and lamentable disasters on the seas, in most parts of the world.* New York: Ezra Strong, 1836.

Tompkins, Jane. *Sensational Designs: The Cultural Work of American Fiction: 1790–1860.* New York: Oxford University Press, 1985.

Torrey, Jesse. *A Portraiture of Domestic Slavery, in the United States.* 1817. Rept. St. Clair Shores MI: Scholarly Press, 1970.

Tyler, Royall. *The Algerine Captive, or, The Life and Adventures of Doctor Updike Underhill.* Walpole NH: D. Carlisle, 1797.

Vanderbeets, Richard. "The Indian Captivity Narrative as Ritual." *American Literature* 43.4 (1972): 548–62.

Van Rensselaer, Cortlandt. "God's Way in the Deep. A Discourse on the Occasion of the Wreck of the Arctic, delivered in the Presbyterian Church, Burlington, NJ, October 15, 1854." Philadelphia: C. Sherman, 1854.

Villiers, Alan. *Men, Ships, and the Sea.* Washington DC: National Geographic Society, 1973.

Wald, Patricia. *Constituting Americans: Cultural Anxiety and Narrative Form.* Durham: Duke University Press, 1995.

Wallace, James D. *Early Cooper and His Audience.* New York: Columbia University Press, 1986.

Warren, Joyce W. *The American Narcissus: Individualism and Women in Nineteenth-Century American Fiction.* New Brunswick: Rutgers University Press, 1984.

Weiss, John. "A Discourse Occasioned by the Loss of the Arctic: Delivered in the Unitarian Church, New Bedford, October 22, 1854." New Bedford: Benjamin Lindsey, 1854.

Welter, Barbara. "The Cult of True Womanhood." *American Quarterly* 18 (1966): 151–74.

Wertheimer, Eric. "Commencement Ceremonies: History and Identity in 'The Rising Glory of America,' 1771 and 1786." *Early American Literature* 29.1 (1994): 35–58.

Wharton, Donald P. "The Colonial Era." Springer, *America and the Sea* 32–45.

———. Introduction to *In the Trough of the Sea: Selected American Sea-Deliverance Narratives, 1610–1766.* Ed. Wharton. Westport CT: Greenwood Press, 1979. 3–27.

———. "The Revolutionary and Federal Periods." Springer, *America and the Sea* 46–63.

Wheelwright, Julie. *Amazons and Military Maids: Women Who Dressed as Men in the Pursuit of Life, Liberty, and Happiness.* London: Pandora, 1989.

Wiget, Andrew. "Reading against the Grain: Origin Stories and American Literary History." *American Literary History* 3.2 (1991): 209–31.

Winthrop, John. "A Modell of Christian Charity." *The Heath Anthology of American Literature.* Ed. Paul Lauter. Vol. 1. Lexington MA: D. C. Heath, 1994. 226–33.

Wolff, Cynthia Griffin. "Passing beyond the Middle Passage: Henry 'Box' Brown's Translations of Slavery." *Massachusetts Review: A Quarterly of Literature, the Arts and Public Affairs* 37.1 (Spring 1996): 23–44.

Zboray, Ronald J. *A Fictive People: Antebellum Economic Development and the American Reading Public.* New York: Oxford, 1993.

Zuckert, Catherine H. *Natural Right and the American Imagination: Political Philosophy in Novel Form.* Savage MD: Rowman and Littlefield, 1990.

Zwinger, Lynda. *Daughters, Fathers, and the Novel: The Sentimental Romance of Heterosexuality.* Madison: University of Wisconsin Press, 1991.

—ᴍ— Index —ᴍ—

Page numbers set in italics refer to illustrations.

abolitionism, xviii, 15, 74, 76, 180n25; art and, 83–84; humanizing black women, 84–89, 179n19; literature and, 80–84, 89–96, 97; motherhood and, 90–94. *See also* The Middle Passage

Adams, John, 41, 43, 155, 175n12

The Adventures of Almira Paul (Paul), 154

African Americans. *See* The Middle Passage

The Algerine Captive, 115

Allen, Eliza, 132

Allen, Sarah, 25–29, 32–33

Alliance (ship), 14

The American Captive, 115

The American Citizen, 10

Americans: behavior modeled in shipwreck narratives, xx, 7–9; capitalism and, 41–44, 53–56; declining emigration in the 1830s, 11; exceptionalism, 3, 43, 55–56, 60, 65, 130, 168n9; as God's chosen people, xi, 3–9, 13, 22–23, 26–27, 49–50, 58–60; held captive in the Barbary states, xv, 107–8, 114–15; national identity and ideals, xi–xii, 60–64, 151–53, 171n18; Native, 13–14, 28, 102; naval ships, 12–13, 140, 188n17; nonconformity of, 50–51; Pilgrims and Puritans as, 3–9; "republican life" and, 131–33; and the Revolutionary War, 12, 133, 134–35; rhetoric of consensus among, 55–56; selfishness, morality and, 41–42, 53–56, 64; social identification with English culture, 101–3, 108, 110–11, 120–21, 127, 129–30; and the Tripolitan War, 107–8; and the War of 1812, xiv, 109, 131, 135, 136; western migration, xii, 57, 154–55, 157, 189n28

"Am I Not a Woman and a Sister," 81, 82

Amistad, ix, 167n1

An Appeal in Favor of That Class of Americans Called Africans (Child), 84

Arbella (ship), 4–5

Arctic (ship), 52–56

art, women portrayed in: black, 81, 82, 83, 91, 93, 97; white, 34, 36, 37, 40, 46–47, 48–49, 119, 128, 129, 173–74n6

Auden, W. H., x
Australian aborigines, 117–21
Authentic Narrative of the loss of the American brig Commerce (Riley), 10
An Authentic Narrative of the Shipwreck and Sufferings of Mrs. Eliza Bradley (Bradley), 99
The Awful Beacon, 139–40

Bailey, Joseph, 10
Balibar, Etienne, xviii–xix, 101
Ballou, Maturin, 154, 155
Barbary states, xiv, 107–8, 114–15
Barber, John W., 30, 31, 173–74n6
Beecher, Henry Ward, 52, 54, 96
Beloved (Morrison), ix, 66
Bercovitch, Sacvan, 8
Berkhofer, Robert, Jr., 14
Bickerstaffe, Isaac, 9
Birkenhead (ship), 51–53
Bonny, Anne, 185n3
Bourne, George, 81
Brackett, Edward Augustus, 40–41
Bradford, William, xiv–xv, 3, 5, 6–7, 13, 27, 138, 169n2
Bradley, Eliza: abolitionism and, 114; attitudes toward captors, 115; experiences in captivity, 105–6; hybridization of English and Anglo-American women by, 110, 130; James Fenimore Cooper and, 113; marriage and travel to Teneriffe, 104; political impact of writing by, 107–8, 115; popularity of, 103, 109, 129; rape implied by, 107; self-characterization by, 105; shipwreck and captivity depicted by, xviii,

xix, 99, 114–15, 129–30, 181n11; the U.S. Navy and, 108
Bradley, James, 104
Brereton, Virginia Lieson, 126
Brewer, Lucy: author of, 186n6; cross-dressing by, 132, 133; on disguises, 135–36; fights in the War of 1812, 135; heroism of, 135; James Fenimore Cooper and, 150, 152; popularity of, 133, 139–40; pregnancy and desertion of, 134; as a prostitute, 134, 135–36; reprinting of, 186nn8–9, 187n10; return to virtue, 137, 162–63; westward expansion and, 153
British Traveller, 123
Brooke, Henry, 19
Brown, William Wells, 67
Bulfinch, S. G., 50
Burnham, Michelle, 101
Burstein, Andrew, 35, 38
Burton's, 11
Bushnell, David, 12
Byron, Lord, 10

The Cabin Boy Wife (Stephens), 154
Caldwell, Patricia, 7
Campbell, Fanny, 132
cannibalism, 121–24, 184n25
capitalism: democratic, 44, 53–56, 65; human selfishness and, 41–42, 43
captivity narratives, xviii, 104–8, 110–14, 116–21, 181–82n1; common characteristics of, 105–6; shipwrecks in, 107, 109, 118; slavery question and, 113; western expansion and, 154

castaways, 73–74, 77–79
Central America (ship), 56–57, 60
Charles (ship), 22
Cherniavsky, Eva, 78
Cherokee Nation v. Georgia, 118
"Chiefly about War Matters"
    (Hawthorne), 66
Child, Lydia Maria, xvii, 77, 80,
    81, 83–84, 87, 98, 132
children, 39–41, 63–64; slave,
    83–84
Christian themes in shipwreck
    narratives: of Ann Saunders,
    125–27; martyrdom and,
    39–41; the Middle Passage and,
    73–74; of Olaudah Equiano,
    18, 20; Providence and, 3–9, 13,
    22–23, 26–27, 49–50, 58–60;
    of Puritans, 3–7, 12; by Thomas
    Shaw, 22; used in sermons,
    34–35; women as models of,
    x–xi, 26–27, 29, 30, 31, 32, 34,
    38–39, 92, 109, 162–64. *See also*
    shipwreck narratives
Clark, Jonas, 10
Clarkson, Thomas, 180n25
Cohen, Daniel, 135
Cole, Emma, 132, 154
colonizers, European: Columbus
    and, 1–2, 171n15; Native Ameri-
    cans and, 13–14; Pilgrim and
    Puritan, xv, 3–7, 22–23, 66
Columbus, Christopher, 1, 13,
    171n15
community and social imaginary,
    170n9
Congreve, William, 9
Constitution (ship), 134, 136, 138,
    152

Cook, James, 124
Cooper, James Fenimore, xi, xix,
    10, 130, 132, 154–55; captivity
    narratives by, 110–14; frontier
    women portrayed by, 158–64;
    Jack Tier by, xix, 154, 158–64; *The
    Pilot* by, 10, 139, 140–44, 149;
    The Red Rover by, xix, 10, 139,
    144–48, 149, 160; *The Water-
    Witch* by, xix, 10, 139, 148–50,
    153; women sailors in stories
    by, 139–40, 150–52
Creighton, Margaret, xi
Crook, Mary, 45
Cross, J. C., 9–10
cross-dressing: by Christian
    morality and, 163; Deborah
    Sampson, 133; decoding and,
    190n30; depicted by James
    Fenimore Cooper, 141, 142,
    143, 146, 156, 159–60; in *Fanny
    Campbell*, 155, 156; by Lucy
    Brewer, 132, 133
Currier, Nathaniel, 34, 36, 37,
    46–47, 48
Curtis, John, 117
Cutter, Barbara, 43, 157

Danforth, Fanny Templeton, 132
Davidson, Cathy, 131
Dean, Jasper, 10
Dean, John, 10
decoding, 190–91n30
DeFoe, Daniel, 22–23
Dekker, George, 149
"Descent into the Maelstrom"
    (Poe), 10
Diedrich, Maria, 68
Dimock, Wai-chee, xiii

Domestic Manners of the Americans (Trollope), 153–54
Don Juan (Lord Byron), 10
Douglas, Ann, 131
Downs, Barnabas, 10
Druett, Joan, xi, xii
Duncan, Mary Lundie, 39, 174n8

Emerson, Ralph Waldo, 50–51
Empress of China (ship), 10
Equiano, Olaudah, xv, 73, 80, 171–72n19; captured in Africa, 15–16; Enlightenment views of, 17; freed to become a seaman, 15, 16; as representative of blacks, 20–21; saves fellow sailors, 16–21; shipwreck narrative of, 16–21, 67
ethnicity: Anglo-American, 101–3, 108, 111, 120–21, 127, 129–30; Australian aborigine, 117–21; Native American, 13–14, 28, 102, 118–19
exceptionalism, 3, 43, 55–56, 60, 65, 130, 168n9

Falconer, William, 10
Fanny Campbell (Ballou), xix, 132, 154, 155–58, 163; Christian themes in, 163; cross-dressing in, 155, 156; Manifest Destiny and, 155; roles of western women and, 155, 157
Federal Union, 58
The Female Marine, xix, 132, 133–39, 150, 152
Finney, Charles, 41–42
Fish, Cheryl, 72, 73, 177n4
Foster, Hannah Webster, 132

Foulke, Robert, 167n3
Frances Mary (ship), 121–22
Fraser, Eliza, xix, 103, 116–19, 119, 120–21, 129
Freneau, Philip, 12–14

Garber, Marjorie, 153
gender roles: cross-dressing and, 132–33, 141–46, 156, 159–60, 163, 190n30; western women and, 154, 155, 157
Gerzina, Gretchen Holbrook, 73
Gilroy, Paul, 70
Godey's Lady's Book (Mcleod), 57
Gossett, Thomas F., 179n22
Gould, Philip B., 131
Graham's Magazine, 11, 154
Grimke, Sarah and Angelina, 80, 84, 87, 98
Guierrere (ship), 134, 136
Gunning, Sandra, 79
Gustavus Vasa, the Deliverer of His Country (Brooke), 19
Gutfeld, Arnon, 55

Hamilton, Alexander, 41
Harris, Sharon M., 15
Hartman, Saidiya, 73–74, 87
Hawthorne, Nathaniel, 66, 67, 98
Hedges, William L., 42
Helen M'Gregor (ship), 39
Herndon, Captain, 58–60
Hesperus (ship), 61–64
Hispaniola, 1
The History of Constantius and Pulchera, 10, 132
History of the Captivity and Sufferings of Mrs. Maria Martin (Martin), 99
Holmes, William, 30, 31, 173–74n6

Home (ship), 39–40
Homeward Bound (Cooper), 110–14

Ickstadt, Heinz, 151
Incidents in the Life of a Slave Girl (Jacobs), xvii, 75–80
In the Heart of the Sea (Philbrick), ix
Irving, Washington, 101
Isaac's Storm (Larson), ix
Isenberg, Nancy, 38
Ito, Akiyo, 171n19

Jack Tier (Cooper), xix, 154, 158–64
Jacobs, Harriet: abolitionism and, 81, 98; allusions used by, 75–80; black women's experiences as Americans and, 81; as a castaway figure, 77–78, 178nn12–13; dressed as a man of the sea, 76; escape, 77, 79, 173n25; experiences similar to slave ship passengers, 76–77; Harriet Stowe and, 96; hypocrisy of Americans depicted by, 68; Middle Passage as a cultural memory depicted by, xvii, 68; Nancy Prince and, 77, 79–81; sexual harrassment of, 177n9; suffering of, 79
Jefferson, Thomas, 41, 175n12
Jerome, Frederick, 45
Johnson, Charles, 67
Johnson, Samuel, 19
Jones, John Paul, 140–44, 188n18

Kadir, Djelal, 2
Kant, Immanuel, 20, 172n24
Kasson, Joy S., 63

Kerber, Linda, 131
Knickerbocker, 11

Ladies Companion, 11
Larson, Erik, ix
Lewis, James R., 106–7
Lexington (ship), 40
The Life and Sufferings of Miss Emma Cole (Cole), 154
Lincoln, Abraham, 10–11, 89
literature: abolitionist, xviii, 80–84, 89–96, 97; American national ideas and identity in, xi–xii, 60–64, 151–53; American westward migration in, xii, 57, 154–55, 157, 189n28; the Barbary states in, xiv, 107–8, 114–15; captivity narratives in, xviii, 104–8, 110–14, 116–21, 181–82n11; decoding cross-dressing in, 190–91n30; dying women portrayed in, 35–36, 40–41; Englishwomen as subjects of, 99–109, 115–16, 129–30; Middle Passage, ix–x, 66–68, 80; motherhood portrayed in, 39–41, 84–85, 90–94; prostitutes in, 134, 135–36; "republican life" portrayed in, 131–33; shipwreck narratives in, 9–11, 22–23, 33–34, 99–100; women sailors portrayed in, 139–53, 162–64; women's roles portrayed in, 33–34, 131–32, 150–51, 162–64. See also shipwreck narratives
Lombard, Anne S., 45–46
Longfellow, Henry Wadsworth, 61–64, 176nn23–24; national ballad, 61–62

Loss of the Centaur man of war, 10

Love for Love (Congreve), 9

Madison, James, 12

Mann, Herman, 133

Mardi (Melville), 10

Marine (ship), 58

Martin, Henry, 103

Martin, Maria, xviii, 129–30; attitudes toward captors, 115, 181n11; Eliza Bradley and, 105; hybridization of English and Anglo-American women by, 110; popularity of, 103, 108–9, 115, 129; published only in the United States, 103; rape and, 107; reprinting of, 99; returned to freedom, 104; self-characterization by, 105; shipwreck narrative of, 99, 103, 113; suffering of, 104, 106, 114, 182n14; the U.S. Navy and, 108

Martin, Robert K., 159–60, 161

martyrdom and suffering, 39–41, 44–45

Mather, Cotton, xv, 2, 5, 7, 27, 170n8

Mayflower (ship), xv, 3–6

Mayflower Compact of 1620, 4, 8

McLeod, H., 57

Melancholy Shipwreck of the Frances Mary from St. Johns, 128

Melville, Herman, xi, 10

men: behavior at sea, 42–43; capitalism, selfishness, and, 41–44; code of "women and children first" and, xvi, 41–42, 51–52, 56–58, 61, 175n17; rescues of women at sea by, 46–49; self-lessness of, 46–50, 58–60; self-made, 43–44, 45–46; "white" manhood and, 88–89, 98

The Middle Passage: dead and dying slaves thrown overboard during, 94, 179–80n24; Harriet Jacobs and, xvii, 68, 75–80, 81, 96, 98; literature and, ix–x, xvi–xvii, 66–68, 80; living conditions on, 76–77; Nancy Prince and, xvii, 68, 69–75, 77, 79–80, 81, 96, 98, 177n4; and the number of Africans taken to America, 67–68, 177n3; Olaudah Equiano and, xv, 15–21, 73, 80, 171–72n19; rape and, 95–96; as a sacred and heroic passage, 79–80; shipwreck narratives and, 10–11; stages of, 177n6. *See also* abolitionism

The Middle Passage (Johnson), ix

mobility of women, 137–38

Moby-Dick (Melville), 10

Montgomery, Benilde, 113, 114

Moore, Marian, 132, 154

Moors, xix, 103–4, 114

Morison, Samuel Eliot, 6, 169n2

Morland, George, 111, 112, 113

Morrison, Karl F., 86

Morrison, Toni, ix, 66, 67

motherhood: black, 84–85, 90–94; white, 39–41, 84–85

"MS in a Bottle" (Poe), 10

Mulford, Carla, 14

murder, 124–26

My Child, My Child (Currier and Ives), 47

Namias, June, 154

Narrative of Arthur Gordon Pym (Poe), 10

Narrative of the Capture, Sufferings and Miraculous Escape of Mrs. Eliza Fraser, 99, 118, 119

Narrative of the loss of the ship Hercules (Stout), 10

Narrative of the Shipwreck and Sufferings of Miss Ann Saunders, 99, 129

A Narrative of the Shipwreck and Unparalleled Sufferings of . . . Sarah Allen (Allen), 25–29, 32–33

A Narrative on the Life and Travels of Mrs. Nancy Prince (Prince), xvii, 69–75

Native Americans, 102, 183n24; defined as noncitizens by the United States, 118–19; Philip Freneau on, 13–14; Sarah Allen on, 28

Nat Turner Rebellion, 118–19

Nelson, Dana D., xi, 88

newspaper accounts: of shipwrecks, 56–60, 121–23; of slaves, 83–84

Newton, John, 95–96

New York Herald, 54

New York Times, 60

Noah, Mordecai M., 108

nonconformity of Americans, 50–51

Norling, Lisa, xi

Nottingham Galley (Dean and Whitworth), 10

Obeyesekere, Gananath, 125

Ocean Monarach (ship), 44–45, 48

O'Connell, Catharine E., 63

Of Plimouth Plantation (Bradford), 139, 169n2

O'Sullivan, John L., 155

Patterson, Mark R., 151

Paul, Almira, 132, 154

Paul and Virginia, 99

Pedersen, Carl, 67, 69–70

Philbrick, Nathaniel, ix

Phillips, Jerry, 171n18

Pierce, Nathaniel, 10

Pilgrims, xv, 3–9, 27–28, 66; hope and faith of, 32–33

The Pilot (Cooper), xix, 10, 139, 140–44, 149, 188n18

Poe, Edgar Allen, xi, 10

poetry. *See* literature

The Portfolio, 10

Portsmouth (ship), 10

Potkay, Adam, 19

Prince, Nancy, xvii; abolitionism and, 74–75, 98; as a castaway figure, 73–74; family history of, 69, 71, 177nn4–5; Harriet Jacobs and, 77, 79–81; Harriet Stowe and, 96; Middle Passage as a cultural memory depicted by, 68, 73, 75; observations of slaves, 70–71; passage to Boston, 70–71, 72–73; shipboard oratory, 71–72

printed shipwreck narratives, 9–11, 22–23; women in, 33–34

prostitutes, 134, 135–36

Pulaski (ship), 46

Puritans: covenant with God, 3–9, 13, 22–23, 26–27, 49–50; Native Americans and, 13–14; shipwreck narratives, xv, 2–9

The Purse (Cross), 9–10

racism, 20–21, 172n23. *See also*
The Middle Passage
railroads, 53
Rankin, John, 86–88
rape, 95–96, 107, 118, 180n26
Read, Mary, 185n3
redemptive womanhood, 43, 157
The Red Rover (Cooper), xix, 10,
139, 144–48, 149, 160
religion. *See* Christian themes in
shipwreck narratives
Religious Emblems (Holmes and
Barber), 30, 31, 173–74n6
*Remarkable Providences Illustrative of
the Earlier Days of American Coloni-
sation* (Mather), xv, 6–7, 8, 27
Remington, Reverend, 44–45,
48, 50
The Reprisal (Smollett), 9
"republican life," 131–33
Revolutionary War, 12, 133,
134–35, 155
Reynolds, David S., 114
rhetoric of consensus, 55–56
Riley, James, 10
Robinson Crusoe (DeFoe), 22–23,
77–78
Rogers, E. P., 32
Romero, Lara, 43
Rotundo, Anthony, 44
Rowson, Susanna, 132

Sampson, Deborah, 133–34,
186n7
Santa Maria (ship), 1
Saunders, Ann, xix, 103, 128, 129,
183n21, 184n26; authenticity
of account of, 183n21; cannibalism by, 121–22, 123–25,

184n28; conversion narrative,
126–28; lower class status
of, 121, 122–23; on murder,
125–26, 184n27; popularity of,
103, 129; shipwreck narrative,
99, 116, 130
Saunders, Virginia, 99
Schaffer, Kay, 118–19
Schriber, Mary Suzanne, 151
Schueller, Malini Johar, 115
The Sea Voyage Narrative (Foulke),
167n3
Second Great Awakening, 41–42
selfishness, 41–42, 53–56, 64
selflessness, 46–50, 58–60
self-made men, 43–44, 45–46,
175nn12–14
"Self-Reliance" (Emerson), 50–51
Sent for You Yesterday (Wideman), ix
Sentimental Democracy (Burstein),
35
Shakespeare, William, 145–46
Shaw, Thomas, 22
ships: American naval technology and, 12–13; Arctic, 52–56;
and the Barbary states, 107–8;
Birkenhead, 51–53; Central America, 56–57, 60; Charles, 22;
of Columbus, 1–2; Constitution, 134, 136, 138, 152; Helen
M'Gregor, 39; Hesperus, 61–64;
Home, 39–40; Lexington, 40;
Marine, 58; Mayflower, xv, 3–6;
Pulaski, 46; of the Revolutionary
War, 12; Swallow, 33–34, 36–38;
in U.S. national narratives, 2–3;
"women and children first"
code on, xvi, 41–42, 51–52,
56–58, 61, 175n17

The Shipwreck (Falconer), 10

Shipwrecked Mother and Child (Brackett), 40–41

shipwreck narratives: American values and behavior modeled in, xx, 7–9; of Ann Saunders, 121–28, 128, 129–30; cannibalism in, 121–24; children in, 63–64; of Columbus, 1; of Daniel DeFoe, 22–23; of Eliza Fraser, 116–21, 130; by Englishwomen, 99–103, 115–16; equating colonies with ships, 4–5; in literature, 9–11, 22–23, 33–34, 60–64, 99–100; manipulated by Puritan leaders, 8–9; of Maria Martin, 103–4; modern, 167n2; murder in, 124–26; in newspapers, 56–60; of Olaudah Equiano, 16–21; in print, 168n8; representations of women in, 33–41; of Sarah Allen, 25–29, 32–33; slavery and, 10–11, 15–21; as a source of information for families, 11, 22–23; suffering and martyrdom in, 39–41, 44–45; in theater, 9–10; victims and, 11–12, 51–56; women rescued in, 46–49. See also captivity narratives; Christian themes in shipwreck narratives; literature

Shipwreck of the Stirling Castle (Curtis), 117

Skeen, C. Edward, 137

Slavers Throwing Overboard the Dead and Dying (Turner), 94

slavery. See abolitionism; The Middle Passage

Slavery Illustrated in its Effects Upon

Woman and Domestic Society (Bourne), 81

Slaves in Algiers, 115

Slotkin, Richard, 105

Smith, Adam, 41

Smith, Valerie, 77–78

Smollett, Tobias, 9

Sollors, Werner, 68

Spelman, Elizabeth, 79

Sprague, William B., 34–35, 36, 174n8

Stephens, Ellen, 132, 154

Sterling Castle (ship), 116

Stout, Benjamin, 10

Stowe, Harriet Beecher, xvii, 89–90, 91, 92, 93, 94–96, 97, 98; anger at the international slave trade, 94; black men portrayed by, 179n22; impact of writings by, 89–90, 98, 178–79n18; portrayals of slave suffering, 80, 84; on the separation of mothers from children, 92–94; on trafficking of women, 95–96

Swallow (ship), 33–34, 36, 37, 38

Thacher, Anthony, 8

theatrical shipwreck narratives, 9–10

They're Saved, They're Saved (Currier and Ives), 48

Thomas and Sally (Bickerstaffe), 9

Titanic, ix

Tompkins, Jane, 35

Torrey, Jesse, 94

Torrey, Mary Anne, 36, 38–39

The Touching and Melancholy Narrative of Marian Moore (Moore), 154

Tripolitan War, 107–8

Trist, Nicholas, 155
Trollope, Frances, 153–54
The True Account of the Loss of the Ship Columbia, 11–12
Turner, J. M. W., 94
Turtle (Bushnell), 12
Twelfth Night (Shakespeare), 145–46
Typee (Melville), 10

Uncle Tom's Cabin (Stowe), 63, 89–90, 91, 92, 93, 94–96, 97, 179n22
Unicorn (ship), 103
U.S. Naval Academy, 59, 60

Van Rensselaer, Cortlandt, 53, 54, 55
Vassa, Gustavus, 19, 20

Wald, Patricia, 171n18
War of 1812, xiv, 109, 131, 135, 136
The Water-Witch (Cooper), xix, 10, 139, 148–50, 153
Weiss, John, 50, 54, 56, 60
Weld, Theodore, 80, 84, 87, 98
westward migration by Americans, xii, 57, 154–55, 157, 189n28
Wharton, Donald P., xv, 8–9
White Captives (Namias), 154
Whitworth, Miles, 10
Wideman, John Edgar, ix
Wiget, Andrew, 170n8
Winthrop, John, 4–5
Wolff, Cynthia Griffin, xvi, 75
women, black: abolitionists' humanizing of, 84–89, 179n19; as castaways, 73–74, 77–79; Harriet Jacobs and, 75–80; heroics by, 92; in literature, 80, 84, 89; motherhood and, 84–85, 90–94; Nancy Prince and, 69–75; portrayed in art, 81, 82, 83, 91, 93, 97; rape of, 95–96, 180n26
women, white: captivity narratives by, xviii, 103–8, 110–14, 116–21, 181–82n11; English, 99–114; heroics by, 28–29, 32, 159; mobility of, 137–38; as models of morality and Christian faith, x–xi, 26–27, 29, 30, 31, 32, 38–39, 55, 162–64; motherhood and, 39–41; portrayed in art, 34, 36, 37, 40, 46–47, 48–49, 119, 128, 129, 173–74n6; as prostitutes, 134, 135–36; rape of, 107, 118; redemptive womanhood and, 43, 157; representations in shipwreck narratives, 33–41; rescues of, 46–49; roles in society, 131–32; as sailors, xix, 139–53, 162–64, 185n3; shipwreck narratives of, 25–29, 32–33, 99–100; as slaves, 104, 105, 114; suffering, martyrdom and, 39–41, 44–45; and western migration, 154–55
The Wreck of the Halsewell (Morland), 111, 112, 113
"The Wreck of the Hesperus" (Longfellow), 61
Wreck of the ship Sydney, 10

Zuckert, Catherine H., 42
Zwinger, Lynda, 63–64